THE MONEY OF INVENTION

THE MONEY OF INVENTION

How Venture Capital Creates New Wealth

∎

PAUL A. GOMPERS

JOSH LERNER

∎

Harvard Business School Press / Boston, Massachusetts

Requests for permission to use or reproduce material from this book
should be directed to permissions@hbsp.harvard.edu, or mailed to
Permissions, Harvard Business School Publishing, 60 Harvard Way,
Boston, Massachusetts 02163.

Library of Congress Cataloging-in-Publication Data
Gompers, Paul A. (Paul Alan)
    The money of invention : how venture capital creates
new wealth / Paul A. Gompers and Josh Lerner.
        p. cm.
    Includes bibliographical references and index.
    ISBN 1-57851-326-X (alk. paper)
        1. Venture capital—United States. 2. New business
enterprises—United States—Finance.
    I. Lerner, Joshua. II. Title.

HG4963 .G658 2001
658.15'224—dc21

                                            2001024747

The paper used in this publication meets the requirements of
the American National Standard for Permanence of
Paper for Publications and Documents in Libraries and Archives
Z39.48–1992.

To Sivan, Annika, and Zoe

To Sunshine and Trixie

Contents

■

Acknowledgments

■

This book draws on our research and case writing about the venture capital industry and the financing of innovation over the past dozen years. Without the cooperation of many investors in, general partners of, and advisors to venture capital funds and organizations, as well as the entrepreneurs that they have financed, we would not have been able to undertake this work.

More directly, the ideas in this volume were refined in many hours of conversations with academic colleagues and practitioners. Some served as informal sounding boards for our ideas as they developed; others commented on early versions of this manuscript. We especially wish to thank Rick Burns, Hank Chesbrough, Ollie Curme, Dwight Crane, Felda Hardymon, Brad Kelly, Michael Klein, Joel Romines, and Bill Sahlman.

The production of this volume was greatly enhanced by research assistance provided by Chris Allen. Our assistants, Marianne D'Amico and Peggy Moreland, were of a great deal of assistance in many stages of the process. Amanda Gardner and Barbara Roth helped steer the production of the final manuscript. The Division of Research of Harvard Business School provided us with financial support.

The project was shepherded from its earliest stage by our agent, Barbara Rifkind, and our editor, Kirsten Sandberg. With a great deal of enthusiasm (but also persistence!), they kept us on track. We owe them a great deal of thanks.

Finally, our families provided a great deal of support while we fretted over writing (and rewriting!) the manuscript. We appreciate their understanding and patience through this entire process.

THE MONEY OF INVENTION

1

The Venture Capital Difference

∎

Innovations fail to create value when they cannot attract the resources required to develop them.

Venture capital has been an important element behind innovation and wealth creation in the U.S. economy for the past thirty years. It has also played an increasing role in developed and developing countries elsewhere around the world. It influences nearly every aspect of business today—yet the manner in which venture capitalists operate has often been shrouded in mystery and cliché.

In some accounts, venture capitalists are master craftsmen who find diamonds in the rough that become monumental successes. On the other hand, the dramatic swings in venture capital activity and the recent dramatic movements of venture capital–backed firms in the public markets have added to the notion that venture capitalists are rapacious investors. It is easy to see how the excesses that were allowed to build up in the venture capital sector ultimately created turmoil. Few commentators, however, have identified the key forces that have shaped—and will shape—the way the venture capital industry operates.

One fact is clear: Young entrepreneurial firms often have problems finding financing for their innovation or idea. Entrepreneurs develop ideas for new business models, products, and services—and hope to one day receive value in return for the sweat, patience, and risk they put on the line to commercialize those ideas. However, innovation, by its very nature, is difficult to finance. Venture capitalists screen entrepreneurial projects, structure financing deals, and monitor their investees' performance after providing the financial backing. Without these activities, many

1

entrepreneurs would never attract the resources they need to quickly turn their promising idea into a commercial success.

Life *without* Venture Capital

We can probably get the most vivid sense of the importance of venture capital by going back in time and examining the experience of U.S. entrepreneurs who had no such financing available to them.

Scene 1: That Cotton-Pickin' Machine

During the nineteenth century, agriculture formed the backbone of the U.S. economy. Not surprisingly, entrepreneurs worked to find new and better ways to increase production of key crops, such as cotton. In the early part of that century, almost all cotton was picked by hand. Inventors recognized the potential benefits of automating cotton harvesting, and by 1850 patents on mechanical cotton pickers had proliferated. However, not one of them proved to be a commercial success and their creators never made money on their ideas.

Agnus Campbell's story is a case in point.[1] A pattern maker from Chicago, Campbell became interested in designing a mechanical cotton picker in 1880. He tinkered with some ideas for a while, and in 1889 developed a prototype spindle picker that he tested in several cotton fields in the South. The results were anything but spectacular: The machine dropped most of the cotton bolls onto the ground and crushed the cotton plants. Over the next twenty years, Campbell experimented with other kinds of pickers, all at his own expense. He generated his ideas in Chicago and then traveled each summer to the South to test them. The process was slow and often limited by Campbell's lack of funding and inadequate resources.

In 1908 Campbell finally received financing from Theodore Price, an affluent cotton dealer, and founded Price-Campbell Cotton Picker Company. As its first goal, the company sought to commercialize the spindle cotton picker that Campbell had labored over. Though the tenacious pattern maker tried a variety of approaches until his death in 1922, Campbell never perfected a commercially viable picker. In 1924 International Harvester bought the patents from Price-Campbell Cotton Picker Company and later launched commercial versions of Campbell's idea. Campbell was clearly limited by his inability to attract financing and get the strategic advice he needed. He worked for nearly forty years on developing a commercially viable product, but never had the resources to fully develop the technology.

Scene 2: The Typewriter That Didn't Type

In 1867, Christopher Latham Sholes, a publisher from Wisconsin, decided to develop a means to automatically add numbers at the bottoms of book pages.[2] Two of Sholes's friends, Carlos Glidden and Samuel W. Soule, convinced Sholes that he should build a device that could produce not only numbers but all the letters of the alphabet as well. The two friends had read an article in *Scientific American* proclaiming that "typewriters" would be in huge demand in the future.

Over the next five years, Sholes and Glidden developed more than thirty experimental models of the typewriter in a small, local machine shop. Sholes and Glidden's first typewriter arranged the keys in alphabetical order. However, the two men discovered that this layout caused many of the more frequently used keys to jam. Eventually, they settled on today's standard QWERTY layout (the sequence of letters in the top-left row of keys), which solved that problem. Their first models typed in capital letters only, but the design was far superior to any other mechanical writing invention of the time.

We might think that Sholes and Glidden became rich from their invention—after all, *everyone* uses QWERTY keyboards and typewriters were once a symbol of corporate America. Sadly, they didn't. Indeed, the partners received only a nominal reward for their ingenuity. A local businessman, James Densmore, purchased all the rights to the Sholes-Glidden typewriter in 1873 for just $12,000. Densmore had convinced Sholes that the invention, while interesting, was not really all that significant. Densmore then signed an agreement with the E. Remington and Sons Corporation to commercialize the new invention. Remington, which produced guns and sewing machines, was looking for new products to manufacture after the Civil War because they believed that the gun market would dry up. They introduced their first typewriter in 1874. Though initial sales proved lukewarm, further refinements in marketing and design propelled sales of the device.

Scene 3: A Job Seeker's Dream?

In late 1994, Neil Banta and Rob Shultz, two entrepreneurs from Chicago, hit on an exciting idea.[3] They were struck by the inefficiencies of the usual job-hunting process—by which job seekers paged through printed help-wanted ads, circled the most promising ones, and then mailed their résumés to the address listed in the ad.

Banta and Shultz felt certain that there was a better way to bring labor-hungry companies and job-hungry workers together. A central online clearinghouse, they decided, could improve the efficiency of the entire process, benefiting all parties. They set up a company and named it Skills On-line. As they saw it, their clearinghouse would let employers post temporary and permanent job openings and evaluate a large database of résumés. Similarly, job hunters could search job postings across the entire country for positions that might fit their interests or skills.

Though the idea had huge potential, Banta and Shultz never raised financing for their company. Why? For one thing, Chicago lacked a vibrant early-stage venture capital sector. Most venture funds in Chicago invested in buyouts (i.e., the purchase of mature, profitable businesses, or late-stage expansion companies, companies that had already attained profitability). Skills On-line was simply outside the "sweet spot" for these groups, and Banta and Shultz ultimately abandoned their idea.

As everyone knows, Banta and Schultz's dream has since been turned into reality—by a number of other firms that have managed to attract venture capital funding. Online companies like Monster.com and Hot-Jobs.com—both of which were founded more than two years after Banta and Shultz conceived the idea for Skills On-line—have scored spectacular successes. For example, Hotjobs.com went public on August 10, 1999, and had a market value of $1.3 billion by the end of that year.

As these examples reveal, innovation and ideas do not generate value all by themselves—no matter how exciting. Inventors and entrepreneurs also need talented management, reliable financial support, and coaching and insight from professionals who specialize in the innovation and commercialization process. Indeed, the very nature of innovation—with its inherent risk and uncertainties—makes it that much harder for entrepreneurs to obtain these essential ingredients for success.

The Money of Invention

In the recent onslaught of articles and commentary on the explosion of communication, software, and medical technologies, one point often gets missed. These discussions rarely mention the critical role of the individuals who have financed these successful firms, whether relatively recent concerns such as Sycamore, Yahoo!, Akamai, and Amazon.com or established giants such as Cisco, Intel, Microsoft, and Genentech. In all these cases, venture capitalists provided funding, contacts, reputation, and advice while these companies were in their formative stages.

But instead of acknowledging these contributions, the business media (as well as entrepreneurs' guidebooks) have perpetuated an unsavory stereotype of venture capitalists, portraying them as scavengers intent on hoodwinking innovators and public-market investors alike. The recent decline in technology stocks has further emboldened critics. Many claim that venture capital excesses were an important contributing factor to the market hype and ultimate decline. While venture capitalists were clearly overoptimistic about certain sectors and funded too many companies in the same markets, they also funded many great companies within this period.

In addition, entrepreneurs have often felt that the terms demanded by venture capitalists are far too onerous for the amount of capital they provide. These claims have little basis in reality, yet they have carried a high price for all manner of businesspeople—not just venture capitalists. While venture capitalists sometimes demand strict control rights and large equity stakes, these measures are necessary ingredients of the venture capital process. Numerous entrepreneurs, for example, have doomed their fledging companies by accepting money from the wrong investors, and countless corporations have squandered millions investing in unrealizable business ideas—because they failed to understand the important elements of the venture capital process.

This book explores why venture capitalists have played an important role in the success of so many high-technology industries. It examines not only how, but also why these investors work as they do. It also highlights the financial and management approaches that have spurred the creation of more than 2,000 publicly traded, venture-backed firms between 1972 and 2000—firms that have an aggregate market capitalization of over $2.7 *trillion*. In addition, the book highlights key lessons for anyone interested in financing innovative activity. More important, however, the book explores the central impact that the venture capital industry has had on innovation, economic growth, and job creation over the same time period—all of which have made the United States a worldwide leader in high technology. Finally, this volume will explore the challenges created by the rapid expansion of venture capital in recent years.

Using This Book

We wrote this book for entrepreneurs, corporate executives, public policy makers, university officials, or anyone who is interested in capturing value from their innovative activities. The lessons and frameworks that we develop in this book examine how innovation is transformed into value and how innovators can bring money and other resources to bear on creating value from their ideas. Anyone interested in understanding that process and applying the lessons of the venture capital "solution" will benefit from these insights.

Entrepreneurs often develop ideas and projects that require external financing but don't understand where they should go for funds or how to assess the relative benefit of venture capital. When choosing among a menu of possible capital sources, entrepreneurs often try to separate fact from fiction in the venture capital market. They often wonder whether the additional restrictions and equity required by the venture capitalist are worth it. These lessons will provide entrepreneurs with a deep understanding of the incentives of venture capitalists, how they operate, and when they can add value. As such, entrepreneurs will become more informed users of venture capital and be able to avoid many potential pitfalls.

Corporate executives are another group that will find the insights presented in this book essential to their strategic initiatives. Many Fortune 500 executives watch nimble young start-ups innovate and grow, often at their own expense. The decline of companies such as Digital Equipment, General Instrument, and Kodak illustrates the road to oblivion for firms that fail to sustain innovation. In an effort to create new value for their shareholders, many of these corporations look to venture capital as a potential solution. These corporations hope that providing capital to young, start-up firms can provide access to innovation and ideas, as well as provide substantial returns on investment. But we show that many of these programs have made substantial missteps. Corporate managers can learn the necessary framework from the independent venture capital sector to help them capture the value of the entrepreneurial process at a pivotal point in their efforts to sustain value.

Public sector officials and university administrators face a similar problem. While governments and universities are not usually associated with maximizing returns, budget pressures have forced these institutions to rethink their role in fostering innovation and to question whether they should undertake large efforts to commercialize their contributions to innovation. As costs continue to increase, laboratories and facilities decay.

It has become increasingly important for public sector and university officials to understand the value-generating ability of venture capital and to share in the gains. And not only do governments and academic institutions benefit; but ultimately the community at large benefits from a greater number of well-paying jobs. Many government organizations and universities have attempted to develop venture capital programs, with little success. The lessons from independent venture organization can be applied in these settings as well.

To that end, readers can approach the various chapters in whatever sequence they wish. However, we've structured them as follows:

Part 1: The Entrepreneur's Challenge

In chapters 2 to 4 we describe the unique challenges facing entrepreneurs who are seeking capital to fuel promising and risky business concepts. Most entrepreneurs are convinced that they have exciting and dynamic ideas. The technological innovation or new marketing idea may have enormous market potential, and competitors often offer poor alternatives.

These entrepreneurs, however, often face a fundamental problem: they rarely have the capital to see their ideas to fruition. If they hope to capitalize on their innovation, they must find outside investors. When they seek financing, however, their business plans are often greeted with skepticism. The investor may demand a large equity stake and onerous control rights in exchange for a relatively modest sum of money, or the investors may turn down the entrepreneur entirely. The phrase "vulture capitalist" accurately reflects many entrepreneurs' view of their financiers. Prior to the growth of the venture capital market, many entrepreneurs were unable to realize the value from their ideas. As the earlier example of Agnus Campbell illustrates, great ideas often make slow progress without outside capital infusions.

What most entrepreneurs do not see clearly, however, are the risks that their business plans pose. Most high-technology entrepreneurial ventures have a number of fundamental problems that make them difficult to finance. In fact, many potentially important innovations have failed to be commercialized in a timely fashion because of these problems. These financing difficulties can be sorted into four critical problems that are explored in chapter 2.

The first of these four problems is uncertainty about the future. Consider the dilemma faced by Banta and Shultz when they tried to launch

Skills On-line. While the number of people hooked up to the Internet in 1994 was growing, it was still relatively small. No one could be certain when a critical mass of people and companies would start using the Internet for business purposes. Similarly, privacy concerns were very large. Would job seekers be willing to post their résumés on the Internet if their current employers might be able to access them? Similarly, would companies want to post jobs for a national audience on the Internet when their competitors might be able to glean information about their future plans? Banta and Shultz also faced uncertainty relative to the development of a platform for delivering their service. Neither Banta nor Shultz had the software background to develop the Skills On-line interface and database functions. Could they find the right technical talent to address their needs? How long would it take and how much would it cost to develop the technology? Dynamic young companies, by their very nature, have high levels of uncertainty.

The second problem, the information gap, is somewhat different. In the case of Sholes and Glidden, the inventors of the modern typewriter, they had knowledge of their invention, but little knowledge of how to value it or what it would take to get the invention to market. This allowed a crafty angel investor to take advantage of them, essentially buying all the rights to the invention for a very small fraction of what it was actually worth. In many settings, potential entrepreneurs, employees, strategic partners, and financiers must make business decisions in which the opposite party knows something that they do not. Fear of such information gaps may render firms incapable of completing transactions that would benefit everybody.

The third problem is soft assets. One of the chief difficulties that Agnus Campbell faced when he tried to attract financing for his cotton picker was that the only assets his company had were the patents that he held for his ideas about developing a new machine. To most potential partners, the patents would have relatively low value before a successful spindle picker had been developed. Campbell had all the knowledge about the development of those patents and the ideas that were tried and ultimately unsuccessful. This knowledge and the patents that were associated with it are soft assets, as opposed to hard physical assets like land, buildings, equipment, and vehicles. Generally speaking, firms with hard assets often have more financing options. They can raise debt financing from banks or have an easier time convincing outside investors that the company has tangible value. Those firms with soft assets, such as trade secrets, copyrights, and patents, often do not.

Market conditions, the fourth problem, also play a key role in determining the difficulty of financing firms. In 1994, when Banta and Shultz were out trying to raise money for their start-up, venture capital fundraising had declined sharply from its peak. Institutional investors had become disappointed in the returns generated by venture investments in the 1980s and reduced their allocation to new funds. Consequently, Banta and Shultz had relatively limited options when they attempted to raise financing. Chicago in particular had suffered drastic reductions in fundraising for young technology-based companies. The external financial market conditions meant that Banta and Shultz could not raise the financing they needed to get their company off the ground. In general, entrepreneurs must consider what the current product markets and financial markets look like when they go out to raise financing and acquire resources. Market conditions play an important role in determining the financing climate and the terms of investment.

Where Do Entrepreneurs Go for Capital?

Entrepreneurial ventures seek capital from a variety of sources. Venture capital, however, is inappropriate for the vast majority of new firms. Only a very small number of the million start-ups in the United States each year attract professional venture capital financing. For example, in 2000, a record year of venture activity, only about 2,200 firms received venture capital for the first time. In order to understand the forces that influence where firms get financing and why venture capital is so critical to the competitiveness of young, innovative companies, the alternative sources of financing need a brief discussion.

Many early-stage companies receive capital from the informal risk capital market, a market that consists of individuals known as "angels." These angels are wealthy businesspeople, doctors, lawyers, or other entrepreneurs who are willing to take an equity stake in a fledgling company in return for providing capital and mentoring.

It is difficult to get accurate data about "angel" activity in the United States. Many of the estimates have been based on surveys, which can be notoriously troublesome. These surveys suggest that between 5 and 10 percent of start-ups (around 50,000 firms) and 300,000 growing small firms require equity capital each year.[4] If the average required investment was $250,000, the required amount of equity capital would be $87 billion, almost twice what the venture capital industry currently invests. Other estimates have placed the annual amount invested by angel investors at between $3 and $30 billion.

Angel investors typically invest in technologies that they understand. One of the recent trends is for groups of successful entrepreneurs to band together to form collective investment pools that find investments in various technologies and industries. In many ways, these new pools of angel capital mimic many of the successful features of venture capital firms that we will explore in the next two chapters.

In addition, angels tend to invest close to where they live. Most do not have the time or resources to dedicate to traveling outside their local markets. As such, angel investing tends to cluster around major business centers. Angels also tend to invest in very early stage companies, with a typical angel financing round being less than $1 million. Finally, and perhaps most importantly for any comparison to venture capital, angels tend to use investment terms and conditions that are more brief and more informal than venture capitalists. As such, many of the important screening and monitoring mechanisms that we will explore in chapter 3 are not present in angel investments. These differences in financing terms and investment tools perhaps explain much of the lower return and poor results that angels appear to typically experience. Perhaps, angels tend to take bigger risks and accept lower returns because they feel that the entrepreneur's idea is attractive for "nonfinancial" reasons, i.e., the idea has the right "bells and whistles."

What is clear from anecdotal evidence, however, is that angels are also a diverse group. Many angel investors may be nothing more than wealthy local doctors, dentists, or businesspeople who have a strong desire to "make a fortune." Many are also naïve about the potential conflicts that can arise and are potentially easy prey for unscrupulous entrepreneurs. On the other hand, some angel investors can provide value to the firm and are critical to its success because of their previous experience building and managing entrepreneurial firms.

The track record, however, shows that angel-backed firms perform substantially worse than professionally backed companies. While both angel investors and venture capitalists have invested in many successful firms, venture capital–backed firms tend to raise more money, grow more quickly, and have substantially higher market shares.[5] The venture-backed companies also have more patents, and venture capital–financed firms are many times more valuable. Venture capital–backed firms, as we will show in chapter 4, also perform significantly better than similar nonventure capital–backed companies after they go public. Venture capitalists select better companies at the beginning and add value to their companies that is sustainable in the long run.

Banks are also an important source of start-up financing for a subset of new businesses. Many firms borrow directly from a commercial bank to build a new plant or facility or to buy new equipment. Companies that lack substantial tangible assets, those that have a large degree of uncertainty about their future, or those that will endure several years of losses prior to earning money are unlikely to receive bank loans. In fact, the amount of bank credit available to young start-ups has dropped dramatically over the past twenty years.[6] Today, most start-up firms face many years of negative earnings and are unable to make the interest and principal payments that would be required on a bank loan. It is difficult for these firms to get the necessary outside financing to fund their projects from any other source of capital than venture capital. It is this inability that hampers growth of new business in many countries. Venture capital can be viewed as a means of overcoming the capital constraints facing these firms.

How Venture Capital Operates

If the four factors that we present are the problems, then what are the solutions? The techniques used by venture groups—from the sharing of investments across different venture groups to the provision of capital in stages, their intensive scrutiny of firms before the investment, and their monitoring of firms afterwards—can be seen as solutions to the four problems. Entrepreneurs often resist these controls, striving to retain ownership of the firm at all costs. However, the venture capitalist can help create a far more valuable company, and, in many cases, entrepreneurs would be far better off owning a smaller piece of a much bigger pie. Chapter 3 examines how venture capitalists structure their investments and why these innovative financing and deal-screening mechanisms can be seen as a direct response to the four factors discussed above.

The venture capital solution to the problems of new, high-potential ventures has several implications for entrepreneurs. First, the entrepreneur must understand the key risks in the venture. Venture capital is a very specialized source of financing, which is appropriate only in certain cases. The corner convenience store is probably not an appropriate venture capital candidate!

Second, as the company evolves, the ideal sources of capital may change, and the speed with which the firm can switch financing sources—for example, by going public or relying more heavily on bank loans—will vary with the evolution of the business. The venture capitalist is a critical link to these other sources of capital that the entrepreneur could not tap on her own. Once they have raised venture capital, start-ups often access other sources of financing quite rapidly. For instance, Bang Networks, an Internet infrastructure start-up, raised nearly $10 million of debt in August 2000, even though it was only a few months old, primarily because of the reputation of Sequoia Capital, its venture capital backer.[7] On its own, Bang Networks would have been shown the door by the potential lenders. With the help of Sequoia, however, they received offers of debt financing from six different lenders. Venture capitalists can be instrumental in providing access to new financing and crafting financing strategies that provide a cushion for future strategic decisions.

Finally, while the controls that venture capitalists demand may be essential, they also create the potential for abuse. A venture capitalist's reputation for fairness is the only assurance an entrepreneur has of being treated with respect. Established venture groups typically care deeply about their reputation for treating entrepreneurs fairly and openly, even in settings where the day-to-day control of the company is ultimately transferred to someone else. Firms like Accel Partners, Battery Ventures, Bessemer Venture Partners, Charles River Ventures, Greylock Partners, Kleiner Perkins Caufield & Byers, Matrix Partners, Mayfield Fund, and Venrock Associates have ascended to the ranks of top venture investors because they have developed a reputation that entrepreneurs value.

The overall importance of the venture capital industry for U.S. economic development is explored in chapter 4. We show that venture capitalists have created nearly one third of the total market value of all public companies in the United States. This value is highly concentrated in technology industries where venture capital financing is responsible for the vast majority of companies, sales, and employment. We also demonstrate that venture capitalists have a positive operational impact on the companies that they finance. These companies grow more quickly, attain greater market share in their industries, and continue to outperform nonventure capital–financed companies even after they go public. We also show that venture capital has dramatically increased the rate of innovation in the economy. Much of the increase in innovation growth rates and commercial applications of technology over the last twenty years can be directly related to the investments made by venture capitalists.

The regional effects of venture investments are also examined. We explore how regions like Route 128 in Massachusetts and Silicon Valley in California have benefited from the concentration of venture investments. These investments have spurred regional growth and have increased the number of highly paid, skilled jobs in the local economy. The efforts by various local and state governments to foster venture capital can, in large part, be tied to the highly visible success of these regions.

Part 2: The Venture Capitalist's Challenge

We then look at the other side of the coin: the challenges confronting venture capitalists. These professionals must find the most effective way to pursue promising opportunities while building a sustainable franchise.

In chapters 5 and 6, we explore the forces that determine a healthy venture capital sector and tease out the dynamics behind the notoriously cyclical nature of the industry. We also take a closer look at the explosive growth that characterized the industry in the 1990s as well as the potential excesses seen in the market by 2000.

In the second part of the book, we examine the essential challenge facing the venture capital groups themselves. We begin in chapter 5 by exploring the determinants of venture capital activity. What are the legal, regulatory, and economic factors that affect the interest of investors to put money into venture capital funds (the supply of venture capital) on the one hand and the desire of researchers and managers to become entrepreneurs (the demand for venture capital) on the other? Understanding the supply and demand implications of regulatory policy decisions and macroeconomic fundamentals provides a backdrop to understand how the U.S. venture capital has enjoyed meteoric growth.

In order to do their job effectively, venture capitalists must build up the "franchise value" of the firm; that is, they must build an organization whose reputation attracts both high-quality young venture capitalists and high-potential entrepreneurial business plans. Building a successful firm also implies growing the size of the money that it manages. Larger venture capital organizations can pay talented young general partners and continue to invest in all stages of a firm's growth. The very process of growth, however, can undermine the effectiveness of the group. This management challenge is only made more intense by the "boom and bust" appetite for venture capital investments on the part of limited partners. Pension funds, which provide the bulk of capital to the industry, have often been erratic and unpredictable in their allocations to new venture capital funds. The state of the venture capital market today and the concerns about the technology sector can be tied to many of these excesses in the venture capital industry. Chapter 6 examines the implications of the boom and bust nature of the venture industry.

Being well known and having a good track record is critical to venture capital success. For instance, Benchmark Capital, which had a string of Internet winners, including eBay, PlanetRx, Scient, CacheFlow, and Juniper Networks, attracted literally hundred of business plans each month. As a premier Internet venture capitalist, their involvement was actively sought out by entrepreneurs. An investment by such a venture group will also open doors for the new firm at top law firms and investment banks.

Success, however, has a downside. As firms have grown rapidly, they have often experienced substantial setbacks. With so much capital to invest, they may feel pressured to "do deals," even if no good investments are to be found. The types of transactions that made the fund successful in the first place may no longer be practical, and the group may find itself drifting into areas where it has little special advantage. In recent years, growth in the demand for investments in venture capital has given venture fund managers more leverage over their limited partners. Venture groups such as Sequoia, Hummer Winblad Venture Partners, Charles River, and Brentwood Venture Capital have raised their take of their funds' profits, and others have imposed burdensome terms on their investors. This type of opportunistic behavior is likely to encourage limited partners to "take back" gains when the market gets smaller.

This apparent contradiction has led many industry observers to conclude that the venture industry is inherently unstable and is destined to be characterized by boom-and-bust cycles. And the behavior of the institutions that invest in these funds has only reinforced this conclusion. All too often, institutional investments have been characterized by a "boom-bust" process, which has made the pressures on venture capitalists even greater.

Finally, to understand the firm's future direction, careful tracking and assessing of the group's performance, both positive and negative, is necessary. In many firms, younger partners do the lion's share of the work, but receive a relatively modest share of the profits. Such scenarios have led to the recent breakup of major venture capital firms, including Burr, Egan, Deleage and Technology Venture Investors, as younger general partners sought to start their own firms.

Part 3: The Emulator's Challenge

In chapters 7 through 9, we raise a question that should interest anyone who manages innovative projects in large companies: Can corporations adapt and benefit from the techniques that have proven so effective for venture investors? After all, large corporations encounter hurdles similar to those of the entrepreneur: How can they bring the necessary resources to bear on exciting business ideas so as to capture value from their innovation? Governments, too, have struggled to stimulate entrepreneurial "clusters" in their economies—knowing that commercializing innovation can spell the difference between mere survival and a dominant position on the global business stage. These chapters also describe the ways in which governments and other public entities around the world have put venture capital principles and processes to work—and the lessons they've learned.

With the increasing visibility of venture capital industry success stories in recent years, a third set of players has emerged: the emulators. Corporations, academic and other non-profit organizations, along with governments in the United States and abroad, have increasingly sought to harness the power of the venture capital model. Yet their efforts, often misconceived, have failed. One example is Boston University, which in the early 1980s tried to harness the creativity of its faculty by establishing a venture fund. The poorly executed effort resulted in the school investing almost $100 million, or one-half of its endowment, in a single, ultimately unsuccessful biotechnology company, Seragen.

The rationale for these efforts is clear. Corporations and academic institutions, like entrepreneurs, want to reap the rewards of their innovations. Traditional corporate planning processes, while able to marshal vast resources for incremental projects, often prove ineffective in these settings. For instance, managers may be reluctant to ruthlessly terminate failing projects because they fear the decision will reflect poorly on them. The venture capital model provides a powerful and disciplined alternative way of approaching investment decisions in settings with substantial uncertainty.

The record of emulators' venture programs, however, has been quite mixed. Most corporate and academic programs are abandoned after only a few years. Even seemingly successful programs such as Xerox Technology Ventures (XTV) have been abandoned. Chapter 7 explores the limitations and constraints placed on corporate venture capital activity. Can these problems, however, be avoided in the future? Is the current interest in corporate venture capital bound to go the way of previous corporate investment waves? Or can corporations utilize and adapt insights from the independent venture capital sector to harness value from their innovations? The answers to these questions are complex, but the insights of the independent venture capital sector provide a benchmark.

Public sector efforts to promote venture capital do not appear to have fared any better than corporate efforts. Most government efforts, as we show in chapter 8, have also proved to be costly failures. In Germany, for instance, more than 600 government programs encouraged venture activity between 1965 and 1995, with few appreciable benefits.[8] In the United States, programs like the Department of Commerce's Advanced Technology Program (ATP) have disbursed over $1 billion to small high-technology businesses over the past ten years, with few tangible results.[9]

The final group of emulators that we explore in chapter 9 is foreign countries. Professional venture capital has its roots in the United States and, until recently, was largely concentrated in North America. In the 1990s, however, a fundamental transformation began taking place around the globe. Government officials and industry leaders began to recognize the importance of harnessing the innovative capabilities of venture capital. The United States had become dominant in many areas of emerging technologies because venture capital proved to be such a potent stimulus for innovation and commercialization of technology. Policies were enacted to lower taxes, ease labor regulations, and develop public markets for emerging companies in an effort to seed an environment that would be conducive to the development of a vibrant venture capital sector. Some of these programs were highly successful. Others, however, have had only minor effects on activity.

In short, venture capital has a major role in transforming the U.S. economy. The desire on the part of corporate and government officials to emulate its workings is understandable, but translating the venture model poses a number of hazards. While being aware of these pitfalls cannot guarantee success, corporations and other emulators can substantially increase their probability of doing well.

The Future of Venture Capital

In the book's final chapter, we speculate on the future of the venture capital industry. In many respects, this industry is rapidly transforming itself from a small, artisan business to a professional service organization. We highlight this transformation and the forces behind this transformation. We examine its implications for the professionals in the industry—and for the people and organizations they serve.

Recent changes in the industry are prompting many venture groups to rethink their organizational structure and strategies. The increasing sophistication of investors and entrepreneurs, the concentration of capital in fewer hands, and the increasing competition in the industry have led many venture organizations to professionalize their activities.

The venture investment process is being transformed by three factors. First, the entry of large state pension funds in large-scale investing has become a major force in the venture industry. For example, the California Public Employees Retirement System's board shifted its allocation to private equity from 4 percent to 6 percent with a 10 percent target in May 2000. Similarly, individual investors have become increasingly interested in investing in venture funds.

The second force driving change in the venture capital industry is the increasing role that intermediaries are playing in the industry. This is the inevitable consequence of inexperienced and widely dispersed investors who need assistance. This has meant that venture fund-raising process is becoming increasingly intermediated and efficient as a result.

The final dynamic is the shifting allocation of investment dollars. Traditionally, during venture capital booms, many inexperienced groups would enter the venture market. During market downturns, however, there was a "flight to quality." The most recent fund-raising boom, however, has been very different: we have seen increasing concentration of venture capital under management, which can only be expected to accelerate in upcoming years.

What are likely to be the successful responses to these changes? We identify three critical responses. First, the importance of building fee income will increase. Second, successful venture groups will need to spend fee income to build the infrastructure needed to provide services to their portfolio companies. Finally, venture capital firms will have to invest in ways to enhance their visibility.

The end result of these forces is that successful venture capital firms must use their fees to create a larger and more institutionalized venture capital organization. This will entail reengineering the venture capital process. Growth in the industry, however, has meant that individual partners are serving on more boards than in past. Intense competition in many industry segments means more demands on the partner from the entrepreneur. The challenge is how to leverage general partners' scarce time and how to improve quality of assistance offered to portfolio firms. We show that the successful venture capital organizations will be those that can invent new ways to manage their businesses and professionalize their operations. What will emerge from this period will be large, branded venture capital organizations that maintain a dominant position in the industry. Fringe venture capital organizations will need to focus on niche markets and will find it difficult to enter these top strata of venture organizations.

With the recent rise in interest in the venture industry, numerous books on the subject have appeared. Most of them have sought to profile venture capital firms, but few actually dig into the fundamental problems inherent in the industry. Similarly, many of the books do not take a critical view of the venture capital process and many of the particular pitfalls that the industry has fallen into over the past several years. By contrast, this book starts by providing a framework by which the financial issues of entrepreneurial firms can be understood. This book also examines the fundamental lessons that can be applied by entrepreneurs, corporate executives, policy makers, and university officials who hope to capitalize on their innovative activities. By taking this fresh approach to the subject, we hope to provide an important reference for practitioners wishing to gain insights into the venture process and who want to put those insights into practice.

PART

I

The
Entrepreneur's
Challenge

∎

Most high-technology entrepreneurs are convinced that they have exciting and dynamic ideas. At the same time, they rarely have the capital to
see their ideas to fruition and must rely on outside financiers. The skepticism with which potential investors approach their concepts, and their
demands for substantial equity and control, are quite disturbing to entrepreneurs. It is no wonder many entrepreneurs try to avoid raising venture
capital, often severely damaging their company's prospects in the process.

What most entrepreneurs do not see clearly, however, are the risks
facing their businesses. In chapter 2, we explore how most entrepreneurial ventures have a number of fundamental problems that make them difficult to finance. These difficulties can be sorted into four critical factors:
uncertainty, information gaps, soft assets, and market conditions.

The first of these four problems, *uncertainty,* is a measure of the array
of potential outcomes for a company or project. The wider the dispersion
of potential outcomes, the greater the uncertainty. By their very nature,
young and restructuring companies are associated with significant levels
of uncertainty. Uncertainty surrounds the question of whether the research program or new product will succeed. The response of a firm's
rivals may also be uncertain.

The second factor is *information gaps.* Because of his day-to-day involvement with the firm, an entrepreneur knows more about his company's prospects than investors, suppliers, or strategic partners. Without
the ability to screen out unacceptable projects and entrepreneurs, investors are unable to make appropriate decisions regarding where and

when to invest. Information gaps may also lead to problems after the investment is made.

The third factor affecting a firm's corporate and financial strategy is *soft assets*. It is much more difficult for an investor to estimate the value of soft assets, such as trade secrets, than hard assets, such as machines, building, or land. Therefore, raising outside financing from traditional sources may be more challenging.

Market conditions also play a key role in determining the difficulty of financing firms. Both the financial and product markets may be subject to substantial variations. The supply of capital from public investors and the price at which this capital is available may vary dramatically. If there is exceedingly intense competition or a great deal of uncertainty about the size of the potential market, firms may find it very difficult to raise capital from traditional sources.

In chapter 3 we explore the various approaches used by venture capitalists in response to these difficulties. By intensively scrutinizing firms before making investments, and monitoring them afterwards with equal intensity, the venture investor can effectively overcome these barriers. Each of the mechanisms employed by venture groups—from sharing of investments across different venture groups to the provision of capital in stages—can be seen as ways to deal with the risks involved in start-ups.

Venture capitalists have had a dramatic impact on the overall economic landscape in the United States. We explore the important contribution of venture capital in chapter 4. The dramatic improvements in performance following venture capital financing for individual firms, the overall impact on innovation, jobs, and wealth, as well as the regional implications of the venture capital industry are documented in detail. The lasting contribution of this industry has far outpaced the impact of large corporate investment.

2

The Problem:
Financing
Entrepreneurial Firms

■

Ninety percent of new entrepreneurial businesses that don't attract venture capital fail within three years.

A software engineer at the government contractor EG&G, Don Brooks had been working on computer systems for the Idaho National Engineering and Environment Laboratory, a Department of Energy facility, when he suddenly had a brainstorm that he knew would help him as well as others solve an all-too-common problem.[1] Using the "gopher" technology that had long made the exchange of files and programs across mainframe devices possible, in 1991 Brooks developed a way for one computer to access data stored on another and to interact with that information. As he publicized his innovation among his fellow employees and across the computing community, people admired the quality of his work. In fact, in head-to-head comparisons, his software program garnered ratings far superior to those of Mosaic, a similar tool then under development at the University of Illinois. Reviewers of Brooks's prototype raved about its ease of use and reliability. The engineer felt certain that, with EG&G's backing, his idea would soon be a major success in the marketplace.

But his hopes were not realized. Four years later, another company working on the same technology went public to great acclaim and fanfare. The firm? Netscape Communications, under the leadership of Marc Andreessen and Jim Clark.[2] Because its new product was based on the Mosaic technology developed at the University of Illinois, Netscape became embroiled in a messy intellectual-property dispute. Despite these challenges, on its first day of trading, Netscape soared to a market capitalization of $2.1 billion.

Why did Andreessen and Clark succeed where Brooks failed? Part of the answer lies in the role of Netscape's initial financiers, the venture capital firm Kleiner Perkins Caufield & Byers. While Brooks struggled to interest EG&G in backing his concept (EG&G considered Brooks's idea outside its core business), Kleiner Perkins moved decisively to fund the fledging Netscape, realizing that market timing was critical to the success of the new venture. In addition to providing financing and advice on product development, marketing, and finance, Kleiner introduced Netscape to key Silicon Valley players, as well as the investment banking teams at Morgan Stanley and Hambrecht & Quist. Even more telling is that Jim Clark, cofounder of Netscape, had been a highly successful entrepreneur at Silicon Graphics and could have easily financed the firm himself. Instead, he understood the value that Kleiner Perkins could bring to Netscape. Lacking such assistance, Brooks soon fell far behind his rivals.

Like Brooks, most high-technology entrepreneurs are convinced that their ideas hold immense promise. Often, their excitement is well founded. An innovative product or new service concept may have enormous market potential and may far outperform competitors' alternatives. Moreover, the intellectual talents of the founding team may be stellar.

However, many of these entrepreneurs discover they need to attract money to fully commercialize their concepts. Thus they must find investors—such as their own employer (if the idea was created while on staff), a bank, an "angel" financier, a public stock offering, or some other source. But potential investors often greet entrepreneurs' business plans with skepticism, or worse, turn them down entirely. Alternatively, some investors demand a large equity stake in the project and tight control rights in exchange for a modest sum of money.

Before the emergence of the venture capital market, the vast majority of entrepreneurs seeking financing from traditional sources failed to realize value from their ideas. Indeed, many product or service innovators privately (and sometimes publicly) referred to investment professionals as "vulture capitalists." These entrepreneurs' frustrations are understandable: Most financiers do not understand the fragile growth process that start-ups experience.

But entrepreneurs themselves have also contributed to their own financing problems. Many of them simply don't have a clear picture of the risks inherent in their business models—risks that pose some serious concerns for potential investors—or they lack a thorough understanding of the four basic problems that can limit financiers' willingness to invest capital, which we outlined in the introduction to this section:

- Uncertainty about the future

- Information gaps

- "Soft" assets

- Volatility of current market conditions

All companies must grapple with these difficulties, but young, emerging enterprises are particularly vulnerable to them, as these problems limit their ability to receive value from their ideas and innovations. This chapter will help both entrepreneurs and potential investors understand these financing hurdles and the various mechanisms that can be used to reduce potential conflicts that arise due to these four factors.

Uncertainty About the Future

There's no getting around it: Innovation is risky business. All entrepreneurial individuals and companies face uncertainty about the future—not only in terms of their own development possibilities, but also in terms of market and industry trends.[3] But a word of caution: Many people who are interested in the investment world confuse *uncertainty* with that which *is unknown* or *unknowable.* In the case of something that is unknowable, no amount of research or analysis will lift the fog. However, for young, entrepreneurial firms, uncertainty doesn't have to mean unknowability. Rather, uncertainty can be viewed as *a measure of the distribution of possible outcomes for a company or project.* The greater the uncertainty, the wider the distribution of potential outcomes.

This distinction between uncertainty and unknowability is critical. A careful analysis of a particular entrepreneurial project can identify key phases of uncertainty, yield a list of potential outcomes of each phase, and provide an assessment of the likelihood of those various outcomes. This kind of thoughtful review constitutes the first step in determining a project's financing alternatives.

A Closer Look at Uncertainty

Bill Aulet had to make a decision when he joined SensAble Technologies in 1995.[4] While completing a Sloan Fellowship at MIT, Aulet had become excited by an opportunity to pursue entrepreneurship with the company, founded by recent MIT graduate Tom Massie. Massie had developed a computer peripheral that simulated physical resistance, a device that might have had applications for some highly specialized areas, such as training doctors in surgical techniques. Aulet, who had served for years as a marketing manager at IBM, had a different idea in mind. He felt that potential investors would be far more excited about the technology if it were used to deliver games to players via the Internet. However, when he began to put together feasible estimates of the size of this online market in upcoming years, as well as the market share that SensAble might be able to capture, uncertainty surfaced at each stage of his analysis. For example, how rapidly would delivery of computer games switch over to the Internet? What would the pricing structure look like? How likely was it that SensAble would capture a significant portion of the proceeds? In order to make a decision that would take into account the uncertainties that SensAble faced, Aulet would need to explore the possibilities of each scenario, assess the range of potential outcomes, and set out a plan for the company.

The Many Shapes of Uncertainty

If we view uncertainty as the range of potential outcomes for a project or idea, then we can get a deeper understanding of the uncertainty faced by a firm by examining the *distribution* of potential outcomes.

There are four possible types of uncertainty distribution. Thinking about an innovation in terms of one of these distributions can provide a useful benchmark for gauging the uncertainty involved:

- Does the potential distribution of outcomes resemble the traditional bell-shaped curve, with a peak in the middle and tails running in either direction? To illustrate, the demand for a new toy being developed by an entrepreneur could be very high or very low. The most likely case, however, would be somewhere in between.

- Is the potential outcome discrete, with a limited number of identifiable outcomes? For example, the potential approval of a new drug by the Food and Drug Administration (FDA) has a discrete distribution. After reviewing all the information, the FDA will either approve the drug for sale or else it will reject it.

Figure 2-1   Potential Outcome Distributions

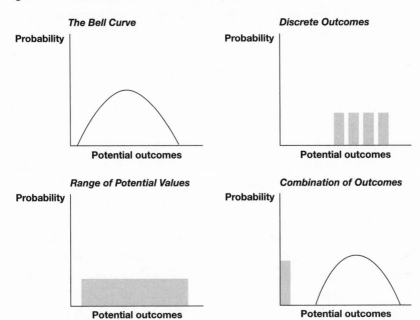

- Is there a range of values for which the potential outcome is equally likely? For example, an entrepreneur who is bidding to supply all or part of the manufacturing required by a major corporation may believe that the likelihood of providing none of the manufacturing is equal to the likelihood of supplying all or half of it.

- Is there a combination of possible distributions? For example, the demand for a new generation of personal digital assistant (PDA) may be zero under certain circumstances, but exhibit a traditional bell curve over another set of circumstances.

Breaking a firm's development into discrete stages of uncertainty can help inventors *and* investors grasp a company's evolving financial needs and market potential. For example, back in 1989, Pascal Brandys, a venture capitalist, and Marc Vasseur, a research geneticist, founded Genset, a biotechnology company.[5] Its goal? To initiate research on the commercial applications of a new genetic technology, polymerase chain reaction (PCR), which allowed scientists to create millions of copies of a single DNA fragment. Although the technology had immense potential, at the time no one could predict with certainty what kinds of commercial markets Genset might ultimately develop, or when commercial applications would be available. Still, Brandys and Vasseur needed to develop a business and financial strategy that would let them learn from their efforts and continue to guide the company as events unfolded. Similarly, potential investors needed to know how to evaluate progress at the firm, limit potential losses, and create enough potential return to justify their investment.

We can break down Genset's uncertainty into several distinct phases. In the first phase, Brandys and Vasseur needed to determine whether the new PCR technology could lead to any viable commercial products. This uncertainty had several discrete outcomes. The initial research would either yield a technology breakthrough that had market potential or it would fail. Nevertheless, Vasseur's technological experience, combined with Brandys's background as a venture capital investor in biotechnology companies, gave the two men confidence that if the technology did have commercial applications, those applications would have great potential value.

In the second phase, uncertainty hinged on government and regulatory approvals. This phase had outcomes over a broad spectrum of possibilities. However, the history of drug approvals in various medical markets helped Brandys and Vasseur estimate the various probabilities; for instance, it is known that once a drug reaches stage III clinical trials, it has a two-thirds chance of approval. By clarifying the types of uncertainty Genset faced, Brandys and Vasseur were able to decide on a strategic direction, one that would poise them to take full advantage of any discovered commercial applications.

Uncertainty may also arise in the form of competitors' responses to the introduction of a new product. For example, Netscape's Jim Clark and Marc Andreessen wrestled over the possible initial response of Microsoft to the introduction of Netscape's browser in the mid-1990s.[6] Netscape had developed a product that ultimately captured nearly 90 percent of the market. They knew that other companies would try to grab some of the action, but their most feared competitor was Microsoft. To develop an effective business and financing strategy, Clark and Andreessen needed to gauge Microsoft's likely response. Would Bill Gates's behemoth ignore the Internet as it had in the past, or would it pounce on the fledgling Netscape? Clark and Andreessen couldn't predict with certainty what shape an offensive from Microsoft would take. This aspect of Netscape's "uncertainty picture" influenced the company's key financial decisions, including their decision to raise a substantial amount of capital in their IPO.

The Financial Implications of an Entrepreneur's Uncertainty

While it's relatively easy to point out the various forms that uncertainty takes, it's far more difficult to quantify their financial implications. Uncertainty affects investors' willingness to contribute capital, suppliers' desire to extend credit, and managers' decisions as they set direction for their company.

Rob Brooker, an American entrepreneur who started a chain of bagel shops in Hungary in the early 1990s, experienced these difficulties first-hand when trying to raise additional capital for his venture.[7] With democracy only just emerging in the country, Brooker couldn't predict what shape Hungary's economic policy would take in the future. Despite the first stirrings of democratic thinking, old bureaucrats still wielded considerable influence in the Hungarian business community. Moreover, various government agencies levied onerous taxes at each stage of the business-development process. Similarly, while the Hungarian market had proved fertile ground for American products such as Levi jeans and McDonald's hamburgers, Brooker couldn't know for certain what kind of appetite for bagels Hungarians might have.

Brooker thus faced a daunting range of possible outcomes—including the large possibility that the venture would fail. The potential upside for just such a business, however, appeared quite limited. The likely market for a chain of bagel shops in Hungary, even for a first mover like Brooker, looked somewhat small. In his search for capital, Brooker got a lukewarm response from the investors he courted. Many of them contributed small amounts of initial capital but dragged their feet about advancing additional funds. They wanted to see Brooker prove the concept first. Similarly, many of Brooker's suppliers, most of whom were located outside Hungary, hesitated to provide credit because of the business's unclear future. Suppliers of capital often look to the achievement of definable milestones as a sign that some of the uncertainty has been resolved. Because Brooker hadn't yet reached those milestones, he couldn't attract as much capital as he wanted. As a result, Brooker ultimately had to sell off the assets of his company at a loss.

Problems can also crop up if outside investors and entrepreneurs perceive uncertainty differently. Though most finance and economic research assumes that people always act rationally and make appropriate decisions given their knowledge about future outcomes, a growing body of research shows that individuals make decisions based on *biased* assessments of information.[8] These assessments are powerfully influenced by people's beliefs about themselves and the workings of business. Most entrepreneurs are certain that their venture will succeed—despite the fact that nearly half of all venture capital–backed companies don't fulfill their potential, and nearly one-third go out of business. For newly launched enterprises without venture capital backing, failure is almost assured: nearly 90 percent fail within three years.

Jack Taub's story is a case in point.[9] A successful pioneer in online data communications, Taub wanted to provide data infrastructure to the developing world. He hoped to use this infrastructure to create a global wireless network that would advance education and business in underserved markets. Convinced that his vision of a global wireless data-communication network would become a reality, he foresaw no significant obstacles to his plans.

Investors, however, were reluctant to fund the venture because of the uncertainties they perceived. For one thing, Taub did not yet have in place elements critical to the success of the technology, such as a network of satellites. What's more, governments in these developing countries would have to adopt Taub's communication standards and be willing to guarantee revenues for each project.

Though Taub met with investment bankers, venture capitalists, and corporate partners, and impressed many with his vision, he didn't see the uncertainties of his venture in the same light as his potential investors, and so did not feel the need to change any aspect of his business plan. The result? He failed to raise the capital he needed to proceed with the venture.

Such exaggerated and unwarranted optimism on the part of entrepreneurs can not only ruin their chances of getting funding, it can also spawn intense conflict over strategy and management policy between investors and innovators. For example, entrepreneurs will almost always choose to continue spending money to market their product or develop their technology—even when the evidence clearly shows that they should abandon their efforts. Similarly, overly optimistic entrepreneurs may feel compelled to expand their firm's capacity beyond its requirements because they overestimate the future demand for their products.

Just as entrepreneurs' oblivion to risk can scare investors away, so can too strong an aversion to risk.[10] In such cases, innovators may avoid making risky but essential decisions because they fear losing what they already have. Many entrepreneurs, for example, invest all their personal resources in their new businesses. When the time comes to commit the firm to a direction that carries substantial risk, entrepreneurs whose sole source of wealth is their ownership in their companies may freeze or adopt a highly conservative stance. Overly cautious decision making can cause outside investors to miss out on potentially valuable new opportunities.

Information Gaps

Young, entrepreneurial firms—along with their potential investors—face another potential pitfall in the capitalization process. This second pitfall comes in the form of information gaps; that is, differences in what various players know about a company's internal workings and prospects, market trends, and other information vital for investment decisions. Entrepreneurs and investors alike risk making unwise decisions because neither possesses a complete picture of reality. Often, the fear of such gaps can render firms incapable of completing transactions that would be beneficial.

Innovators' Informational Advantages

In the natural course of running a company, entrepreneurs learn more about a particular technology than outsiders can hope to glean. They also know more about what happens inside their company on a day-to-day basis. They may choose to keep this information private for several reasons. Perhaps they hope to keep proprietary information from finding its way into competitors' hands. Or they want to protect the benefits they receive from managing their own companies, including the prestige and perks that come with the job. Such entrepreneurs may even try to inflate their firm's performance reports to present an attractive package to investors.

The story of Ovation Technology vividly captures what can happen when innovators withhold or distort information about their firm's progress.[11] In the early 1980s, Tom Gregory and a group of his colleagues from a minicomputer software company decided to enter the personal computer software market and compete head-to-head with Lotus and Microsoft. The company they founded, Ovation Technology, raised over $6 million in venture capital financing. Gregory and his founding team possessed extensive marketing backgrounds but scant technical skills.

So, perhaps not surprisingly, Gregory's team decided to spend substantial resources on marketing—at the expense of research and product development.

Out of the gate, Ovation began spreading the word about major improvements in functionality that their program would offer over their competitors. Its polished advertising campaign excited the imaginations of potential customers and investors, and gave them the impression that the company was thriving. Current investors, however, found it difficult to gauge the progress of the company. Although Ovation gave them glowing reports of the company's supposedly significant strides, they never presented a completed prototype. In fact, the company never finished developing its product—and never made a significant sale. If the founders had shared the necessary information with investors, perhaps Ovation's venture capitalists could have guided Gregory along the development path and this failure could have been averted.

In addition to inside knowledge about a company, entrepreneurs may have far more knowledge about market dynamics than investors—a situation that can lead to unnecessary and unfortunate conflict between the two parties. Hira Thapliyal, president, CEO, and founder of Arthrocare, a medical devices company, experienced this phenomenon firsthand.[12] In 1997, Thapliyal had received market feedback from his company's first product launch. The product, a laser-based surgical scalpel, had not penetrated the orthopedic market as successfully as Arthrocare had hoped. In order to succeed, the company needed to price the base units more aggressively and continue to invest heavily in the research and development needed to expand Arthrocare's product line into new surgical markets.

Though he was convinced that this strategy made sense in the long run, Thapliyal also knew that it would cause a temporary decline in earnings. Arthrocare had recently gone public, and Thapliyal tried to calm shareholders' anxiety about the potential decline. Over the long haul, he maintained, the new strategy was in their best interest. When news of the earnings shortfall came out, however, many investors sold their shares. The price of Arthrocare stock plummeted.

Thapliyal had failed to convince outside investors that his strategy made sense for several reasons. First, the investors did not have in-depth knowledge of the market and thus could not understand Arthrocare's strategy. Second, Thapliyal withheld other vital information—such as what Arthrocare's marketing and pricing program would look like—to avoid compromising Arthrocare's market position. Thapliyal's inability to credibly bridge this information gap ultimately cost him his job as president and CEO of Arthrocare.

In addition to inside knowledge about a company's workings and market trends, innovators also know much more about their firm's prospects than outside investors do. Daily contact with the market provides constant feedback about how likely it is that the firm's research will bear fruit, what plans competitors have up their sleeves, what customers think of a product, or who might offer to finance the firm in the next round of capitalization. Outside investors can't easily obtain or verify this kind of information.

In other instances, a venture's milestones are difficult to identify; thus potential investors have no way to judge the firm's progress. For example, there may be no clear method for gauging the likelihood of market acceptance of a new product. Similarly, evaluating the qualitative differences between a start-up's new product and its existing offerings may be difficult until a large number of customers have used the product for a long period of time. In these cases, entrepreneurs and investors must rely on their own subjective assessments to gauge the firm's progress. And just as innovators and financiers can disagree over what kind of uncertainty is facing a new firm, they can also define a company's progress in radically different ways.

A recent lawsuit between a high-tech company and its venture capital investors illustrates what can happen when disagreement over how to define a firm's progress arises.[13] The founder of the company—a telecommunications switching firm—was an engineer with years of experience researching new designs for faster switches. He had raised financing from a venture capital firm to develop a prototype of a new communications switch with the promise of a second, more substantial round of financing upon completion of a working prototype. Several months later, the engineer claimed to have built a working switch, and the venture capitalist provided the second-stage financing. As it turned out, each party had a different definition of "working prototype." When the venture capital firm realized that the founder's definition differed from its own, it began investigating the actual performance of the founder's prototype. The disagreement between the founder and the venture capital firm ended up in a lawsuit. A significant amount of money and precious managerial time were lost due to the parties' failure to establish a common definition of success.

Investors' Informational Advantages

Information gaps can hamper entrepreneurs' efforts as much as investors'. Investors know more about their own resources or ability to add value than an entrepreneur can discover. And despite a financier's claims that he has substantial contacts in the industry or important knowledge of the market in question, innovators can't always verify these claims. As the following example shows, this creates the risk of entering into a bad deal.

In 1992, Michael and Richard Weissman, founders of the day care franchiser Tutor Time, attracted the attention of a potential business partner at a childcare trade show.[14] Tutor Time had been looking for a strategic partner to help in expanding to other markets around the country. This potential partner claimed that he was involved in a number of businesses, including childcare and real estate development. He produced financial statements that indicated he was worth several million dollars. He also claimed to have an interest in one of the nation's twenty-five largest real estate development companies. Tutor Time's founders believed that their new partner could provide the capital and real estate expertise they needed for Tutor Time to go national quickly. Within weeks, the Weissmans and the investor had formed a joint venture to develop and market Tutor Time childcare centers across the country.

As it turned out, many of the investor's prior projects were teetering on the brink of insolvency, and his financial statement was a sham. Before the Weissmans discovered the deception, they had been saddled with a number of poorly bid lease build-outs for new day-care centers. Some of these sites were several hundred thousand dollars over budget before the Weissmans grasped the extent of the disaster. The fallout from the ill-advised partnership included lawsuits between Tutor Time affiliates and employees and between the unscrupulous investor and his associates.

Problems as a Result of Information Gaps

The problems that can arise from information gaps inhibit many traditional investors from funding entrepreneurial ventures. Entrepreneurs might take potentially harmful actions that investors are not aware of. For example, the entrepreneur may undertake a riskier strategy than initially suggested or may not work as hard as the investor expects. The entrepreneur might also invest in projects that build up her reputation at the investors' expense. Alternatively, even if the project has negative expected returns, the private benefits of "running his own show" may inspire an entrepreneur to continue.[15] For this reason—and others—an entrepreneur may, at times, try to inflate performance to avoid closing down his firm.

The example of Kendall Square Research illustrates how difficult it is to monitor the performance of start-up companies. A company founded in Cambridge, Massachusetts, Kendall Square Research raised over $100 million to develop a new generation of parallel computers.[16] The company fraudulently booked sales to "boost" performance in order to maintain the image of solvency and robust growth during a slowdown in government and university purchases of large, expensive machines. In July 1993, the company announced sales of $24.7 million. By the end of the year, it had restated the first nine months down to $10.6 million. At the same time, it revised its net loss for 1992 to $17.2 million from $12.7 million. When the company announced these changes, the stock price, which had been trading near $25 per share, dropped precipitously. Ultimately, the company was forced into liquidation. Entrepreneurs have considerable ability to manipulate the information that investors evaluate.

Information gaps exist in all aspects of business. Sometimes those gaps are purposeful because management or investors do not wish to disclose information that would compromise their position. Other times, the information cannot be easily and persuasively conveyed to another party. Even if the entrepreneur wanted to share such information with investors, outsiders might well misinterpret the information.

The experience of Rob Utschneider, founder of Torrent Systems, a Boston-based software start-up, illustrates this problem.[17] Torrent received early funding from the Department of Commerce's Advanced Technology Program (ATP). ATP funds precommercial, highly risky research and development, with the stipulation that *all* funding be used for direct research expenses. None of the grant money can be used for expenses that might have ties to commercial activity. Torrent had tried to make a clear distinction between the two areas and had raised additional money from North Bridge Venture Partners, a prominent Boston-based venture fund, to cover the project's other costs (including commercial activities).

Torrent made substantial progress developing its software and forged an agreement with IBM about future sales of the product. When the company casually announced the agreement in a press release, officials at ATP were alarmed, and wondered whether Torrent had used some of the ATP funding to engage in commercial activity. ATP's concern was understandable; that year, its administrators had come under intense scrutiny from a Republican Congress, which had its antennae out for "corporate welfare." If Congress thought that ATP was funding commercial ventures that could have been funded by private investors, it might cut off future funding.

Because ATP officials did not have day-to-day contact with Torrent, Utschneider failed to convince them that Torrent had acted in accordance with the rules of the program. The outcome? ATP sent a team of auditors to Torrent, and ultimately ceased its funding. The Torrent story shows how difficult it is for investors to distinguish between competent and incompetent (or trustworthy and untrustworthy) entrepreneurs—and how this difficulty can spawn inappropriate decisions.

Whatever the source, information gaps reduce investors' willingness to provide funds, increase the unease that suppliers have about extending credit, and hinder a firm's ability to recruit new employees. In addition, information gaps affect the types of financing investors give and the corporate control that investors require. Understanding these effects is a second critical step in understanding the financing hurdles facing young, technology-intensive companies.

Soft Assets

The value of all firms is dependent upon the assets it owns today and the investment opportunities it can undertake in the future. Assets in place today are either hard, physical assets such as buildings, machines, or real estate, or they can be soft, intangible assets such as patents, trademarks, or the collective ability of a company's employees, sometimes referred to as human capital. The availability of financing and the terms under which financing is provided depend heavily upon the nature of the firm's assets.

As hard assets are, in general, easier to value than soft assets, firms with hard assets often have more financing options than those with only soft assets. Most hard assets have active secondary markets for resale that allow the value of an asset to be easily determined. For example, real estate values can be assessed by looking at comparable buildings or parcels that have sold recently. Banks, leasing companies, and other lenders provide financing based on these simple hard-asset rules, with an eye toward how much they could recoup if they had to sell all the hard assets of the firm piecemeal. Most banks or financial lenders use strict formulas to determine how much money they are willing to lend a particular company—formulas based on a firm's physical assets rather than its potential value. An entrepreneurial firm outside Chicago, efficient market services (ems), offers a prime example of how this works.[18] ems was founded to provide consumer goods companies with information on how well their products were selling in grocery stores around the country. The company sought to leverage the information-technology revolution by providing an unprecedented service: timely, accurate, and store-specific inventory and pricing information on products sold through individual supermarkets. It believed that such information would help its customers optimize inventory levels, avoid backorders, establish appropriate pricing, and align promotional efforts with sales.

Though ems was clearly a technology-based start-up, its operations still required substantial physical assets, as it had to put one of its own computer workstations in every one of its thousands of partner supermarkets. Owing to this large, hard-asset investment, ems succeeded in raising almost $10 million in lease financing early in its development. The leasing company, Comdisco, felt confident in its ability to estimate the value of the computers that it was lending against, even if ems itself was a risky start-up.

Soft assets rarely have active markets that list their value. Each soft asset is unique—looking at the value of a recently sold patent would not provide much information about the value of another patent. For example, the 7-Up trademark, while similar in many ways to the Coke trademark, clearly does not have the same value. Drug patents, while related, are not perfect substitutes for one another. Because the value of a soft asset is difficult to estimate, lenders are less willing to provide credit against such an asset. Moreover, soft assets provide little cushion in case a company crashes.

Patents and Trademarks

Although more tangible than an idea, patents and trademarks themselves are not enough to enable a company to obtain financing from most lenders. A soft asset such as a patent may have value only when it is combined with other assets, such as an entrepreneur's knowledge of a particular process or technology that the patent involves. Similarly, the particular process or service embodied by a soft asset may be intimately related to the entrepreneur's reputation. In either case, if any other company tried to use the soft asset, its value would plummet.

The trouble with using patents as collateral can be seen in the example of RhoMed, a New Mexico–based medical-technology firm that had been spun off from the Los Alamos Laboratory, a U.S. Department of Energy national laboratory. RhoMed had few assets aside from several patents it had won for its diagnostic radiology testing and treatment technology.[19] After an intense quest for funding, RhoMed found a financier, Aberlyn Capital, which was willing to make a loan secured by a key RhoMed patent. Unfortunately, a key alliance fell through, and the firm was unable to repay its obligation to Aberlyn. When Aberlyn tried to recover its loss by marketing the patent, it ran into difficulty. Many firms regard a single patent as far less useful than a patent that is part of a broader portfolio. Other firms, correctly guessing that Aberlyn had little appetite for undertaking costly litigation to defend its patent, began using the technology without a license agreement. Aberlyn was left holding an asset that ultimately had no value.

Another problem with soft assets is that their value is often linked to the overall value of the company. For example, the trademark for a particular restaurant chain may retain its value only if the company remains in business. If the restaurant chain ceases operations, the trademark may lose its value due to the bad image of the company now in the customers' minds. No lender would be willing to bet on such a trademark.

Human Capital

The collective skill set of a firm's employees constitutes a vital competitive edge. But, how does a potential lender evaluate that skill set? Moreover, how does a lender recoup its losses through capturing the value inherent in a firm's workforce in the event of a business failure? Unlike buildings or machines, people can walk out a company's doors, go to work for a competitor, or start their own firm.

The story of Cambridge Technology Partners (CTP) is a case in point. In late 1998, Cambridge Technology Partners was considered a darling of the information technology-services world. Jim Sims had taken over as president and CEO of the company in 1991 and had built it into one of the premier IT consulting firms. He had assembled and nurtured a group of highly trained, highly motivated computer-science professionals who consistently delivered top-notch services to large clients. CTP's revenue exploded from less than $50 million in 1992 to more than $600 million in

1998. At the same time, its net income soared from $2.2 million in 1992 to $57 million in 1998.[20]

During 1999, however, the firm stumbled. Owing to some operational problems and difficulties integrating acquisitions, revenues plateaued in 1999 and earnings dropped to a little over $3 million that year. Investors took notice, and CTP's stock price, which had approached $60 per share in 1998, fell to just $10 per share. Employees with stock options that had exercise prices substantially above the prevailing stock-market price began leaving in droves, alarmed by the dwindling value of their compensation packages. In fact, the *best* employees were the first ones out the door. New, high-flying start-ups had courted them with jaw-dropping salaries, signing bonuses, and irresistible equity-ownership stakes. The value of Cambridge Technology Partners evaporated along with its consultants.

Future Investment Opportunities

Future investment opportunities, also known as real options, often constitute tremendous value. Genset, the biotechnology company discussed earlier, is a prime example. Pascal Brandys and Marc Vasseur entered the genetics industry in its early days without knowing what direction their company would take. However, they *did* know that by launching a research program in genetics, they would generate future investment opportunities as Genset's technology matured. By getting into the business early, they could accumulate essential competitive and market intelligence.

From the beginning, Genset brilliantly leveraged its early entry into the genetics arena. By focusing on genetics right away, Brandys and Vasseur learned about future commercial opportunities, eventually focusing the company's efforts on genomics, the mapping and study of human genes. Being the first to market let Genset take a global leadership position in genomics, even though no one could have predicted that any company would make money in the industry back in 1989, when Genset was founded. Early investors recognized Genset's unique positioning and future growth potential, and voted with their checkbooks—providing Genset with $2 million in seed financing and substantially more as it grew.

Not all companies are as lucky as Genset was, however. Like other soft assets, growth options are difficult to quantify, and thus to finance. Because they represent a firm's *future* ability to invest in new projects, the company cannot guarantee that such possibilities will translate into hard cash. Similarly, a specific growth option may have value only in the eyes of the innovator who proposed the original idea.

Firms that enter various industries may have little choice about the asset structure of the business. Some industries have a need for large, physical assets while others rely on softer, more ephemeral assets. What emerges from the discussion above, however, is that the nature of the firm's assets will have a large impact on the supply of financing and its terms.

Financial- and Product-Market Conditions

Financial and product markets can be alarmingly fluid. The supply of capital from public and private investors and the price at which this capital is available may vary depending on regulatory edicts or changes in investors' perceptions of future profitability. Thus investors' interest in a particular product or service idea may evaporate overnight, as in the case of business-to-consumer and business-to-business Internet start-ups. And the vitality of product markets may change with shifts in the intensity of competition or in the attitudes of customers. The competitive landscape may also change in an instant, as it did when more than a dozen pet retail sites were founded on the Internet in a short period of time, affecting a firm's current value and its potential profitability. Entrepreneurs must constantly evaluate the status of financial and product markets today and the direction they may take in the future.

Financial-Market Flaps

The experience of BioTransplant, a Boston-based firm, illustrates financial-market dynamism.[21] When the firm considered going public in 1994, everything looked on track. Its product developers had proposed some impressive technologies, and biotechnology stocks were trading at an all-time high. Under the leadership of Elliot Lebowitz, the company had raised several rounds of venture capital financing, had signed strategic alliances with major pharmaceutical companies, and had forged research-collaboration agreements with top transplantation research teams around the globe. The company had followed its strategic blueprints perfectly and had hit all its major milestones on target.

But everything changed later that year when Hillary Rodham Clinton began pursuing health care reform ideas and several high-profile drug failures sent biotechnology stock prices into a tailspin. Many private companies that had been waiting to go public were told by investment bankers that investors wouldn't touch their stock at any price. The opportunity to issue public equity had evaporated for BioTransplant, and the firm's future looked at best uncertain, at worst, grim. In the face of a funding drought, Lebowitz was forced to reevaluate both the firm's financial- and product-market strategies. Lebowitz learned a valuable lesson: Even the best-performing companies can have difficulty raising funding if their sector falls out of favor with the public market.

The decline in the stock-market value of many Internet companies in the spring of 2000 is another striking example of financial-market dynamism. Many Internet retailing companies attracted huge valuations before the severe market correction that came later in March and April 2000. The sudden dive in Internet stocks slammed this public market window shut.

This swing in market conditions had radical consequences for Internet retailers. Those who survived the correction now had no choice but to move from an exclusively growth-focused strategy (which had little regard for profits) to one that tried to generate true value. Many firms, including well-known firms like Pets.com and eToys, were forced to close their doors.

The Product-Market Pendulum

In additional to financial-market shifts, swings in product markets—primarily changes in competition—can hamstring start-ups' ability to establish market share, earn profits, and boost their value. Competition may also force start-ups into an escalating race of product enhancements that require tremendous research and development expenditures.

Regulatory intervention may also hamper a start-up's ability to enter a new market or expand its existing ones. Regulators may mandate price ceilings or insist on costly product features, both of which make profit generation more difficult. Similarly, although mergers among competitors may improve economies of scale, government regulations may prohibit them in the name of antitrust legislation. Finally, governments often actively seed competition in various markets through investment and tax incentives with the hope of increasing consumers' choices and decreasing their costs.

Star Cablevision illustrates the importance of product-market shifts in determining corporate value and financing decisions.[22] In 1990, Star's founder, Don Jones, had entertained bids from potential buyers. He had received several impressively large valuations and was deciding whether to sell part or all of the company. However, during this time several events occurred that drastically eroded Star's valuation. First, in response to consumer complaints, Congress introduced legislation to further regulate cable television rates. The new laws led many in the industry to lower their expectations of future cash flow forecasts. Second, several competitive threats appeared in the form of two satellite television companies offering programming through small, affordable dish antennae. The combination of these threats and the new, restrictive legislation turned buyers bearish, and Jones saw the acquisition price of his company fall by nearly 40 percent in a matter of months. His ability to attract future financing, both debt and equity, also suffered.

The Four Pitfalls of Capitalization: How Much Do They Matter?

The ability of a young company to grow rapidly and respond swiftly to changing competitive conditions is a key source of its competitive advantage, if not its survival. However, this ability is hindered by the four pitfalls that we've discussed: uncertainty, information gaps, soft assets, and changing market conditions. Entrepreneurs can go only so far in addressing these difficulties. But they need not be helpless. Among the steps they can take to overcome these obstacles are:

- Get a better sense of the risks in their industry and business and communicate these to investors.

- Enumerate and set clear goals and timelines to reduce information gaps.

- Communicate clearly what the firm's assets, both hard and soft, are.

- Think critically about financial and product market cycles and the challenges that they pose to the company's business model.

But in many cases, these steps won't be enough to access financing from banks and other traditional sources. To surmount capitalization roadblocks, innovators must therefore look to other investors—in particular, venture capitalists. As we'll see in the next chapter, this particular class of investors has some unique characteristics that make it especially qualified to overcome innovators' investment woes.

3

The Financing Solution: Venture Capital

■

In today's entrepreneurial environment, finding the right financier is a key element of building a sustainable enterprise.

Imagine a promising innovation or new product in its earliest stages, when it's just an intriguing idea in an entrepreneur's mind or a business plan in her briefcase. At no other time will the uncertainty surrounding that idea be so high. The innovator does not know whether a market for the final product will even exist, or whether the necessary technology can be developed. And what about the founding team's management abilities? Perhaps these individuals, though talented, have never worked together in this way or on this kind of project before.

And the challenges don't stop there. The information gaps between the entrepreneurial team and their potential investors are more like chasms than gaps. Investors haven't had a chance to thoroughly test the technology. Nor do they know nearly enough about the project's potential pitfalls. And either party may possess only limited knowledge about any competitor's progress. Moreover, the only assets at this stage are soft assets. The firm is little more than an idea that may not be protectable, and the liquidation value of the firm's assets may amount to nothing. Finally, the product- and financial-market dynamics are at their most turbulent point. No one can predict how customers' needs may change or which way the regulatory or financial winds might be blowing by the time the idea becomes an actual product.

It's at this early stage that innovators will face their biggest difficulty in finding much-needed financial backing—and potential investors their greatest risk in granting their support. How can both parties move past these obstacles?

In early 1996 Felda Hardymon, a venture capitalist with Bessemer Venture Partners, a Boston-based venture capital firm, was scouring the market looking for a potential investment in the telecommunications industry, an area in which he had enjoyed previous investment successes.[1] An opportunity for investment in Networks Northwest came to his attention. The business plan for Networks Northwest highlighted its role in a joint venture, developing business software for wireless carriers. However, Hardymon could spot potential flaws in the investment. Securicor Telesciences, the other joint venture partner, was in an old-line business. The entrepreneur proposing the transaction, John Hansen, had not been successful as an entrepreneur in the past. And perhaps most important, Networks Northwest would have few assets other than its stake in the joint venture and, as such, the value of an investment in Networks Northwest was difficult to estimate and perhaps quite tenuous.

Hardymon turned to his network of contacts to understand the market potential for the business. He called the CEO of one of his previous investments to check out the economics of the proposed plan. Based on what he learned, he crafted a financing agreement that limited Bessemer's risk and provided the greatest incentive for Hansen. The deal Hardymon was ultimately able to negotiate entailed an investment not in Networks Northwest itself but directly in Securicor Wireless, the joint venture.

As Felda Hardymon's story shows, the venture capital industry is uniquely positioned to surmount the obstacles presented by the uncertainty, information gaps, soft assets, and volatile market conditions that so often plague entrepreneurial firms' efforts to raise money.

Why? Venture capital firms realize that they make money by identifying promising innovations early, investing capital to build the venture, and aiding the entrepreneur with growing her business. Unlike traditional lending institutions, venture capital firms specialize in collecting and evaluating information on start-up and growth companies. Also, most venture firms are focused on a particular set of industries, which allows them to better evaluate a start-up's growth potential. Additionally, venture capitalists are active investors, becoming intimately involved in the companies they finance so as to offset the substantial risk they take on when they choose to fund a new enterprise. They monitor their investees' progress, serve on their boards, and contribute financing based on the firms' achievement of milestones. They may even retain the right to appoint key managers and remove members of entrepreneurial teams. These investors often have been successful entrepreneurs or have extensive operating experience. Venture capitalists provide support to investees in numerous forms, including capital, ongoing strategic advice, and contacts with potential customers or strategic partners.

These differences between venture capitalists and other kinds of investors are manifested in a specific set of techniques that venture firms use to manage risk and to encourage the success of their investees. These techniques include:

- a thorough screening and due diligence process that occurs before the decision to invest;

- staged financing—contributing financial support in discrete stages over time;

- syndication of investments (i.e., bringing in other venture capital investors and diversifying commitments);

- compensation contracts—including the use of stock grants and options, particularly convertible preferred equity—that align investors' and managers' incentives;

- covenants and restrictions that protect new ventures from potentially damaging decisions by entrepreneurs; and

- the strategic composition of investees' boards of directors.

Taken together, these techniques provide a powerful mechanism for the efficient, smart financing of young, high-growth companies. Thus, venture capitalists not only bring financial backing to the table; they provide an essential competitive advantage for promising new enterprises—the very organizations that most need such an edge. To be sure, some innovators may chafe against the controls and other terms that their venture capital investor insists on. Yet those very terms and controls, along with a venture capitalist's expertise and financial strength, translate into a well-financed and well-managed company—a company that stands a much better chance of succeeding in the marketplace.

Let's take a closer look at venture capitalists' most important "tools," including the rationale behind each and the ways each party benefits.

Screening and Due Diligence:
Picking the Hottest Investment Opportunities

The first step in overcoming the obstacles facing both the investor and the entrepreneur is the screening and due-diligence processes that venture capitalists implement.[2] These investors possess highly specialized knowledge about the industries they support; have access to vast networks of experts who can help them evaluate people, markets, and technology; and know how to craft agreements that keep uncertainty to a manageable level, close information gaps, and reveal the most promising opportunities among the thousands that come their way.

Specialized Knowledge

By virtue of their partners' education, previous employment, or years of investment experience, most venture capital firms acquire a deep understanding of a particular set of industries. For example, Benchmark Capital achieved a track record investing in Internet-related companies in 1998 and 1999. Benchmark built this record by assembling a group of individuals who had technological and investment backgrounds. With their specialized understanding of communications, software, and computer hardware, the general partners at Benchmark had an ability to see where the Internet might exert its most dramatic impact long before other business professionals and investors could distinguish such patterns.

Specialized knowledge lets a venture capital firm gauge an opportunity's promise. For example, a healthcare venture firm will know how to discover the number of potential patients affected by a particular disease, estimate the cost of conventional treatments to combat that disease, and assess the potential of alternative treatments. Further, this analysis allows the venture firm to judge the credibility of an entrepreneur's proposal and estimate the potential value of an investment in it. The experience of HealthCare Investment Corporation (HIC), founded by Wallace H. Steinberg, aptly illustrates the power of specialized knowledge.[3] HIC was one of the largest venture capital firms devoted exclusively to investments in the healthcare industry, and Steinberg had earned a reputation for astutely recognizing the potential commercial applications of healthcare technology. He had spent twenty-one years as research director at

Johnson & Johnson and kept close tabs on research conducted at the National Institutes of Health (NIH). In 1991, Steinberg became aware of pathbreaking research in transplantation technology then being performed by Dr. David Sachs at the NIH. Steinberg spotted the market potential of the new technology and moved to quickly build a management team around Sachs and form BioTransplant. With the reputation of Sachs and the management teams' business skills, BioTransplant soon established major strategic alliances with Sandoz and several major research universities and hospitals. These alliances greatly aided BioTransplant in its pursuit of new transplantation technology. Without Steinberg's specialized industry knowledge, this particular opportunity would not have arisen.

Specialized knowledge supports the due-diligence and screening process in other ways. Once a venture group develops a track record of identifying hot opportunities in particular industries, entrepreneurs with promising ideas for that market segment will flock to that firm to present their business propositions. This ability to attract a steady stream of business plans in a particular area has several key benefits. The venture capital firm will likely be the first to see all the best deals, and can thus evaluate those proposals against alternative investments. As such, the firm will likely capture most of the "big fish." This achievement in turn sets up a reinforcing cycle that further benefits both the venture capitalist and potential investees. Specifically, the steady stream of business plans lets the venture group keep its finger on the pulse of the marketplace. The firm thus accumulates better information than any other market player because it sees a much larger portion of the available opportunities. The result? A sharp sense of market potential.

A Network of Experts

Through previous employment, their experience screening business plans, and by constantly seeking information on new technologies, venture capitalists build a web of contacts in universities, major corporations, other entrepreneurial companies, and professional-services firms—and call on these contacts to provide critical reviews of potential new investments. Though a venture capitalist may know a lot about a particular technology and its business applications, he may not have the ability to critique the design of a new semiconductor or software program.

In this case, he might turn to experts for advice. Similarly, contacts in other corporations or entrepreneurial firms can provide feedback on the proposed project's management team, particularly its members' skills and experience.

As a related benefit, this large network of experts generates a pipeline of "deal flow" that the venture capitalist can screen for potential investment opportunities. Most venture capital firms wade through literally thousands of business plans every year. Many of these firms refuse to even consider supporting a plan unless it comes with a personal recommendation from someone in their network of experts.

The experience of Jonathan Guerster at Charles River Ventures vividly illustrates this network effect.[4] Guerster joined Charles River as an associate in late 1997 with an explicit mandate to invest in e-commerce-related businesses. One area in which he focused was Internet bill presentment—that is, the ability to deliver and pay bills online—which he knew held tremendous market potential. Before joining Charles River, Guerster had worked at OpenMarket on Internet bill presentment and recognized the technology's promise. Once at Charles River, Guerster spent some time surveying the landscape and identified three potential investment targets: Just-in-Time Solutions (JITS), Bluegill, and edocs, all of which were focusing on this particular market and seeking first-round venture financing in early 1998.

To support the due-diligence process, Guerster contacted Jim Moran, senior vice president of sales for CheckFree, a company that processed electronic payments via the Internet. Moran knew each of the three companies in question and had actually met the founders of both Just-in-Time and edocs. When he and Guerster conferred about the three firms, Moran made a strong pitch to invest in edocs. He felt that edocs had a far superior approach to the online bill-presentment market. In addition, he expressed a willingness to leave his position at CheckFree to join edocs. He thus bet his credibility and career on the future of the company. As a result, Guerster and Charles River subsequently invested in edocs, and the company grew rapidly.

Deal Screening: No One Right Approach

While all venture firms perform due diligence, not all use the same approach. This diversity of approaches is illustrated by the successful methods employed by three founders of the modern venture capital industry:[5]

- Tom Perkins, cofounder of Kleiner Perkins Caufield & Byers in Silicon Valley, looked at the technological position of a company. He assessed whether the new technology a company had developed was superior to existing alternatives, and decided whether that position was proprietary and protectable. In essence, he looked for defensible barriers-to-entry.

- Arthur Rock, father of the venture capital industry in Silicon Valley and investor in Intel, Fairchild Semiconductor, Apple Computer, and Scientific Data Systems, emphasized the quality of a project's management team. He asked himself if the team's members were committed to the project and if they were "intellectually honest." To him, this focus on the management team and their personal integrity was far more important than the actual market or technology.

- Don Valentine, founder of Sequoia Capital, assessed the market for the proposed product or service first. Is the market large and growing? Is it well defined?

The views and experiences of these three venture capitalists point out that multiple deal identification strategies and techniques may ultimately be successful. The important lesson is that venture investors utilize these methods to reduce the initial uncertainty and information gaps that exist at the earliest stages of a firm's development.

Staged Financing: Supporting Milestone Achievement

One of the most common features of venture capital investing is staged financing.[6] Rather than giving the founding team all the money up front, venture firms typically stage the investment based on their receipt of new information about the project and the achievement of certain project milestones. For example, investors may give a company just the amount of capital it needs to finish programming a beta version of its software product. Once the company produces the preliminary version, the venture firm then evaluates the merits of the product and defines terms for possible additional rounds of financing. In particular, the investors will ask themselves and their network of experts the following kinds of questions:

- How innovative is the product, and how superior is it to existing alternatives?

- How likely is it that the technology can be developed into a commercial product?

- Are there stages of development that can be delineated up front?

- Who are the entrepreneurs' competitors?

- What products do these competitors offer?

Staged financing gives the venture capitalist the opportunity to gather information at each milestone and monitor a firm's progress—as well as the ability to pull out of a project if the management team proves incompetent or market conditions no longer favor the firm's product. This technique plays a critical role in controlling potential conflicts between the entrepreneurial team and investors.

Why doesn't the venture capitalist keep closer tabs on their portfolio companies by writing checks every week and looking over entrepreneurs' shoulders daily? A simple reason: The process is expensive and time consuming. Costs include lost opportunities associated with generating and analyzing reports, as well as the significant time and legal expenses that each new round of financing entails. Additionally, most companies take months or sometimes even years to achieve a milestone. Major reviews of progress, due diligence, and the decision to continue funding are generally done at the time of refinancing.

Still, most venture capitalists periodically check up on entrepreneurs between rounds of financing, primarily to manage the information gaps that naturally develop in the course of day-to-day business and to ensure that entrepreneurs are not behaving in a way that might jeopardize their investment. The lead venture capitalist—the one who had identified the company and dictated the financing terms—might visit the entrepreneur once a month, on average, and spend four to five hours per visit—increasing the frequency during times of crisis or when concerns over meeting milestones arise.[7] Venture capitalists also receive monthly financial reports from their investees.

Firms that fail to make milestones or have particularly big information gaps normally are put on a shorter leash. The time between evaluations decreases and the frequency of reevaluation increases as the venture capitalist expects there to be greater potential conflicts with the entrepreneur. For example, early-stage investments are usually associated with greater potential for disagreements between venture capitalists and entrepreneurs about the feasibility of continuing the operation. The motivations and goals of the venture capitalist and entrepreneur are likely to be most at odds at this point in the company's development. As such, most early-stage venture rounds are smaller and are intended to last for a shorter time than later-stage investments.

The examples of Apple Computer and Federal Express illustrate how venture capitalists use staged investment to periodically evaluate these firms' progress—and intervene in strategic development if necessary.[8]

Apple Computer received three rounds of venture capital financing:

1. January 1978: $518,000, at a price of $0.09 per share.

2. September 1978: $704,000 at $0.28 per share—an increase that reflected the progress Apple had made.

3. December 1980: $2,331,000 at $0.97 per share (which recognized Apple's additional achievements).

Ultimately, Apple was able to go public in an initial public offering on December 12, 1980—at a price of $22 per share. At the end of the first day of trading, Apple had a market value of $1.15 billion dollars.

Like Apple Computer, Federal Express received three rounds of venture capital financing—but the two firms developed in markedly different ways. Federal Express's capitalization rounds looked like this:

1. September 1973: $12.25 million, at $204.17 per share.

2. March 1974: The firm's performance was well below expectations, prompting another round of financing—but this time in the form of $6.4 million at $7.34 per share.

3. September 1974: Performance had continued to deteriorate. At this stage, the venture capital investors intervened extensively in the strategy of the company and provided just $3.88 million, at $0.63 per share.

Ultimately, Federal Express's performance improved, once operating and logistical problems were worked out. The company went public in 1978 at $6 per share. Without the staged-investment structure, Federal Express may never have embarked on its successful strategy.

Using Staged Financing to Align Interests

A principal concern for venture capitalists is whether interests and incentives of the investors and the entrepreneurs are aligned. For example, an entrepreneur may feel compelled to continue running a project that he knows investors would abandon—perhaps because he believes that this is his only shot at building a company.[9] His investors, on the other hand, care primarily about the return they will get from their investment and hence may push to liquidate the company if it isn't performing well. Or to enhance her reputation in the field, an entrepreneur may insist on developing a semiconductor that is technologically superior to existing ones but that costs so much that investors worry whether it will yield profits in the future. Finally, because an entrepreneur has limited downside but gains handsomely from success, he might want to pursue highly risky strategies, such as rushing a product to market when further testing may be warranted. By contrast, investors tend to advocate a more methodical approach to product development and business strategy.

When a firm consists mostly of soft assets, the potential for conflict between innovators' and investors' interests increases. Venture capitalists can recover less of their investment in liquidation and expected losses due to poor management decisions are greater. This makes tight monitoring and reduced funding durations necessary.

Staged financing offers a way for venture capitalists to align their investees' interests with their own, encourage the efficient management of resources during the entrepreneurial firms' development, and protect the venture firm's investment. For example, when investing in industries that are heavily weighted toward research and development, that are subject to greater discretionary investment by the entrepreneurs (i.e., it is more difficult for investors to determine whether the entrepreneur is investing in the appropriate projects), or that carry an increased risk of worthless assets after a liquidation, a smart venture capitalist will shorten the time interval between funding rounds. This strategy inspires the entrepreneur to work hard to meet milestones and increase value while limiting the ventures capitalists' losses.

On the other hand, firms whose value hinges almost entirely on future growth options might call for a different staged-financing strategy. To ensure that entrepreneurs are making the proper investment choices, venture capitalists might stage their investment rounds at critical points in the firm's development, such as the production of a beta version of the product or reaching Phase III clinical trials. When the time comes to invest in a firm's growth opportunities, the venture capitalist will be able to control its direction.

Syndication of Venture Capital Investments: Sharing the Risk

Most entrepreneurial companies funded through venture capital receive financing from more than one firm. How? The venture firm originating the deal brings in other venture capital investors to share in the investment and oversight. This syndication of investment offers several benefits.[10] First, it lets the venture capital firm diversify and thus reduce the risk inherent in any individual investment. To illustrate, a typical venture capital fund may have $200–$400 million to invest. In any one round of financing, the firm might contribute just $5–$10 million to each company, but if the firm agrees to four rounds of venture financing, it would have to come up with $20–$40 million dollars per company in order to finance its portfolio. If the venture firm originating the deal were to make the entire investment, it could thus invest in only five to ten companies—not a diverse enough portfolio to sufficiently reduce risk. By bringing in syndicate partners, a typical fund can invest in fifteen to twenty companies.

Syndication offers another advantage as well: It improves the due-diligence process by letting venture firms gather additional opinions on investment opportunities—and thus reducing their risk even further. This is particularly valuable when the opportunity in question is in the earliest stages or hinges strongly on technology—and thus involves considerable uncertainty and large information gaps. Syndication can also serve as a check on the venture capitalist's behavior. Without it, unscrupulous investment firms could more easily take advantage of their investors or other venture capitalists. For example, they might be tempted to keep a greater share of the good investments and, in later rounds of funding, push new investors to accept larger stakes in their less attractive portfolio companies. Or, they may invest in future rounds of their portfolio companies at inflated prices to boost interim fund returns in order to fool their investors and raise new funds. Syndication with other venture groups thus controls avarice and imposes pricing discipline.

Additionally, syndication puts other experienced venture capitalists on investees' boards of directors. Thus these enterprises gain the advice and networking power of multiple investment firms. To illustrate, one critical step in building any successful company is the recruitment of a skilled senior-management team. Most venture capitalists maintain contact with former top-level executives who worked at companies the group has financed in the past. Having several networks of management talent from which to recruit can make the difference between stumbling and succeeding for entrepreneurs. In fact, in today's business environment, finding the right talent may be one of the most difficult—and important—elements of building a sustainable company.

This quest for management talent strongly motivated the syndication between Battery Ventures and Polaris Venture Partners when they invested in Akamai Technologies in October 1998.[11] The founders of Akamai had relatively little hard-core business experience. Tom Leighton was a distinguished MIT computer scientist; Danny Lewin, a promising Ph.D. student with a brilliant idea for managing Internet traffic. Neither man knew much about how to forge business relationships or cut deals. The only person on the team with business experience was Jonathan Seelig, an M.B.A. student at the MIT Sloan School of Management. Though Seelig had several years' experience in the telecommunications and data-communications industry, he didn't have enough to serve as CEO.

To turn the promising technology into a company, the venture capitalists had to have the right senior-level management team. At the time Lewin, Leighton, and Seelig were getting Akamai off the ground, Battery Ventures was working with Paul Sagan on several due-diligence projects. With almost a decade of experience in the media business, Sagan had served as president and editor of Time Inc. News Media, an affiliate of global media and entertainment giant Time Warner, Inc. Before that, he had been a vice president and senior vice president of Time Warner Cable, a division of Time Warner. At the request of Battery, Sagan agreed to become president and Chief Operating Officer of Akamai.

Though Sagan had the media experience necessary to build relationships with various online content providers, he did not have the kind of operational experience Akamai would need to succeed. Battery decided to bring Polaris Venture Partners into the deal because George Conrades—who had years of operating experience—was a venture partner at Polaris. Conrades agreed to serve as chairman and chief executive officer of Akamai. His experience included top-level service at GTE and GTE Internetworking, an integrated telecommunication-services firm; BBN

Corporation, a national Internet-services provider and Internet-technology research and development company; and IBM. The combination of Sagan and Conrades transformed a superior technology into a company that established a dominant position in an exploding market.

Each venture capital firm also brings a network of previous investments to the table. These contacts can prove valuable to start-ups that wish to develop strategic relationships with these companies. Establishing a funding relationship with that venture capital firm can often be an effective first step to forging the desired alliance. The venture capitalist can introduce the two firms and broker an acceptable deal for both parties.

For example, the legendary success of Kleiner Perkins Caufield & Byers is due primarily to its ability to cultivate relationships with other companies. One of the oldest and most successful venture capital firms in the United States, Kleiner Perkins has routinely made substantial bets in specific technology sectors over the past thirty years. Each time it targets a particular industry, Kleiner Perkins's general partners attempt to forge relationships between its portfolio companies, previous investee companies, and large strategic partners that can help each firm become even more successful—thus benefiting the individual firms as well as itself.

This "focused industry" model has been adopted more recently by Softbank Ventures, a subsidiary of Softbank Holdings. Softbank has been making very large investments in the Internet sector since 1995, and was an early backer of some of the most successful Internet companies including Yahoo!, US Web, Verisign, Net2Phone, and eLoan. When trying to convince entrepreneurs to take capital from them, Softbank explicitly markets to prospective entrepreneurs its ability to connect them to these types of companies. Most young start-ups might find it difficult to strike a deal with a market leader like Yahoo!. An investment from Softbank, however, can open the door. Focusing on a single industry, however, exposes the venture group to substantial risk if the industry moves out of favor.

Incentive Compensation: Encouraging Commitment and Performance

In large, public companies, many senior-level managers' compensation consists primarily of a fixed salary that is not affected by major shifts in the firm's performance. In situations like this—where managers have little ownership in the firm—conflicts between managers' and investors' interests can loom. Without strong alignment of both parties' incentives, top managers may make decisions that erode investors' returns. These conflicts especially pose problems in start-up firms. Because the information gaps are so large in these young organizations, investors can't easily oversee and thus influence managers' decisions. Similarly, in the face of such extreme uncertainty, the firm's leaders may tend to embrace more conservative strategies as they set future business goals. Linking the incentives of all parties is essential, not only to protect investors' stake in the firm but also to support the firm's success.

Venture capitalists explicitly tie the fortunes of top managers to the future of the company. How? By reducing the level of fixed salary for the firm's management team and increasing the level of stock and option grants. In one sample of venture capital–backed companies, the sensitivity of the CEO's pay-for-performance is almost sixty times higher than it is in large, mature public companies.[12] Such leaders clearly have a strong incentive to enhance their firms' success. Venture firms also use compensation controls to reduce potential abuse by entrepreneurs. For example, they might stipulate that the stock or options vest over three or four years. This discourages entrepreneurs from leaving the firm for new opportunities and taking their shares—and their talents—with them. Similarly, venture capitalists can significantly dilute entrepreneurs' stake in subsequent financings if a firm fails to hit its targets. This provides additional incentives for innovators to meet the agreed-upon milestones. For instance, an entrepreneur may own 50 percent of the firm's equity after the initial venture capital financing round. Because of the staged nature of venture capital investing, the entrepreneur knows that she will need to raise several more rounds of financing before the company can go public. If the entrepreneur fails to achieve the milestones specified in the business plan at the time of the initial investment, subsequent financing will come at a lower price per share. With this lower price per share, the entrepreneur will lose equity in subsequent financing rounds—another strong incentive to meet the agreed-upon goals.

Venture capitalists also pay attention to how a particular investment is structured. The entrepreneur's human capital is critical to the success of the firm. If the equity stake given to the entrepreneur is used to provide the proper incentives, he will need a large fraction of the firm to induce the proper effort level. The value of the entrepreneur's input may be so large that he retains the majority equity stake. As the previous section makes clear, a large equity ownership is necessary to align incentives when the entrepreneur's input is critical.

Covenants and Restrictions: Protecting Venture Investments

Although large equity ownership by entrepreneurs can boost their commitment to their company's success, it reduces investors' control when conflicts of interest arise. To protect their stake in the company, venture firms thus often make their investments in the form of *convertible preferred equity* or *convertible debt,* which have higher priority than common stock.[13] In the event of a company's sale or liquidation, owners of this type of equity get paid before common stockholders do. This gives entrepreneurs, who generally own common stock, a much greater incentive to help their company succeed, because if things don't go well and the company gets liquidated, the investor—not the entrepreneur—will be paid first. The entrepreneur might well receive nothing by the time the dust has settled. Buying convertible preferred equity lets the venture capitalist shift much of the risk to the entrepreneur.[14]

To get a better sense of the power of convertible preferred equity to align entrepreneurs' and investors' incentives, let's discuss the typical terms and conditions associated with venture investments. Most venture contracts state a conversion price at which the preferred stock becomes common stock. This conversion price is usually set to the purchase price of the convertible preferred stock. This strategy ensures one-for-one conversion; that is, the venture firm receives one share of common stock for each share of convertible preferred stock purchased. Some contracts adjust the conversion ratio so as to influence future rounds of financing. For example, the agreement may contain provisions that automatically adjust the conversion price down if the company sells stock below the share price that the investor has paid. The rationale behind these provisions is that the company is presumably selling at a lower price (a "down round") because of underperformance. Through an automatic adjustment, the original venture firm is less likely to oppose or forestall a smaller round of financing at a time when the company most needs capital or when the venture capital market itself is sluggish.

Most contracts also contain antidilution protection which keeps the entrepreneur from performing stock splits, issuing special dividends, or selling equity to other parties, particularly friends and family, at a lower price than the venture firm paid. Any of these activities would dilute the stake of the venture firm.

The terms typically include terms that list explicit events—such as an initial public offering (IPO)—that would trigger automatic conversion of the preferred equity into common stock. An IPO above a certain, specified size almost universally triggers conversion. That's because if a company has built a successful enough track record to go public, much of the uncertainty and information gaps that motivated the use of the convertible equity will have been resolved. Thus the venture firm would be more willing to convert to common stock.

In addition to automatic conversion at IPO, numerous contracts include provisions for conversion upon the achievement of other milestones. Many of these goals are accounting based, such as income or revenue targets. Like barometers, they measure how much uncertainty about the company's potential has been resolved. By surmounting these predetermined hurdles, the entrepreneur demonstrates the objective success of the company.

In addition to conversion provisions, preferred-equity agreements also contain numerous covenants and restrictions that limit potentially detrimental behavior by the entrepreneur. The provisions also let investors control aspects of the company such as major investment decisions or the sale of assets. These contractual features decouple the allocation of control from the allocation of the company's returns, thus balancing the impact of having the management team own a large stake in the company, thus having voting control.

Many contracts give additional consideration to the preferred stock. For instance, they might require that if the preferred stock is not converted to common stock and the company is sold or liquidated, then the venture firm would receive the entire face value of the preferred stock first.[15] Any additional return would then be split between the preferred shareholders—that is, the venture firm—and the entrepreneur. (This specific feature is known as "participation.") Some contracts give venture firms a multiple of their shares' face value before common shareholders receive anything. This sort of arrangement prevents entrepreneurs from making early liquidation decisions. If the venture firm had invested in common stock that had the same priority as that of the entrepreneur, the company's founder might want to liquidate early and receive his percentage of the investment. As just one example, if a venture firm invested

$2 million in the common stock of a start-up in which the founder retained 75 percent ownership, the founder could liquidate the company on day two of business and walk away with $1.5 million.

Many contracts also contain mandatory redemption rights. These enable the venture firm to force the company to repay the face value of the investment at any time. Investors can also use this mechanism to compel the liquidation or merger of the company. Finally, this mechanism limits entrepreneurs' ability to extract value from soft assets because the entrepreneur cannot continue the company indefinitely. In sum, the mandatory redemption provisions help venture investors determine exit decisions if an entrepreneur declines to go along with their recommendations.

Some contracts restrict sale of any of the company's assets as well. Most of the time, this restriction limits the sale of assets above a certain dollar value or percentage of the company's book value without the approval of venture investors. This technique prevents entrepreneurs from increasing the risk level of the company by making a big bet on a new market segment or technology that is not in the interest of outside investors. It also keeps the entrepreneur from making "sweetheart" deals with friends by transferring substantial value outside the firm. Finally, the prohibition on asset sales prevents the firm from changing its intended focus. The entrepreneur cannot sell a factory or research facility to enter a new line of business without the approval of the venture firm.

Venture investors also have some say over changes in control of the company. After all, in deciding to invest in a particular company, a venture capitalist has backed a particular management team. Accordingly, the investment contract may state that the founders cannot sell any of their common stock without investor approval. Or it may require the entrepreneur to sell his equity back to the venture firm if he chooses to leave. Transfer-of-control restrictions are important because they influence venture capitalists' investment in that all-important human capital: the management team.

Finally, these contracts usually contain provisions affecting a firm's ability to raise additional, higher-priority financing without investor approval. (In cases where a firm raises several rounds of financing from the same venture firm, these restrictions get waived because each subsequent round typically has higher priority than the previous round.) Restricting entrepreneurs' ability to raise additional financing may seem onerous at first, but it decreases their ability to exploit information gaps and transfer value away from the venture capitalist. For example, an entrepreneur may take on extensive loans that could jeopardize the venture capitalist's return if they needed to be paid off before the venture capitalist received any payments. Alternatively, selling additional preferred or common stock at substantially lower prices than the venture capitalist paid could dilute the venture firm's ownership stake in the firm and reduce its return.

The Board of Directors:
Balancing Investors' and Innovators' Interests

Venture capitalists play an active role on their investees' board of directors. The primary role of any board is to provide guidance and strategic advice about the direction of the company; to offer a network of contacts; and to hire, fire, and compensate senior management, including the CEO.[16] The board acts as the central nervous system of a venture capital–backed company. By serving on the board, a venture capitalist can reduce information gaps and periodically assess the levels and kinds of uncertainty affecting its investment.

A well-structured board balances the need for oversight and the potential for conflict between investors and entrepreneurs. Indeed, the majority of venture capital investment agreements specify the size of the board of directors—ideally, five to seven individuals. With a five-member board, the entrepreneurial team typically names two directors, the venture firm names two (both of whom are usually representatives of their firm), and all parties mutually name the fifth director—often an industry representative who will enhance the company's credibility.

In many venture investments, the contract allocates control of the board to the outside investors, even if they don't own more than 50 percent of the equity. This discourages managers from trying to extract value from minority shareholders as someone is closely monitoring the entrepreneur's decisions. Similarly, in an initial public offering, domination of the board by outsiders lends additional credibility to the company.

Finally, the best boards change their composition depending on what's going on at the company. For instance, during times when management oversight is critical, more venture capitalists might join the board.[17] This might include times when the company decides to replace the CEO or when the firm is performing poorly. And if management turnover increases to an uncomfortable level, adding investors to the board can ensure that the company gets the advice and oversight it needs during such vulnerable times.

The Venture Capital Solution

The funding that venture capitalists provide can make or break a struggling young company. But investment firms offer much more than just money. Their specialized knowledge of their target industries, active involvement in the companies they support, and use of strategic techniques to align their own and their investees' interests all help ensure that promising companies allocate resources effectively and have the best opportunity to succeed.

Any potential investor making investments in young, entrepreneurial companies or any entrepreneur raising capital needs to be aware of the way that venture capital investments mitigate the difficulties arising from uncertainty, information gaps, soft assets, and changing market conditions. Good investment strategies should utilize:

- Detailed due diligence and deal screening based on intensive industry knowledge and important networks of experts.

- Staging of investments to explicit milestones that are carefully thought out to correspond to the resolution of uncertainty.

- Syndication of investments to gather more information and diversify risk.

- Equity ownership and incentive compensation for senior management to directly link the interests of investors and the entrepreneur.

- Selective use of covenants and restrictions in critical areas that limit the potential conflicts that may arise.

- Carefully thought out boards of directors that provide oversight, strategic advice, and credibility to the company.

The investment process used by venture capitalists enhances the potential value innovators can receive from their ideas by mitigating the difficulties arising from uncertainty, information gaps, soft assets, and changing market conditions. The impact that venture firms have on the companies they finance and the industries they shape has been profound. We take up this impact in the next chapter.

4

The
Venture Capital
Economy

■

Even after they go public, companies backed by venture capital continue to outperform their rivals in the same industries.

If you had asked the average U.S. citizen in 1970 what venture capital was, you probably would have received a blank stare or a shoulder shrug in response. Yet in the decades since, both the venture capital industry and the media attention that it has received have experienced explosive growth. Today, venture capitalists and the CEOs of the companies they finance regularly make newspaper headlines and grace the covers of major business magazines. What's more, radio and television news programs often profile the meteoric rise of high-technology companies, their founders, and the investors who helped put them there. But while many such companies—including Microsoft, Intel, Cisco Systems, and Genentech—have attracted widespread attention, the *cumulative* impact of venture capital has not.

How exactly has venture capital shaped the economic landscape in this country? To answer that question, we need to look at the ways in which the venture financing process influences economic activity in four arenas:

- Individual firms

- The larger economy, including job creation, revenues, and earnings across numerous industries

- Innovation

- Geographic regions

The Impact on Individual Companies

Perhaps the first step in assessing the impact of venture capital firms is to examine the experience of the companies they invest in. Does venture funding actually change the future direction of start-ups and influence their success? As we'll see, this unique form of capital helps entrepreneurial firms invest more than they would otherwise, grow more quickly, and sustain performance in the long run—even after going public. This cycle of success begins by smoothing out the investment and spending experience.

Smoothing out the Capital Formation Process

As discussed in chapter 2, many young companies can't get debt financing because they lack the tangible assets, impressive operating history, and positive cash flow that traditional lenders insist upon; those that do receive bank credit find that it can dry up during even modest economic downturns. The 1980s and 1990s were particularly difficult for entrepreneurial firms due primarily to government regulation. Laws stipulating a larger capital base for commercial banks caused the number of small loans extended to plummet.[1] To illustrate, $192 billion of loans under $1 million in size were granted in 1981, while only $92 billion in similarly sized loans were made in 1994. In addition, small firms' ability to access the public markets for financing has been exceedingly uneven.

Venture capitalists can act as a buffer between the volatile suppliers of capital and the hungry entrepreneurial firms that need it—smoothing out the capital formation process so that innovators can implement their ideas. Venture capitalists typically expect to supply future funding for their existing portfolio companies from commitments to their existing fund. For example, if a venture firm makes a first-round investment in a young wireless company, then it usually reserves enough cash in its existing funds to completely fund the wireless start-up until it matures. The result? Firms that receive venture capital financing can grow more quickly and uniformly because the assurance of future financing if they reach their milestones releases them from having to track down new money.

Catalyzing Fast, Uniform Growth

With reliable, predictable financial support from venture capitalists—no matter what the economic climate—start-ups can invest in the research, market development, marketing, and strategizing needed to attain the scale to go public. As a result, venture-backed firms tend to be consider-

Table 4-1   Age of Venture Capital– and Nonventure Capital–Backed IPOs

Comparison of average (median) age at initial public offering date for a sample of venture capital–backed and nonventure capital–backed firms.

Industry	Venture-Backed Firm Age at IPO (in months)		Nonventure-Backed Firm Age at IPO (in months)	
Oil and Gas	109.1	(81)	80.1	(42)
Chemicals	44.9	(43)	111.0	(49)
Metals	180.5	(115.5)	195.9	(145)
Machinery	67.2	(56)	122.7	(67)
Electronics	93.2	(65)	144.6	(97)
Instruments	62.5	(50)	104.1	(75)
Airlines	39.4	(48)	81.9	(50)
Communications	67.9	(54)	108.9	(53)
Wholesale/retail	72.2	(51)	126.2	(101)
Restaurants	42.4	(40)	107.0	(68)
Finance	66.2	(49)	145.2	(77)
Software	73.1	(54)	95.8	(93.5)
Computer Services	100.6	(89)	70.7	(43.5)
Research Services	48.1	(57)	95.7	(56.5)
Consulting Services	67.2	(69)	95.5	(72)
Repair Services	90.8	(49.5)	91.8	(77)
Health Services	46.7	(41.5)	51.6	(29)
Social Services	28.0	(28)	44.0	(44)
Other Services	70.2	(57.5)	184.1	(120)

Source: Adapted from Paul A. Gompers and Josh Lerner, "Venture Capital and the Creation of Public Companies: Do Venture Capitalists Really Bring More Than Money?" *Journal of Private Equity* 1 (Fall 1997): 15–42.

ably younger at the time of their IPOs than nonventure-backed companies. (See table 4-1.) Clearly, venture capitalists speed the development of companies by allowing companies to pursue effective strategies without worrying about access to capital.

Akamai, the Internet infrastructure success story, is a particularly vivid example.[2] After several months of development, Akamai raised $8.3 million of venture capital financing from Battery and Polaris Ventures in November 1998. The round placed a post-money valuation on the company of $27 million. However, Akamai needed additional capital to construct the network of servers that would manage the company's content delivery over the Internet, and in April 1999 it raised another $20 million in venture financing from Battery and Polaris Ventures.

To differentiate itself from rivals and solidify its competitive advantage in the marketplace, Akamai began cultivating technology partnerships, targeting Apple, Cisco, and Microsoft as potential players. Battery Ventures's investment in Akamai enhanced the firm's credibility in the eyes of these possible partners. Here's how Akamai's partnering efforts played out:

- *April 1999:* Akamai negotiates its first technology partnership—a two-year arrangement with Apple Computer. Under the terms of the agreement, Apple Computer pledges to make a minimum payment of $12.36 million for Akamai's FreeFlow service. In return, Akamai promises to be the exclusive network provider of Apple's standard and streaming QuickTime TV content.

- *June 1999:* Akamai issues Series D convertible preferred stock for $12.5 million to Apple.

- *August 1999:* Akamai forms a strategic alliance with Cisco Systems to jointly develop new content routing, switching, and caching technologies to improve the performance of Internet content delivery. The company also issues Series E convertible preferred stock for $49.0 million to Cisco Systems.

- *September 1999:* Akamai enters into a strategic partnership with Microsoft Corporation to integrate Microsoft technologies (in particular Microsoft Windows Media) into the Akamai network. Microsoft agrees to prepay $1 million in fees to the company for its services, and Akamai issues Series F convertible preferred stock for $15 million to Microsoft.

Each of these deals directed a flood of capital into Akamai, earned it credibility in the marketplace, and prepared it for its IPO in October 1999. Throughout the deal making, Battery's general partners helped recruit Akamai's senior managers and introduced key players to one another.

Sustaining Long-Run Performance

Venture capital clearly makes a difference in a new firm's early progress, but what about the long-run performance of such companies—*after* they've gone public?[3] The evidence suggests that the early participation of venture firms—including their guidance, monitoring, shaping of management teams and boards, networking, and credibility—helps innovators sustain their success long after their company issues an IPO.

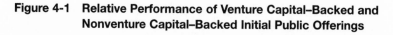

Figure 4-1 Relative Performance of Venture Capital–Backed and Nonventure Capital–Backed Initial Public Offerings

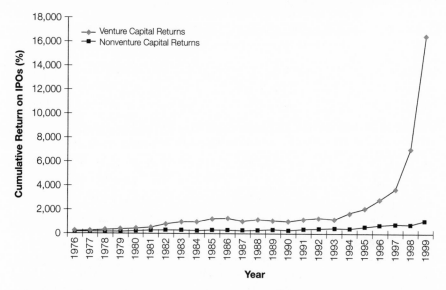

Source: Calculated from Securities Data Company and the Center for Research in Security Prices databases.

Figure 4-1 bears this out. The return shown for each year represents the average return, in percent, on all companies that had gone public within the previous five years. In this way, the figure compares the relatively recent performance of newly public venture capital and nonventure capital–backed companies for each year.

The results demonstrate the superior long-run performance of venture-backed firms. As just one example, if an investor chose to put $1 in 1976 into nonventure capital–backed IPOs, she would have had $11.02 at the end of 1999. If that same investor had put that $1 in venture capital–backed IPOs instead, she would have accumulated $164.43 by 1999. As chapter 3 discussed, the better management and monitoring systems venture firms put in place create more long-run value in the companies and build stronger relationships with investment banks and other intermediaries. It is surprising, however, that the market does not seem to anticipate it at the time of IPO. Investors earn substantial returns after the IPO by investing in venture capital–backed companies.

Clearly, venture capitalists play a critical role in the creation of public companies and dramatically influence their future growth and development. Firms backed by venture capitalists grow more quickly and reach the public market sooner than similar nonventure firms. Finally, venture-backed companies continue to outperform nonventure companies long after they go public.

Impact on the Larger Economy

Venture capital investment exerts a major impact on an individual company's performance. But does all this fund-raising and investing influence the overall economic landscape as well? How would we even determine whether such an influence exists? After all, investments made by the entire venture capital sector for most of the period from 1970–2000 totaled less than the research-and-development and capital-expenditure budgets of large, individual companies such as IBM, General Motors, or Merck. On the face of it, we might conclude that the business press has exaggerated the importance of the venture capital industry. After all, high-tech start-ups make for interesting reporting, but do they really redefine the U.S. economy?

One way to explore this question is to examine the impact of venture investing on wealth, jobs, and other financial measures across a variety of industries. Since consistent information on venture-backed firms that were acquired or went out of business simply doesn't exist, we can track only those companies that have gone public.

Post-IPO Companies

Investments in companies that eventually go public yield much higher returns than those in firms that get acquired or remain privately held.[4] And indeed, venture capitalists have achieved spectacular successes in taking firms public. Figure 4-2 shows the history of venture-supported IPOs from 1972 to 2000. Much like the growth in the venture capital industry itself, venture-backed IPOs shot up in that time period. While the overall IPO market has seen similar growth, the share of IPOs that had venture capital backing has expanded dramatically. In 1980, only 20 percent of all IPOs were venture-capital financed. Twenty years later, that had increased to more than 50 percent. From 1972 through 1980, seventy-eight venture-backed companies went public—while in 2000 alone, as many as 221 venture capital–backed firms entered the public-equity markets for the first time.

Perhaps even more dramatic, these firms have had an unmistakable effect on the U.S. economy. From 1972 through 2000, 2,180 firms went public after receiving their private financing from venture capitalists.

Figure 4-2   Venture Capital–Backed Initial Public Offerings by Year

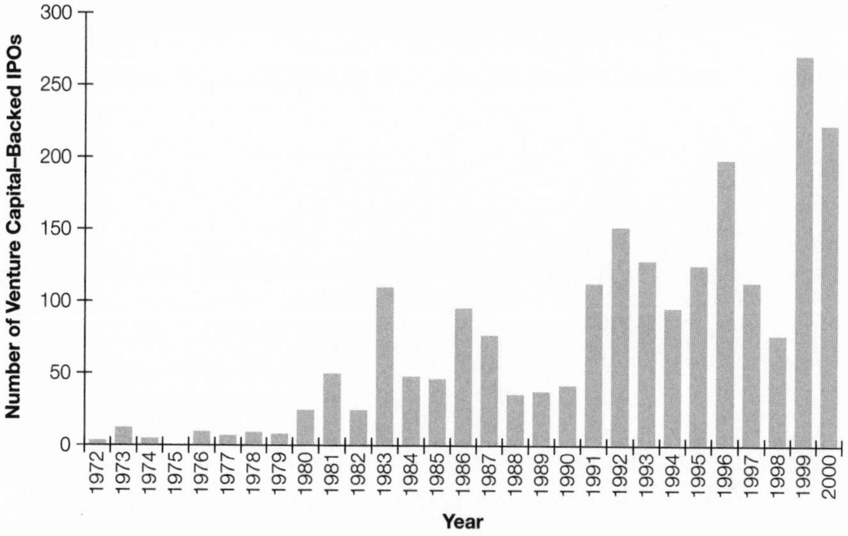

Source: Compiled from Securities Data Company databases.

As table 4-2 shows, certain industries have a large number of companies that were still publicly traded after having received venture capital financing while other industries have had very little venture capital involvement. In the energy, environmental, financial, and transportation industries, roughly a dozen or fewer companies remaining public at the end of 2000 had received venture capital backing. Venture-backed companies in the energy, financial, and transportation sectors represented only about one percent of the total market value, sales, and profits of venture-backed companies. These industries tend to be dominated by mature companies. The relatively low importance of venture capital in these sectors reflects the lower propensity for major innovations. What is clear from the table, however, is that the overall impact of venture capital on the U.S. economy has been quite large.

Another way to assess the overall impact of the venture capital industry is to look at the economic "weight" of venture-backed companies in the context of the larger economy. Table 4-3 reveals some startling numbers. By the end of 2000, venture-backed firms that had gone public made up over 20 percent of the total number of public firms in existence in the United States. And of the total market value of public firms ($8.25 trillion), venture-backed companies came in at $2.7 trillion—over 32 percent.

Table 4-2 Venture Capital–Backed Public Companies within Various Industries in 2000

Industry	Number of Venture Capital Public Firms	Market Value of Venture Capital Public Firms ($ millions)	Total Sales of Venture Capital Public Firms ($ millions)	Total Profits of Venture Capital Public Firms ($ millions)	Total Employment of Venture Capital Public Firms (in thousands)
Aerospace	1	215.67	33.27	6.75	4.36
Biotech	169	265,353.41	13,297.39	2,620.13	54.21
Communications	137	185,206.08	24,286.44	8,668.73	111.97
Computer Hardware	81	820,933.38	135,980.12	9,291.32	280.25
Computer Software	353	746,238.89	62,358.88	12,026.97	102.56
Consumer Goods	36	14,578.61	18,724.64	3,593.42	89.70
Consumer Services	89	32,109.70	49,920.55	-2,886.08	50.32
Electronics	56	29,215.44	9,564.50	2,543.23	34.17
Energy	4	2,352.83	629.71	235.92	0.27
Environmental	5	615.73	403.91	104.15	4.14
Financial	14	18,877.31	8,871.37	1,352.03	11.18
Industrial Goods	55	19,992.51	11,267.91	2,258.13	49.54
Industrial Services	78	25,694.72	17,821.03	2,420.82	25.54
Medical Devices	76	6,784.21	4,462.34	1,993.06	28.86
Medical Services	27	21,724.07	16,304.12	2,670.18	274.97
Other	13	131,312.00	9,298.72	796.30	63.98
Semiconductors	64	352,026.81	67,791.95	15,817.08	207.51
Transportation	6	557.33	1,976.08	310.91	6.89
Computer Services	54	29,248.91	7,662.28	712.87	17.69
Total	1,318	$2,703,037.61	$460,655.21	$64,535.92	1,418.11

Source: Compiled from Compustat and Securities Data Company databases.

Table 4-3 The Impact of Venture Capital in 2000

	Number of U.S. Public Firms	Market Value of Firms ($ millions)	Sales of Firms ($ millions)	Profits of Firms ($ millions) (after-tax margin)	Number of Employees (in thousands)
Total	6,403	$8,252,143	$4,186,193	$513,078 (12.3%)	25,325
Venture Capital–Backed	1,318	$2,703,038	$460,655	$64,536 (14.0%)	1,418
Venture Capital % of Total	20.6%	32.8%	11.0%	12.6%	5.6%

Source: Compiled from Compustat and Securities Data Company databases.

Venture-funded firms also made up over 11 percent and 12 percent, respectively, of total sales and profits of all U.S. public firms at the time. And contrary to the general perception that venture-supported companies are not profitable, after-tax profit margins for these companies hit an average of 14 percent—substantially higher than the average public-company profit margin of 12.3 percent. Finally, those public firms supported by venture funding employed 5.6 percent of the total public-company workforce—most of these jobs high-salary, skilled positions in the technology sector.

Venture investing not only fuels a substantial fraction of the U.S. economy, it also strengthens particular industries. It has relatively little impact on industries dominated by established companies because the venture investor's mission is to capitalize on revolutionary changes in an industry and mature sectors often have a relatively low propensity for radical innovation. But contrast those industries with highly innovative ones, and the picture looks completely different. For example, companies in the computer software industry that received venture backing during their gestation as private firms represented more than 75 percent of the software industry's value. In the computer hardware industry, such firms represented 78 percent of the industry's market value, more than 60 percent of the industry's sales and profits, and almost half of all the industry's employees. Venture-financed firms also play a central role in the biotechnology, computer-services, industrial-services, and semiconductor industries. All of these industries have experienced tremendous innovation and upheaval in recent years. Venture capital has helped catalyze change in these industries, providing the resources for entrepreneurs to generate substantial return from their ideas.

A further testament to the impact of venture capital can be seen by examining the twenty largest venture capital–backed companies by market value at the end of 2000 shown in table 4-4. These twenty firms represent a broad number of industries and most are the dominant player in their sectors. Cisco Systems, with a market value of $467 billion, dominates the market for network switches, which provide the communication backbone of the Internet. The second largest company on the list, Microsoft, which had a market value of $422 billion, has a dominant position in operating systems and application software for personal computers. The rest of the companies in the top twenty carry dominant places in their industry. As these statistics suggest, venture capitalists create whole new industries and seed fledgling companies that later dominate those industries.

Table 4-4 Top Twenty Venture Capital–Backed Companies by Market Value as of December 31, 2000

Company	Market Value ($ millions)	Sales ($ millions)	Profits ($ millions)	Employees	SIC Code	Industry
Cisco Systems	467,096.47	18,928.00	2,668.00	34,000	3576	Computer Hardware
Microsoft	422,640.00	22,956.00	9,421.00	39,100	7372	Computer Software
Intel	202,046.70	33,726.00	10,535.00	86,100	3674	Semiconductors
Sun Microsystems	145,227.99	15,721.00	1,854.00	38,900	3571	Computer Hardware
America Online	122,051.43	6,886.00	1,232.00	15,000	7812	Motion Picture Production
Amgen	66,329.28	3,629.40	1,138.50	7,300	2836	Biotech
Dell Computer	65,563.45	31,888.23	2,310.15	40,320	3571	Computer Hardware
Genentech	42,826.37	1,645.95	−74.24	4,460	2834	Biotech
Juniper Networks	40,098.43	673.50	147.92	1,250	3576	Computer Hardware
Ariba	35,503.75	279.04	−792.78	1,680	7372	Computer Software
Veritas	34,377.88	1,207.33	−619.79	4,730	7372	Computer Software
Sycamore Networks	30,203.79	198.14	20.40	5,230	3661	Communications
Ciena	30,121.57	858.75	81.39	2,780	3661	Communications
Solectron	27,413.76	14,137.50	497.20	65,270	3672	Semiconductors
Compaq Computer	25,419.45	42,383.00	569.00	70,100	3571	Computer Hardware
Brocade Communications	25,302.29	329.05	67.93	610	3576	Computer Hardware
Tellabs	23,062.34	3,387.44	730.80	7,000	3661	Communications
Linear Technology	20,151.15	705.92	287.91	2,820	3674	Semiconductors
Maxim Integrated Products	19,212.53	864.92	280.62	4,180	3674	Semiconductors
Yahoo!	16,884.35	1,110.18	70.78	3,260	7370	Computer Software
Total	$1,861,532.99	$201,515.33	$30,425.77	434,080		

Source: Compiled from Compustat and Securities Data Company databases.

Table 4-5   Composition of Venture Capital Investment by Industry and Stage

Panel A: Dollars Invested by Industry ($ millions)

Industry	1980	1981	1982	1983	1984	1985	1986	1987	1988	1989
Online-specific	0.0	0.0	0.0	0.0	0.0	0.0	0.0	0.0	0.0	0.0
Communications	70.8	165.7	224.7	458.3	474.9	548.6	548.9	469.3	895.7	720.8
Computer Software and Services	18.0	50.5	153.7	366.0	452.4	412.5	464.9	472.0	432.8	482.1
Other Products	83.0	122.2	122.8	197.2	211.8	251.0	563.3	530.0	904.0	789.5
Medical- and Health-related	49.5	103.5	113.9	271.3	310.0	344.8	363.8	520.8	552.8	756.4
Semiconductor and Other Electronic	74.2	163.0	202.2	329.4	444.5	437.5	477.4	451.6	433.8	331.2
Consumer-related	52.3	51.5	131.4	280.2	249.4	254.0	517.9	764.5	808.9	865.1
Computer Hardware	152.2	361.3	608.4	1,169.8	995.2	747.2	769.2	580.8	534.8	428.9
Biotechnology	48.9	100.0	83.9	144.6	116.2	141.4	271.6	284.2	326.1	332.1
Industrial and Energy	152.7	272.6	250.8	265.2	326.4	458.8	314.8	353.8	305.8	447.3
Total	701.6	1,390.3	1,891.8	3,482.0	3,580.8	3,595.8	4,291.8	4,427.0	5,194.7	5,153.4

Panel B: Dollars Invested by Stage of Development ($ millions)

Stage	1980	1981	1982	1983	1984	1985	1986	1987	1988	1989
Early	286.7	643.4	650.1	1,286.0	1,356.8	1,045.7	1,393.3	1,339.8	1,412.8	1,307.7
Expansion	197.2	417.4	654.9	1,290.5	1,311.3	1,302.5	1,326.8	1,570.2	1,757.7	1,760.7
Later	55.6	107.8	255.0	436.0	474.2	622.1	583.5	631.6	452.8	558.9
Buyout	162.3	221.6	332.0	469.5	438.4	625.5	988.0	885.6	1,571.4	1,526.2

Source: Compiled from various issues of the *Venture Capital Journal.*

The Changing Focus of Investments

The focus of venture capital has also shifted over time, stirring up some interesting results in the economy. Table 4-5 presents a breakdown of venture capital investments by industry and by stage of development. In Panel A, the industry pattern shows several clear trends. For example, online (Internet-related) investments were so modest that Venture Economics, publisher of the *Venture Capital Journal,* did not break them out until 1994, when a total of $61 million was invested. By 2000, however, online related investments totaled $25.2 *billion.* Two other industries, communications and computer software services, both took off in the late 1990s as well. In the early 1980s, computer hardware and semiconductor electronics received a large fraction of venture capital investments. Medical and health related investments surged in the late 1980s and again in the late 1990s.

These waves of venture capital activity focusing on various industries at different times are driven by two factors. On the one hand, venture

1990	1991	1992	1993	1994	1995	1996	1997	1998	1999	2000
0.0	0.0	0.0	0.0	60.9	242.5	778.8	1,440.0	3,284.7	18,513.1	25,246.1
421.4	295.8	1,107.2	694.2	957.4	1,081.2	1,669.0	2,396.4	3,318.5	8,335.4	17,627.8
615.6	459.2	646.2	1,370.9	722.0	801.9	1,783.2	2,698.6	3,834.7	7,500.9	14,374.3
468.0	284.4	778.7	524.2	420.9	575.8	1,320.3	1,406.8	2,443.7	4,551.9	6,279.4
497.0	308.3	812.1	609.9	837.5	823.6	1,085.0	2,236.7	2,392.2	2,457.0	3,613.7
264.6	210.1	231.0	183.1	247.5	340.7	463.4	699.9	827.0	1,740.2	6,098.8
435.0	350.0	359.4	704.4	748.9	774.3	1,061.1	1,236.0	1,083.7	1,710.4	1,665.6
277.1	232.4	251.1	150.9	252.5	345.9	351.8	427.9	556.2	1,303.8	2,279.2
284.3	272.8	503.9	441.8	423.9	396.7	1,013.0	949.6	1,030.1	1,182.2	2,763.8
227.0	153.2	162.7	175.8	192.7	338.1	423.4	551.8	441.1	751.1	1,423.8
3,490.0	2,566.2	4,852.3	4,855.2	4,864.2	5,720.7	9,949.0	14,043.7	19,211.9	48,046.0	81,372.5

1990	1991	1992	1993	1994	1995	1996	1997	1998	1999	2000
1,092.9	770.9	1,106.8	2,070.1	1,493.5	2,167.1	3,150.2	3,502.3	5,278.7	10,776.5	18,634.3
1,525.2	1,118.8	1,848.6	1,527.8	1,292.0	1,981.6	3,620.9	6,024.7	7,985.8	26,380.8	44,266.6
416.1	462.8	1,137.1	783.5	1,235.0	980.0	2,117.0	2,801.3	3,661.8	8,764.0	16,274.5
455.8	213.6	759.8	473.7	843.6	592.1	1,060.9	1,715.5	2,285.5	2,117.7	1,871.6

capitalists are opportunistic, always trying to find the latest technological breakthrough that might have an important market. Because technological innovation proceeds at different paces and with different results in the various industries, venture capital activity can become focused on different markets at different times.

A less kind picture, however, has to do with herding by venture capitalists. Venture capitalists often look around at other investors to determine what is "hot." If a venture capitalist suddenly notices that a market segment is quite active, he might invest in that segment as well. This can lead, as we will see in chapter 6, to overfunding in certain industries while other industries with attractive growth opportunities remain underserved. The explosive growth of Internet investing in the late 1990s is just such an example. Such overinvestment may serve to create short-run problems for the market.

Just as venture investing has focused on different industries over the years, it has also varied in terms of which lifecycle stage its target companies are in. For instance, in the early 1980s, venture firms primarily targeted early-stage companies. However, as venture capital funds have grown larger—some of them now contain as much as $1 billion in committed capital—many firms have begun making larger, expansion-stage investments because they can put more capital to work for the same amount of effort. As we discuss in chapter 10, these changes towards larger venture capital funds may have important implications for entrepreneurs and investors. The message is clear: The venture capital revolution served as the driving force behind the transformation of the U.S. economy in the late twentieth century.

The Impact on Innovation

How much does venture capital financing actually influence the innovation rate of companies and industries? There are two schools of thought. Some feel that venture capitalists find innovation and bring it to the commercial markets, not influencing the rate of innovation, but only its ability to reach the market. Others feel that the venture capitalist's ability to free innovators from the concerns of raising capital unleashes innovation.

Unlike sales, profits, market value, or number of employees, however, innovation is difficult to measure. Nevertheless, there is one metric that can help us measure the rate of innovation in an economy, region, or company: the number of patent applications.

Patterns in Patenting

Why choose patenting as a measure of innovation? Companies use patents to protect their new ideas, so assessing how often they apply for patents can give us a sense of how many potentially valuable new ideas they're generating.[5] Figure 4-3 shows some interesting relationships among trends in patenting, R&D expenditure, and early-stage venture capital disbursements. According to patenting statistics, American firms became considerably less innovative from 1965 through 1985, during which period patenting rates dropped by nearly 35 percent. During this same period, many critics in the public sector and business community claimed that U.S. businesses had lost their competitive edge—that is, their ability to develop new technologies and markets. After 1985, however, patenting rates took off.

Figure 4-3 Patenting Rates in the United States

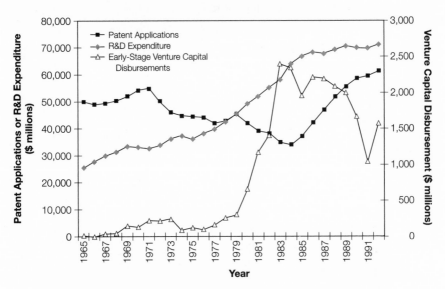

Source: Compiled from Samuel Kortum and Josh Lerner, "Assessing the Contribution of Venture Capital to Innovation," *Rand Journal of Economics* 31 (2000): 674–692.

What explains this decline and rebirth of innovation? As figure 4-3 reveals, the drop in patenting from 1965 to 1985 paralleled a steady increase in corporate expenditure on research and development. Therefore, the decline in innovation didn't stem from reduced spending on innovative *activity*. Rather, it occurred as a result of a general decline in the ability of U.S. corporations to innovate. Then, in the late 1970s and early 1980s, early-stage venture capital disbursements shot up, mainly as a result of the high returns that venture capital had been earning in the late 1970s, a time when the overall stock market had increased very little. Soon after, the number of patent applications began to soar.

Table 4-6 shows the ratio of venture capital investment to R&D spending for U.S. manufacturing firms. While the total venture capital invested might make up only a small portion of overall spending on research and development, compared to overall expenditure on research and development, it has increased by a factor of 200. Early-stage venture capital investing has increased even more, by a factor of 250.

Though these trends are compelling, the real question remains: Did venture capital cause the explosion in innovation, or did the increase in

**Table 4-6 The Ratio of Venture Capital Investment to R&D Expenditures
for U.S. Manufacturing Firms**

| | *Ratio of Venture Capital to R&D* | |
Year	All Venture Capital (%)	Early-Stage Only (%)
1965	.05	.02
1966	.01	.00
1967	.08	.07
1968	.12	.08
1969	.45	.38
1970	.38	.24
1971	.69	.41
1972	.62	.44
1973	.65	.30
1974	.22	.13
1975	.33	.24
1976	.22	.10
1977	.35	.21
1978	.60	.37
1979	.66	.28
1980	1.30	.80
1981	2.20	1.39
1982	2.52	1.29
1983	4.12	1.97
1984	3.70	1.95
1985	2.92	1.42
1986	3.23	1.62
1987	3.24	1.57
1988	3.01	1.54
1989	2.83	1.56
1990	2.40	1.11
1991	1.48	.71
1992	2.22	1.05
1993	2.79	1.05
1994	2.79	1.96
1995	2.80	1.42
1996	3.29	2.06
1997	5.73	2.99
1998	8.08	3.32
1999	11.06	5.01

Source: Compiled from Samuel Kortum and Josh Lerner, "Assessing the Contribution of Venture Capital to
Innovation," *Rand Journal of Economics* 31 (Winter 2000): 674–692.

innovation jump-start venture capital investing? The evidence suggests
strongly that venture capital increased innovation, not the other way
around. In fact, according to the statistics, each dollar of venture capital
appears to stimulate patenting three times more than a dollar of tradi-

tional corporate research and development does. This finding suggests that venture capital, even though it averaged less than 3 percent of corporate R&D from 1983 to 1992, drove a much greater share—about 8 percent—of U.S. industrial innovations over that decade. Given the continued rise in venture funding since 1992, and assuming that the potency of venture funding remained consistent with the measured impact of venture capital in patenting rates, the calibrations imply that, by 1999, venture capital investments accounted for about 18 percent of U.S. innovative activity.

Nevertheless, this still doesn't explain the exact *mechanism* by which venture capital increases patenting. One possible explanation is that such funding forces entrepreneurs to protect their intellectual property with patents rather than other mechanisms such as trade secrets. Venture capitalists may just know more about protecting innovations and, hence, utilize the ability to apply for patents. If this is true, we might infer that venture-backed patents, because they represent more marginal inventions, would be lower quality than nonventure-backed patent filings.

How could we investigate this question of patent quality? One possibility is to check the number of patents cited by other patents. Higher-quality patents should be cited by other innovators more often than lower-quality ones. Similarly, if venture-backed patents are lower quality, then companies receiving venture funding would be less likely to initiate patent-infringement litigation.

When we measure patent quality with these criteria, we find that the patents of venture-backed firms are more frequently cited by other patents and are more aggressively litigated—thus we can conclude that they are high quality. Furthermore, the venture-backed firms more frequently litigate trade secrets, which suggests that they are not simply patenting frantically in lieu of relying on trade-secret protection. These numbers reinforce the finding that venture-supported firms are more innovative than their nonventure-supported counterparts.

How Does Venture Funding Drive Innovation?

It is one thing to see the fruits of venture capital financing, but why does such investing produce this particular result? One possible explanation is that the screening process that venture capitalists use in selecting investment opportunities is more efficient than the process that corporate research and development departments use. One metric important for all venture capitalists is whether a particular business proposal has a sustainable competitive advantage. In the technology industries that venture capitalists target, sustainable competitive advantages normally derive from intellectual property and innovative ability. Unless a venture firm sees the potential for patents or some other form of protected intellectual property, it isn't likely to invest. By contrast, most large, mature corporations tend to look at their existing lines of business when choosing projects to fund. Technologies outside the firm's core market, or projects that raise internal political tensions, often get shelved. In fact, many successful venture-backed start-ups are launched by employees who leave when their companies decline to pursue a promising new technology.

In addition to the initial selection process, the advice that venture firms provide to entrepreneurs, as well as the post-investment monitoring and control, support top-quality innovation. Adding key managers and providing contacts for critical strategic partnerships is highly value-added and potentially allows the entrepreneur to be even more inventive and creative than she would otherwise be. Venture capitalists also tend to spot more potential future applications of technology than larger, mature companies do, perhaps because older companies focus on narrower markets. The insights of the venture capitalist may help focus the creative energy of the entrepreneur on fertile areas of innovation.

Finally, the staging of investments also improves the efficiency of venture capital funding. In large corporations, research and development budgets are typically set out at the beginning of a project, with few interim reviews planned. Even if projects do get reviewed midstream, few of them are terminated when signs suggest they're not working out. The venture capitalists' use of staged financing provides strong incentives to see results for the capital provided. Also, industrial R&D managers typically have little incentive to tightly monitor expenditures or explore new areas, as their compensation bears little or no relation to the outcome of the research projects managed. The particular difficulties that corporations face with trying to implement venture capital solutions are explored in chapter 7.

Impact on Local Economies

Almost everyone in business knows about California's Silicon Valley or "America's Technology Highway" (Route 128 in Massachusetts)—two hotbeds of high-tech innovation that have seen their economies transformed by local venture investments. Seeing the benefits local economies have gained from this activity, other regions around the country have also tried to promote venture capital programs, but often with far from satisfactory results. State and local governments have set up venture funds targeted at particular firms in their region, or have provided tax incentives to promote private investment. Similarly, universities and local governments have established high-technology "incubators" in hopes of drawing venture investment into the local economy. These incubators typically offered office space, computer support, and limited administrative resources to get the potential new companies off the ground. The example of these two regions shows us the value of venture activity, but also raises several critical questions: How can we judge the impact of venture capital on a particular region's economy? What determines the magnitude of the economic spillovers from such investment?

Patterns of Regional Venture Capital Action

To answer these questions, we first need to look at patterns of regional venture capital activity. During the period 1978–1999, California raised the most venture capital of any state. The total pool of venture capital started at $19 million in 1978 and hit $34.9 billion by 1999—representing 397 distinct venture funds. These numbers represented about 30 percent of the total venture capital generated in the United States, and 31 percent of the total venture funds. Massachusetts and New York (which has served as a base for many venture capital funds even if this capital has traditionally been invested elsewhere) also account for a large fraction of venture capital fund-raising.

Together, these three states accounted for 63 percent of the total number of U.S. venture capital funds and 68 percent of the total venture capital raised during that period and represent the historical centers of venture capital activity in the United States. Venture capital grew up in Silicon Valley and Route 128 because of each region's ties to research universities and other high-technology companies. Universities like MIT and Stanford have served as the source for many new innovations. Similarly, the success of companies like Fairchild Semiconductor in Silicon Valley and Digital Equipment Corporation on Route 128, two early venture capital–backed success stories, showed other would-be entrepreneurs that starting a new venture could be highly profitable.

Relatively few other states have even a moderate venture capital presence. For example, Connecticut, Maryland, New Jersey, Pennsylvania,

Illinois, Minnesota, and Texas each have only between 2.5 percent and 6 percent of the funds raised. In the first four of these states, many funds invest in deals outside their own state. When we measure funds invested in states outside venture firms' home states, we see similar patterns. Once again, investments in California dominate the overall picture. Venture capital companies *outside* that state poured almost $20 billion into 6,000 California-based companies between 1987 and 1995. These figures represented 35 percent of the total capital invested and 33 percent of the total number of companies financed in the United States, respectively. Massachusetts, New York, Connecticut, New Jersey, Pennsylvania, Texas, and Illinois also have relatively active venture capital markets on the investment side as well. Each of these states received at least $1.5 billion of venture capital investment during this same time period.

Another metric of the venture capital intensity of various states is the fraction of the state's economic activity that venture capital represents. The top-ranked state according to this measure is Massachusetts where venture capital investments equal .62 percent of the state's economic activity. This measure demonstrates the importance of venture capital for new business formation and jobs within any state. The second-ranked state is California, which has a ratio of venture capital to gross state product of .50 percent. While California's venture capital market is larger, so is the state's overall economy. Investment in most other regions was relatively minor over this period of time even though many state and local governments sought to promote greater venture capital activity. Venture capital has not been a dominant force in the economic development of most states.

Venture Capital's Impact on States' Economic Health

Clearly, venture capital activity is concentrated in a small number of states in this country. But does this activity significantly affect the health and competitiveness of the local economy? A 1999 report by the Progressive Policy Institute rated each state's ability to compete in the "new economy" and participate in the entrepreneurial revolution.[6] The report examined key areas of the economy that would make a market receptive to innovative activity and commercial applications of technology. The Institute ranked states in these five areas:

- Number of knowledge jobs (as measured by office, managerial, and technical jobs, and educational attainment of the state's workforce)

- Globalization

- Economic dynamism (as measured by turnover—that is, number of births and deaths of companies, and ability to turn innovation into commercial opportunities)

- Transformation to a digital economy

- Technological innovation

Not surprisingly, the report ranked Massachusetts and California as the top two states according to these criteria. Next came Colorado, Washington, and Connecticut. Four of these five states rank at the top in terms of venture capital intensity. Venture capital can play a role in spurring the growth of new jobs, the employment skill base, and entrepreneurial activity.

The report provides quantitative measures of the impact that venture capital can have on a particular state. To measure the importance of knowledge jobs within the state economy, the report looked at office, managerial, and technical jobs as well as the educational attainment of the workforce. In Massachusetts, the top-ranked state in terms of knowledge jobs, nearly 35 percent of the labor force holds a managerial, professional, or technical job. Venture capital creates an environment that fosters increases in these types of high-salary, high-skill jobs.

Economies that are favorable towards entrepreneurship and innovation usually have significant economic dynamism. In order for the creative activity of innovators to have commercial impact, an economy must be receptive to new firms. By the same token, trying to realize the value of an innovation through new companies is risky and uncertain. Many firms trying to capture this value will fail. California and Colorado rank number two and three on the list of company births and deaths. More than 3.5 percent of the companies in those states are born or die in a given year. Venture capital sows the seeds of future economic development in these highly dynamic markets.

In addition, states that promote dynamic economies must have a capacity to innovate and turn innovation into commercial opportunities. One element of this raw material is the human capital, or skill, base of the economy. The states that are well positioned to take advantage of venture financing have large high technology labor forces and an ability to generate intellectual property through innovation. Colorado, Massachusetts, and California are among the top five states in terms of percentage of the labor force that works in the high-technology sector. Between 7 and 9 percent of the states' workers in all three states are employed in high-technology jobs. These economies are positioned to take venture capital and create new wealth. Similarly, as discussed earlier in the chapter, patents are often used as a measure of the innovation potential of a company or region. When the patent rate per employee is examined, Connecticut and Massachusetts are once again represented in the top five states.

Generation of Venture-Support Industries

As yet another way to assess venture investing's overall impact on a state's economy, we can measure the development of industries that support venture-backed firms' growth and prosperity. These include law firms that specialize in the fund-raising and investing sides of the venture capitalization process. Wilson Sonsini Goodrich & Rosati in Silicon Valley and Testa, Hurwitz & Thibault in Boston are two examples of such firms. Both firms are active investors in and advisers of entrepreneurial firms as well as providers of legal advice. Accounting firms that understand the challenges faced by high-tech start-ups, as well as banks that can provide these firms with financial services, are also essential. Silicon Valley Bank is a pioneer in providing lending and financial services to young, entrepreneurial companies.

These resources also tend to cluster around a small number of major research institutions. The synergistic relationships among these service providers, the local labor force, academic institutions, and venture capital firms has helped drive both venture and entrepreneurial activity in these regions.

And last, many of these service providers expand to new markets. For example, Silicon Valley Bank now has offices in Los Angeles, Seattle, Portland, Boston, Orlando, Denver, Atlanta, Virginia, Chicago, Philadelphia, Austin, Dallas, Phoenix, Minneapolis, and the Research Triangle in the Raleigh-Durham, North Carolina area. Each of these cities currently boasts a rapidly growing venture capital sector. In other cases, new firms crop up and fill the void in states or regions that previously lacked venture capital activity. Educational initiatives at leading law and business schools have yielded talented lawyers, accountants, and service providers who have been attracted to the venture capital sector. These changes point to additional growth of the venture sector in the future—and a more even distribution of innovation hotbeds across the country.

Catalyzing Economic Growth

No matter how we look at the numbers, venture capital clearly serves as an important source for economic development, wealth and job creation, and innovation. This unique form of investing brightens entrepreneurial companies' prospects by relieving all-too-common capital constraints. Venture-backed firms grow more quickly and create far more value than their nonventure-backed firms. Similarly, venture capital generates a tremendous number of jobs and boosts corporate profits, earnings, and workforce quality. Finally, venture capital exerts a powerful effect on innovation.

The success of the venture capital industry is highly visible. Until now, we have focused on the interaction of venture capitalists with their portfolio companies. But the organization of venture capital funds themselves is also critical. In the next section, we highlight the important aspects of venture capital organizations and how they cope with the dramatic market movements and changing investor appetites. We explore the boom and bust nature of venture capital and try to understand the virtues as well as the pathologies of this important industry.

The
Venture Capitalist's
Challenge

■

Let's now shift our perspective from how venture capital firms finance and develop start-up firms to the challenges facing venture capital organizations themselves. A reader of the popular business press might walk away with one of two conflicting impressions: Either these groups are like merchant banks, making fast money by "flipping" short-term investments, or they resemble rock-and-roll bands, for whom success derives directly from the partners' oversized personalities.

The reality is more complex. As shown in the preceding chapters, many aspects of the venture-investment process are designed to address the special problems plaguing young growth companies. Institutional investors such as pension funds or university endowments that are trying to decide which venture groups to commit to also grapple with numerous similar problems. Many elements of the venture capital organization, including the limited partnership structure and unique compensation and contractual strategies, have evolved to facilitate that end of the investment process. In chapter 5, we explore these features and the reasons they have evolved.

At the same time, however, the evolution of the venture capital industry has been far from steady and harmonious. Rather, the industry has endured extreme swings in the amount of capital it has raised. These variations have created a boom-and-bust cycle that can spawn real problems within the industry. We explore the impact of this cycle in chapter 6, as well as strategies that can help venture groups address this variability and sustain their success.

5

How Do
Venture Organizations
Work?

■

The limited partnership has been a critical element in the venture industry's success.

Although venture capital firms serve as a valuable driver for economic growth and innovation, investing in a venture capital fund in some respects requires a leap of faith. Most institutional investors—pension funds, university endowments, and foundations, for example—typically have small staffs and thus can't do a lot of research into the various choices of where to invest their money. At the larger institutional organizations, as few as a dozen professionals may be responsible for investing several *billion* dollars each year. And venture capital, by its very nature, focuses on risk: These funds invest in new, untried firms pursuing complex, innovative technologies or novel business strategies.

Yet many venture capital funds still manage to raise money, and the venture sector endures. The firms have addressed their investors' concerns by experimenting with a series of organizational structures, and by systematizing and refining the ways in which they manage their investment activities. In this chapter, we take a closer look at:

- the evolution of venture capital organizational structures, particularly the emergence of the dominant structure, the limited partnership;

- the special challenges associated with the publicly traded venture fund, an alternative structure;

- the key challenges facing all venture organizations, regardless of their structure; and

▪ the compensation, organizational, and management strategies that these firms have developed in order to surmount these challenges.

The Evolution of Venture Funding

The venture capital industry began as a predominantly North American phenomenon. It had its origins in the United States, in the offices that managed the wealth of financially successful individuals in the late nineteenth and early twentieth centuries.[1] Families such as the Phippses, Rockefellers, Vanderbilts, and Whitneys invested in and advised a variety of business enterprises, including the predecessors of AT&T, Eastern Airlines, and McDonnell Douglas. As their investments grew, these families began involving outsiders in the selection and oversight of these holdings.

Then in 1946, the first truly modern venture capital firm was born. Named American Research and Development (ARD), the company was founded by MIT president Karl Compton, Harvard Business School professor Georges F. Doriot, and several local business leaders. These men sought to make high-risk investments in emerging companies that based their innovations on technology developed for the war effort.

Raising ARD's first venture fund proved challenging. Most institutional investors approached by Doriot and his compatriots shied away from what they saw as an overly risky opportunity. Many of them questioned whether backing a small, unproven fund that specifically sought high-risk investments was consistent with their fiduciary responsibilities. As a result of these difficulties, ARD's founders ultimately structured the company as a publicly traded, closed-end fund and marketed it mostly to individuals.

The closed-end fund structure offered some significant advantages. Instead of the venture capitalist having to repay funds to investors who had lost interest, such investors simply sold their shares on a public exchange to other investors. This provision allowed the fund to invest in illiquid private firms, secure in the knowledge that it would not need to return its capital to individual investors. Most important, because shares in the fund constituted a liquid investment that could be freely bought or sold, according to Security and Exchange Commission regulations anyone could hold them. Even so, ARD had trouble finding an underwriter to sell the offering. (Some institutions, including MIT and John Hancock Mutual Life, did purchase significant blocks of shares.)

The few other venture organizations launched in the decade after ARD's formation were also structured as publicly traded, closed-end funds. A precedent had been set—largely because public investors were pretty much the only ones willing to bet their resources on venture efforts.

Soon, however, it became clear that the publicly traded structure had some significant drawbacks. In a number of cases, unscrupulous brokers sold the funds to inappropriate investors; for example, elderly people who needed high current income rather than long-term capital gains. When the immediate profits promised by these brokers failed to materialize, the investors vented their frustration not on their broker but on the venture capitalists themselves. For instance, during much of the mid-1950s, Georges Doriot spent most of his time being harassed by investors who had lost substantial sums on their shares of American Research and Development. Something had to change.

The Rise of the Limited Partnership

In 1958, a new structure arose that was intended to address the limitations of the publicly traded funds: the venture capital limited partnership.[2] As before, investors (known here as limited partners) provided capital for venture capitalists (the general partners) to invest. But unlike the earlier structure, limited partnerships were not publicly traded.

The first limited partnership venture capital fund, Draper, Gaither & Anderson, was designed to be exempt from securities regulations, including the exacting disclosure requirements of the Investment Company Act of 1940, which entailed the detailed disclosure of holdings and limited involvement with portfolio firms.[3] In order to be exempt from these regulations, the funds needed to (1) accept capital from fewer than 100 "accredited investors" (those with high annual income or significant net worth) and (2) intend to remain privately held. (In venture capital circles this exemption is often referred to as the "Rule of 99.") In 1996, this requirement was amended to allow these partnerships to accept funds from an unlimited number of "superqualified" investors (those with more than $5 million in assets).

The Draper partnership and similar funds that began to crop up at this time emulated other limited partnerships that were then commonplace, such as those formed to develop real-estate projects and explore oil fields. These partnerships had predetermined, finite lives (usually ten years, though this period usually could be extended). Thus, unlike closed-end funds, which often had indefinite lives, partnerships had to return their funds' assets to investors within a set period.

At the same time, venture capital limited partnerships differed from other kinds of limited partnerships in a crucial way: They made distributions in the form of stock. Rather than selling successful investments and returning cash to their investors, the venture capitalists would simply give investors their allocation of the stock. In this way, investors could choose when to realize the capital gains associated with a fund's investment. This feature benefited individuals and corporate investors enormously, as they could arrange the sale of their shares in a manner that would minimize their tax obligations. For instance, they could choose to hold onto the stock until a year in which they sold an investment that had substantial losses. They could then use the losses to offset the gains from the venture investment.

Though other venture funds soon copied the structure of the Draper fund, limited partnerships made up only a minority of the venture capital pool even as late as the early 1970s. Most venture organizations continued to raise money through closed-end funds or through what were known as Small Business Investment Companies (SBICs)—a program of federally guaranteed risk capital pools established by the U.S. government in 1958 after the launch of the Soviet Union's *Sputnik* satellite triggered widespread fears about the United States' relative technological standing.[4] To boost the United States' stature in this area, the government encouraged would-be venture capitalists to establish pools of risk capital, and provided matching funds and loan guarantees.

Many SBICs raised impressive funds through the 1960s, but the sector's performance soon proved problematic. The combination of federal guarantees and limited scrutiny of SBIC applicants led to unsavory scenarios that foreshadowed the savings-and-loan crisis of the 1980s. All too frequently, unscrupulous or naïve operators were granted SBIC licenses. Many of them invested in firms with poor prospects or backed fraudulent enterprises.

After a robust market for initial and follow-on offerings by high-technology firms in the late 1960s and early 1970s, SBIC performance reached new lows during the market downdraft of the mid-1970s. In part, this shift was triggered by external events: The OPEC oil shock and ensuing recession slashed the growth prospects of firms across the board. Valuations of public and private firms plummeted, reflecting the now meager cash-flow expectations to which businesspeople everywhere had resigned themselves.

Figure 5-1 captures the swings in public-market conditions during this period. The graph depicts the volume of initial and follow-on offerings in

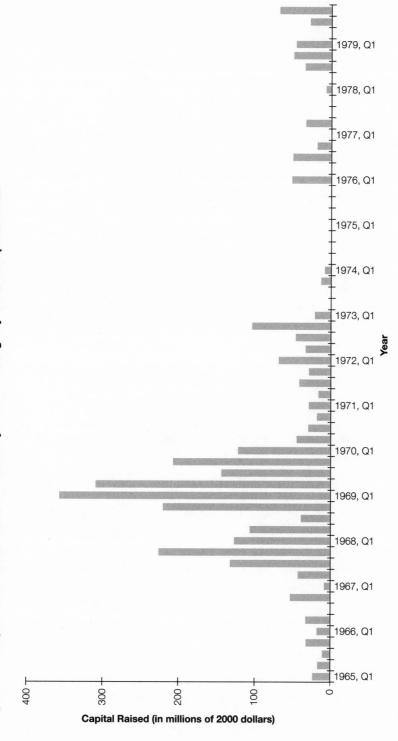

Figure 5-1 Capital Raised in Initial and Secondary Public Offerings by Small Computer Firms

Capital Raised (in millions of 2000 dollars)

Year

Source: Compiled from various issues of *Investment Dealers Digest*.

the sector that saw the greatest concentration by venture investors in these years: computer and computer-related firms. As you can see, the dizzying highs of 1968 and 1969 (the amount raised in these two years totaled $1.5 *billion* in today's dollars) rapidly ebbed in 1970 and later years. From early 1973 to mid-1978, total offerings reached only about $200 million; and during some quarters, *no* financing was raised.

What explains these swings? To be sure, many firms that raised capital during the boom years had business plans that were poorly thought out, or were engaged in doomed battles with entrenched giants such as IBM. Investors may have soberly concluded that these firms had limited prospects. But other firms with "winning" technology also found it difficult to raise capital. For instance, companies seeking to commercialize the personal computer and networking technologies that would exert such a revolutionary impact in the 1980s and 1990s also struggled. The sharp decline in valuation levels and in the receptiveness to new offerings during the mid-1970s perhaps reflected shifts in sentiment from boundless optimism to dark pessimism as well. The well-publicized difficulties of the SBICs—along with those of novice venture organizations—raised red flags for investors. Fund-raising by venture organizations rapidly dwindled, reaching its nadir in 1975. That year, no new venture capital funds were raised.

The Modern Era

This gloomy outlook evaporated once again in the late 1970s and early 1980s—the result of several policy shifts that changed both the willingness of institutions to supply venture capital and the demand for such funds.[5]

Specifically, in 1979 the U.S. Department of Labor clarified what was known as the "prudent man" rule stipulated by the Employee Retirement Income Security Act (ERISA) of 1974. The rule stated that pension managers had to invest their funds' resources with the care of a "prudent man"; that is, carefully and conservatively. Consequently, many pension funds avoided investing in venture capital entirely; it was just too risky for them. In early 1979, however, the Department of Labor ruled that pension-fund managers could take into account portfolio diversification in determining the prudence of an investment. Thus, the ruling implied that the Department of Labor would *not* view allocation of a small fraction of a portfolio to venture capital funds as imprudent, even if a number of companies in the venture capitalist's portfolio failed. That clarification flung the door open for pension funds to invest in venture capital.

Table 5-1   Fund-raising by Venture Capital Partnerships

First Closing of Funds	Number of Funds	Size ($ millions in 2000 dollars)
1978	23	482
1979	27	546
1980	57	1,407
1981	81	1,934
1982	98	2,359
1983	147	6,159
1984	150	5,466
1985	99	4,733
1986	86	5,001
1987	112	6,075
1988	78	4,199
1989	88	3,905
1990	50	2,831
1991	34	1,727
1992	31	2,271
1993	46	2,888
1994	80	4,171
1995	84	4,710
1996	80	7,924
1997	103	9,385
1998	161	19,717
1999	209	38,240
2000	228	69,741

Source: Based on information published in the *Venture Capital Journal* and *Private Equity Analyst,* as well as unpublished databases compiled by Venture Economics and Asset Alternatives.

The first institutions to contribute large investments in venture capital were the endowments of private universities and foundations. These institutions, under less regulatory scrutiny than other institutional investors, had previously led the way into other asset classes as well, such as public equities. Next in line were some of the most sophisticated corporate pension funds, such as those of General Motors and IBM. The 1990s saw the emergence of yet another set of investors in venture capital: public pension funds that managed retirement accounts for teachers, firemen, and other public employees. Though these last investors typically allocated a smaller share of their assets to venture capital than the endowments, their sheer size meant that even minimal allocations could profoundly shape the venture capital industry.

Table 5-1 depicts the substantial rise of capital under management during these years, as well as the growth in the average fund size. Table 5-2 shows the changing mixture of investment sources, especially the

Table 5-2   Sources of Venture Capital Fund-raising

Sources of Funds

Year	Private Pension Funds (%)	Public Pension Funds (%)	Corporations (%)	Individuals (%)	Endowments (%)	Insurance Companies/ Banks (%)	Foreign Investors/ Other (%)	Independent Venture Partnerships as a Share of the Total Venture Pool (%)
1978	15	a	10	32	9	16	18	c
1979	31	a	17	23	10	4	15	c
1980	30	a	19	16	14	13	8	40
1981	23	a	17	23	12	15	10	44
1982	33	a	12	21	7	14	13	58
1983	26	5	12	21	8	12	16	68
1984	25	9	14	15	6	13	18	72
1985	23	10	12	13	8	11	23	73
1986	39	12	11	12	6	10	11	75
1987	27	12	10	12	10	15	14	78
1988	27	20	12	8	11	9	13	80
1989	22	14	20	6	12	13	13	79
1990	31	22	7	11	13	9	7	80
1991	25	17	4	12	24	6	12	80
1992	22	20	3	11	18	14	11	81
1993	59	a	8	7	11	11	4	78
1994	47	a	9	12	21	9	2	78
1995	38	a	2	17	22	18	3	c
1996	43	a	13	9	21	5	8	c
1997	40	a	30	13	9	1	7	c
1998	37	10	18	11	8	3	13	c
1999	43	a	14	10	17	16	b	c
2000	40	a	4	12	21	23	b	c

Source: Based on information published in the *Venture Capital Journal* and *Private Equity Analyst*, as well as unpublished databases compiled by Venture Economics and Asset Alternatives.

[a] In these years, public and private pension fund commitments are reported together.
[b] In these years, foreign investments are not tabulated separately (e.g., investments by foreign individuals are tabulated in the individuals category).
[c] In these years, the share data are not available.

emergence of pension funds as the dominant investor in the late 1970s and early 1980s. While the actual dollars contributed by individual investors actually increased during these years, their percentage of total contributions fell sharply. And though they continued to play an important role, they often lost out in the competition for the ninety-nine investment slots that each fund offered to institutional investors.

The Emergence of Intermediaries

This same period saw the emergence of yet another offshoot of the venture industry: intermediaries who aimed to make the venture capital market more efficient.[6] Investment advisors, or "gatekeepers," have been fixtures in the venture capital world since the early 1970s. The initial intermediary organization was born in 1972, when the First National Bank of Chicago established an advisory group as part of its trust department. These organizations provided advisory services to some clients (who still made the ultimate decision as to where to invest) while exercising discretionary control over other clients' assets. These advisors set up separate accounts for larger investors but commingled the assets of smaller investors into what became known as "funds-of-funds."

The 1990s saw a startling jump in the number of funds-of-funds, as well as the increasing specialization of such funds. Major investment banks, in particular, raised multibillion-dollar funds-of-funds from their wealthiest clients. Other funds—for example, the Common Fund (for university and other educational endowments) and FLAG Venture Partners (for well-off families)—were geared toward certain classes of investors. Some targeted investment niches such as international venture capital funds, minority-managed funds, and those based in a particular state. In the late 1990s, some funds-of-funds were even established to invest in a single fund. Whatever the fund-of-funds' focus, the fund organizers typically charged investors an annual management fee—often 1 percent—based on capital under management. In some funds, managers also received a share of the capital gains generated by the funds (carried interest) in addition to the annual fees.

Just as advisors arose to help investors, placement agents emerged to assist the general partners of venture funds. These agents represent venture capital groups that are in the process of raising funds. Traditionally, placement agents worked only for private equity groups undertaking leveraged buyouts and other later-stage investments. In recent years, however, as venture organizations have begun raising considerably larger funds from a more diverse base of investors, these agents have provided them with services as well. They thus maintain close ties to large investors and have a keen sense of the market. Placement agents range in size from major investment banks such as Merrill Lynch to specialist boutiques (for instance, the Monument Group) to one-person shops.

The Reemergence of Publicly Traded Venture Funds

By the end of the twentieth century, publicly traded venture capital funds were gaining more attention.[7] These organizations included pure venture funds, such as the Internet Capital Group, along with hybrids that combined a venture fund with operating companies (e.g., CMGI and its subsidiary @Ventures) or with an "incubator" for new firms (e.g., Divine Interventures).

The emergence of these funds was accompanied by much hoopla, and many traded up to unsustainably high valuations in 1999 and early 2000. The severe beating that many of them have subsequently taken in the turbulent markets is thus not surprising. At the same time, we believe that this organizational structure will become increasingly common. Our enthusiasm may be surprising, given this structure's troubled historical record and the Securities and Exchange Commission's (SEC's) increasingly severe enforcement of regulatory provisions related to such funds, but it is rooted in a fundamental shift in the U.S. economy. Much of the growth that the venture industry enjoyed during the 1980s and 1990s was fueled by investments from traditional pension, or defined benefit, plans. Pension plans became more and more comfortable with trusting their money to venture capital endeavors, and made increasingly larger allocations to these funds. Moreover, the *size* of the pension funds themselves had swelled as the baby boomer generation aged. Therefore, they had more capital than ever to invest.

During these same decades, more and more younger workers were shifting from these defined benefit plans to managing their own savings in the form of 401(k) plans and other defined contribution plans. Unlike pension funds, defined contribution plans don't mingle individual employees' investments.

For these younger investors, gaining access to limited partnership venture funds was virtually impossible. Securities regulations restricted venture funds to individuals who met stringent criteria based on levels of net worth and income well beyond the average middle-class family. The minimum investment level for any given fund typically was in the millions or tens of millions of dollars. Many established funds did not accept any capital at all from new investors. They had sufficient demand from existing investors, who had the first option to invest in subsequent funds raised by their venture group.

As access to such funds narrowed to just a few elite investors, frustrated ordinary investors found the idea of public venture funds more and more attractive. As the pool of individually managed retirement savings grows ever larger in the years to come, we believe public venture funds will likely play a major role in individual investing. But before that can occur, publicly traded funds must overcome two obstacles: the regulatory climate and pitfalls in valuation.

The Regulatory Challenge. The Investment Company Act of 1940 is one of the most complex and extensive of all U.S. federal securities statutes.[8] One of the four major securities acts enacted during the New Deal era initiated by President Franklin D. Roosevelt, the 1940 Act sought to regulate mutual funds and other instruments for pooled investments in securities. It spelled out detailed regulations governing almost every aspect of investment companies' operations, including reporting, governance, and record keeping. Furthermore, it required that investment companies hold no more than a 10 percent stake in their portfolio companies and forbade their general partners from serving on the firms' boards. These requirements would have made venture capital investing, with its substantial equity stakes and intensive board service, impossible.

Anticipating that investment companies might seek to avoid these requirements, the drafters of the act developed a strict definition of what constituted an investment company. A company would be regarded as an investment firm, the law stated, if it engaged "in the business of investing, reinvesting, or trading in securities" *or* if investment securities represented 40 percent or more of the firm's assets.

Sensitive to the sweeping nature of these requirements, the drafters of the act (and of its subsequent amendments) established a number of exceptions to these rules. One of these relates to private, limited partnerships, such as those seen in traditional venture capital funds. But the 1940 Act has posed some vexing problems for some of the new, publicly traded venture funds. Internet Capital Group (ICG) is an apt example.[9] Before its May 1999 IPO, this organization had fewer than 100 shareholders and was exempt from the 1940 Act requirements. But after the offering, it could no longer remain exempt. Indeed, it was in danger of being designated an investment company because over 96 percent of its assets (other than government securities) were minority positions in companies. In a filing with the Securities and Exchange Commission, however, ICG argued that it still qualified as exempt, because the *bulk* of these assets were in the form of companies that it controlled, even if it had a minority interest. In its filing, the group highlighted its role in the governance of these companies, its active encouragement of intercompany synergies, and other fund-management actions. The appeal succeeded, but these requirements continue to present a major challenge to this new class of funds.

The Valuation Challenge. As if government regulations aren't thorny enough, public venture funds also face a problem endemic to the investment market itself. In many instances, these funds' shares have traded at values strikingly at odds with that of their underlying assets. Despite the fact that in many cases publicly traded venture funds have taken an intentionally conservative stance in their valuation of their portfolio companies (for instance, some retain the valuation at the time of the last venture round, even if the company has had several successes since that date), frequently these funds have traded at huge premiums or discounts to these values. While small, private companies are difficult to value, these considerable deviations suggest that more than just investor confusion is at work.

Similar patterns have emerged among closed-end funds more generally.[10] Even the share price of those funds that hold only public securities (whose market value can be readily observed) will deviate from the value of their underlying holdings. In one often-observed pattern, funds initially trade at a premium to the underlying value of the funds' assets, but soon begin to trade at a discount. Financial economists have offered various explanations for these discounts. In some periods, investors seem to assign a "franchise value" to the investment group, believing that it will generate hefty returns in the future. At other times, they seem to assume that a fund will perform poorly in the future. The extent of the discount seems to be associated with bearish versus bullish sentiment in the market as a whole.

During periods of bearish sentiment toward high technology, the poor price performance of these funds has made it difficult for the funds to access capital. They've thus had to husband their funds (e.g., eschew new investments) and have been unable to make aggressive follow-on investments in portfolio companies. In fact, during the period in the 1960s when technology companies traded at depressed valuations, venture groups such as Boston Capital came under the scrutiny of hostile investors, who proposed to purchase a controlling stake in the funds and liquidate their assets.[11]

Thus, before the public venture model can truly work, there's a great need for education—both of regulators and of public investors. But the powerful economic forces behind the push for such investments suggests that it's only a matter of time until these funds emerge as important actors on the venture stage.

A Closer Look at the Venture Capital Limited Partnership

The limited partnership structure has not only allowed venture funds to raise capital, but also to choose and manage investments successfully. And because this structure has dominated the evolution of the venture capital market, it makes sense to take a closer look at how the different elements of such a partnership function together, as well as why they have evolved as they have.

The structuring of limited partnership venture funds may initially seem complex and technical—perhaps better left to legal experts than to general managers. But the subject of partnership structure is a critically important one. Why? The structural features of these limited partnerships—whether management fees, profit-sharing rules, or contractual terms—profoundly shape the decisions of many individuals, including investors, the entrepreneurs they back, bankers who are underwriting a firm backed by venture capital, corporate-development officers who have invested alongside venture capitalists in a young company, and pension fund and other institutional managers who are entrusting their organizations' capital to a venture fund.

An example may help to illustrate this point. Almost all venture funds are designed to be self-liquidating, that is, they must dissolve after ten to twelve years. This scheduled termination imposes a healthy discipline on everyone involved in the fund. For one thing, it forces investors to take the necessary but painful step of "pulling the plug" on underperforming firms in their portfolios.

However, the self-liquidation structure can also prompt venture capital organizations to rush young firms' IPOs in order to demonstrate a successful track record—even if the investees aren't ready to go public. This "grandstanding" can damage the long-run prospects of entrepreneurial firms.[12]

The experience of Illinois Superconductor, a spin-off from Argonne National Laboratory, makes this danger all too clear.[13] The firm's venture capital backer, ARCH Venture Partners, had raised its initial fund in an unusual way: It had received the funds from the University of Chicago, with the mandate to encourage the establishment of new firms based on discoveries at the school and at Argonne (which the university managed).

The venture capitalists at ARCH were, however, eager to change their status from that of university employees to that of independent venture capitalists—and gain the greater autonomy and compensation that the latter enjoy. To do this, they would need to raise a fund from outside investors. ARCH's partners knew that it would be difficult to raise such a fund without first demonstrating a success. Therefore, they urged Illinois Superconductor to go public—which it did in October 1993. ARCH launched fund-raising for its $30 million second fund a few weeks later.

While it's difficult to say for certain that an IPO has occurred too early, with the benefit of hindsight we might conclude that Illinois Superconductor went public too soon. The firm suffered relentless losses and ultimately had to raise equity through a variable convertible preferred security that proved costly to the existing shareholders. As a result, the share price took a dive, and the firm was delisted from the Nasdaq National Market System.

The various elements of the limited partnership fund structure—particularly the general partners' incentive compensation and contractual restrictions—strongly influence the outcome of a fund. Limited partners choosing between venture funds—just like the venture capitalists themselves when considering business plans—are subject to the same stumbling blocks that we explored in chapter 2: uncertainty, information gaps, soft assets, and market dynamics. The structures of incentive compensation and contractual restrictions aid in negotiating those obstacles.

General Partners' Incentive Compensation

The compensation earned by the general partners of a limited partnership venture fund takes two forms:

1. The management fee that the general partners charge investors

2. The share of the profits, or carried interest, that the general partners receive when the investments are liquidated.

Management fees range from 1 percent to 3 percent, though most hover around 2 to 2.5 percent. Typically, the percentage is based on the capital raised by the fund, though in some cases it may depend on the value of the fund's assets or some other measure. This fee is intended to defray the day-to-day expenses of fund management, from travel to office expenses to partner salaries. In many cases, the fee is lowered in the later years of the fund, when the portfolio is being wound down and the amount of partner involvement is expected to decrease accordingly.

Carried interest provides an incentive for the partners to work hard. When an investment is liquidated, the capital gains are divided among the general and limited partners. In this way, investors can be certain that they are benefiting from their "leap of faith" in the same ways the general partners are. This provision can help ease investors' concerns about their limited ability to oversee the fund managers' day-to-day activities.

Originally, fund managers received a share of the profits only *after* the investors had recouped their capital. Thus, if a fund raised $100 million from investors, the venture capitalists themselves would not see any proceeds until stock or cash totaling $100 million had been returned to the investors.

Over time, however, investors realized that this compensation scheme could lead to opportunistic behavior on the part of fund managers. Consider a case where a venture group that has raised $100 million holds the securities of two firms in its portfolio, each of which is valued by the market at $100 million. Suppose the venture group knows about significant weaknesses in the business model of the first firm, an Internet portal for dog lovers, that aren't apparent to outsiders, while it believes the second firm, a networking equipment manufacturer, has excellent prospects and that its stock is likely to appreciate. With the older compensation scheme in place, the venture group would be strongly tempted to distribute the shares of DogGoneIt.com (the overvalued firm) first, so that their investors would get all the shares. The fund partners would then receive a 20 percent stake of profits of the fund—shares of the second, undervalued security. When all the investments were ultimately sold in the marketplace, the venture capitalists would likely end up with more than 20 percent of the capital gains: the value of the shares of the dog portal may have fallen considerably by the time they were sold by the limited partners.

Because of this danger, an alternative profit-sharing scheme emerged. With the new structure, the venture group receives a share of each distribution, even if the investors have not yet recouped their capital in full.

The part of the distribution that represents the original cost of the investment is returned to the investor. All the capital gains are then divided according to the partnership's sharing rule.

Consider the case in which a fund with a 20 percent carried interest invested in a start-up at $2 per share, and sold the company for $12 per share. The first $2 of the cash from the sale of each share, representing the original cost, would be returned to the investors. The $10 of capital gains would then be divided, with 20 percent ($2) going to the venture capitalists, and an additional $8 going to the investors.

For many years, this 20 percent carried interest sharing rule prevailed in the industry. Numerous other partnerships, such as hedge, oil-and-gas, and buyout funds use this rule as well. In fact, investment organizations as far back as the British maritime partnerships of the seventeenth century and the Venetian and Genoese merchant agreements in the twelfth and thirteenth centuries used this same calculation.[14]

Nevertheless, from the earliest days of the venture industry, there has been a variety of ways firms have handled the distribution of carried interest. Though almost all less-experienced funds rely on the 20 percent rule, older and more established venture groups have displayed more diversity. Some managers of top-tier groups have demanded—and received— higher carried interests, as much as 30 percent.

What explains this variety? In first-time funds, a venture capitalist will work hard even without strong compensation incentives. That's because he primarily wants to establish a reputation for selecting attractive investments or adding value to the firms in his portfolio. Once he builds this track record, he'll be able to raise additional funds and sustain his organization's success. But as he becomes a more seasoned fund manager, the "career-concern" incentive becomes much less important to him. An experienced investor will then need other reasons to work hard—namely, a bigger share of his fund's profits.

In recent years, these disparities between new and established funds have widened. More and more seasoned venture groups have successfully demanded carried interest of 25 to 30 percent. For instance, the venture firms Accel and Matrix raised their profit share to 30 percent around the end of 1999, after having hiked their partners' share from 20 percent to 25 percent just a few years before.[15] Both firms had enjoyed substantial investment returns, and had risen to the top echelon of the venture industry.[16] (See figure 5-2.)

Figure 5-2 Level of Carried Interest for Venture Funds of Various Sizes, 1995–2000

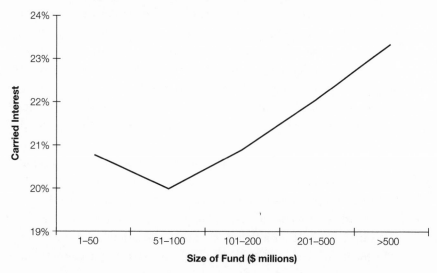

Source: Based on the authors' study of over 1,000 partnership agreements and private placement memoranda held by a variety of large institutional investors.

Contractual Restrictions

The incentive of carried interest helps protect investors from the damage to their returns that can result if venture capitalists do not apply themselves to managing their fund. But investors seek to protect themselves in other ways as well. The partnership agreements governing venture capital funds specify acceptable and unacceptable behavior on the part of everyone involved. The covenants are motivated primarily by investors' desire to mitigate conflicts of interest, to make sure that the general partners "feel the pain" if the fund is unsuccessful, and to limit excessive risk taking by fund managers.

Conflicts of Interest. Many venture organizations manage multiple funds, formed several years apart. This situation can lead to conflicts of interest as the fund managers try to balance the needs of the overall fund family (and themselves) against those of the investors in a particular fund. For example, a venture capitalist by the name of David Silver raised two funds, Santa Fe Venture Partners I and II, from a large number of pension funds and insurance firms.[17] The first fund made a series of investments in technology companies. Much of the capital from this fund went to a computer retailer that soon suffered huge losses as it attempted to gain a foothold in a highly competitive market. The offering memorandum for the second fund stipulated that the fund was intended to support medical-technology companies. However, the capital from the second fund went in large part to shore up the failing retailer backed by the first fund. Though the investors ultimately sued and wrested control of the funds from Silver, there were few assets left to salvage by that point.

This isn't the only conflict of interest that can occur.[18] The possibility of distorted valuation in follow-on investments is also high. Many venture funds will write up the valuation of firms in their portfolios to the price paid in the last venture round. By having the second fund invest in one of the first fund's firms at an inflated valuation, the original fund can (temporarily) inflate its reported performance. This move may allow them to more readily raise a third fund. So even if it makes sense for a venture capital group to invest in an enterprise that another fund has already backed, it might do so at too high a valuation.

To guard against these sorts of conflicts, partnership agreements for subsequent funds frequently require that the fund's advisory board review such follow-on investments or that a majority (or super-majority) of the investors approve these transactions. Contracts may also require that the earlier fund invest simultaneously with the second fund at the same valuation. Alternatively, the limited partners may allow the new investment only if one or more unaffiliated venture organizations simultaneously invest at the same price.

Another way to address potential conflicts of interest is to curb the ability of venture capitalists to invest personal funds in firms. After all, if fund managers contribute personal wealth to selected firms, they may devote excessive time to these firms and may resist terminating funding if the firms stumble. Thus many partnership agreements limit the size of the investment that a fund's venture capitalists can make in any of the fund's portfolio firms. In addition, investors may require venture capitalists to seek permission from the advisory board or the investors themselves before investing their own funds in a private firm. Other agreements require venture capitalists to invest a set dollar amount or percentage in every investment made by the fund. This mechanical rule limits the danger that venture capitalists will exploit their inside knowledge by investing their own money—instead of the funds'—in the most promising transactions or favor firms where they have a larger personal stake.

Limiting Changes to the Compensation Scheme. To ensure that the compensation scheme laid out in a venture fund agreement provides adequate incentives to manage the fund, limited partners may further restrict the general partners' ability to control it.

The most direct way for venture capitalists to control their compensation is to sell their interest in the general partnership. Granted, these interests are not precisely comparable with investors' stakes. (For instance, as we've seen, many venture capitalists receive distributions only after their investors recoup their capital.) Yet these interests may still constitute attractive investments—especially if they're offered at the right price. Investors, who may worry that such sales will reduce venture capitalists' incentives to monitor their investments, often prohibit these sales.

Some venture capitalists may also try to ensure an attractive return for themselves by raising a large follow-on fund. The new fund boosts the management fees that these venture capitalists receive. But as they manage more and more capital, they often have less energy and time available to devote to existing funds. Partnership agreements may prohibit venture capitalists from raising a new fund until a set percentage of the portfolio has been invested or until a given date.

Finally, some venture capitalists try to secure more compensation by engaging in outside activities such as managing a firm or another investment fund. Because these activities take away from the attention that a venture capitalist can pay to his fund's investments, partnership agreements may require venture capitalists to devote a specified amount of their time to managing the partnership's investments. Alternatively, the contract may restrict the venture capitalists' involvement in businesses outside the venture fund's portfolio. These limitations often apply only to the first years of the partnership, or before a set percentage of the fund's capital is invested. During this period, the success of the fund hinges tightly on the venture capitalists' undivided attention.

The following shows how one investor experienced the problem of shifting compensation. The Iowa Public Employees' Retirement System (IPERS) wanted to encourage venture capital activity in that state.[19] To do this, IPERS gave $15 million to a California-based venture organization, which agreed to manage a new fund, Heartland Seed Capital Fund, L.P. Heartland's purpose was to invest in promising ventures in Iowa. After three years, however, the fund had made only one investment, using only $1 million of the available capital. Meanwhile, the partners had collected $1.4 million in management fees, and were demanding another $500,000 in fees from IPERS. In the litigation that ensued, the pension fund alleged that its new partners had devoted most of their time to investment activities involving their funds on the East and West coasts, and had virtually ignored the Heartland funds.

Excessive Risk-Taking. Many investors in venture funds worry that the fund's managers will take excessive risks with their capital. Because these managers receive a share of the profits if the investment succeeds but do not absorb any losses beyond the small amount of capital that they themselves invest in the fund, they can gain disproportionately by putting the portfolio at extreme risk.

Venture agreements employ several tools to limit such risk taking. They often restrict the amount that the venture capitalists can invest in any one portfolio company. Moreover, they may limit the venture capitalists' use of debt (prohibiting both leveraging the fund and guaranteeing the debt of the portfolio companies).

General partners may also be tempted to choose investment opportunities in industries in which they have little expertise in the hopes of gaining experience. For instance, during the 1980s, many venture funds began investing in leveraged buyouts. Those that developed a successful track record proceeded to raise funds specializing in LBOs; many more, however, lost considerable sums on these forays.[20] Similarly, numerous buyout groups invested in venture capital transactions in 1999 and 2000. Only a handful succeeded in this class of investments. Not surprisingly, limited partners often restrict the fund's choice of investments to those about which the general partners have some knowledge.

When Are Restrictions Used? There are some aspects of venture capitalists' behavior that limited partnership agreements *don't* address.[21] For example, the vesting schedule of general partnership interests is typically not discussed. Such details are usually spelled out in agreements between the venture capitalists themselves, not between these managers and their limited partners. Another instance where limited partners have little input is the agreements among general partners regarding the division of the profits. It is up to the venture firm to decide how much of the fund's profits accrue to the senior venture capitalists, who may focus on setting the fund's overall direction and fund-raising, and how much accrue to the younger partners, who undertake the bulk of the day-to-day management work. It is likely that the input that limited partners have into these questions will grow, as the imbalance between supply and demand in the venture capital market eases in the next few years.

All the restrictions we've explored certainly increase the complexity of venture dealings. As groups build up reputations for probity and caution in their dealings, however, the need for investors to protect their interests through convoluted partnership agreements diminishes. Even if investors wanted to restrict the behavior of the most established funds' managers, they likely wouldn't succeed. There is so much demand for funds raised by top-tier venture organizations that a single potential investor's insistence on dictating certain terms will probably fall on deaf ears.

Raising Venture Funds: Problems and Strategies

All venture capital organizations face the challenge of raising funds, and this task becomes easier or harder depending on what's going on in the economy at large and in various industries. Nevertheless, first-time funds and established funds each experience the fund-raising process in markedly different ways.

First-Time Funds

For first-time funds, the fund-raising process can prove painfully time-consuming. Many investors are reluctant to bet on an unproven team. Even if the general partners have successful individual track records, if they haven't worked together before as a team, investors get nervous.

The experience in the early 1990s of Michael Cronin and Michael Lazarus, general partners of Weston Presidio Capital, provides an apt example.[22] Each of the two men had extensive experience in private equity—Cronin as an investor with Security Pacific Capital for fifteen years, and Lazarus as director of the private placement department of Montgomery Securities, a California investment bank specializing in technology and growth firms. Both men had made or recommended investments that had yielded attractive returns. They now wanted to set up a new fund that would focus on later-stage venture capital investments across a variety of industries.

Despite their impressive backgrounds, the partners found it virtually impossible to find institutional investors to commit to their fund. Some pension funds they approached were initially receptive, but they informed Cronin and Lazarus that the partners would need to demonstrate the attractiveness of the investment opportunity to their investment advisors before they would see any capital. Many of these advisors required numerous meetings with the two partners and their associates, during which they scrutinized their track records and their proposed strategy. The two partners stepped through hoop after hoop—but to no avail. The investment advisors—many of whom shunned first-time funds as a matter of policy—ultimately turned them down.

First-time venture groups thus face a frustrating dilemma: How can they raise a fund without a track record, when to obtain a track record they need to have raised a fund? New venture capital organizations recommend addressing this conundrum in several ways:

- *Strategy #1:* Contribute more of the capital. U.S. tax law formerly stipulated that general partners must invest at least 1 percent of the venture capital raised by a limited partnership.[23] Though the government later relaxed this requirement, most general partners still contribute only 1 percent. General partners of first-time funds who feel the need to establish credibility with potential partners may supply a larger share of the capital. This helps the fund achieve a critical mass and signals the general partners' commitment to its success. But in many cases, general partners of first-time funds don't have enough liquid resources to provide even their 1 percent share (in this case, they may provide notes rather than cash). Thus, they may be unable to signal potential investors in this way. Furthermore, some investors view such large commitments with skepticism, believing that the seemingly generous venture capitalists may shy away from risky but attractive investments.

- *Strategy #2:* Identify investors who aren't motivated only by financial returns, but who instead seek to gain some strategic benefit from contributing to the fund. For instance, in the hopes of stimulating local economic development, a state pension fund may reserve a certain portion of its venture capital allocation for funds based solely in the state. Similarly, a corporation with extensive activity in an industry not well served by existing venture funds, such as advanced ceramics, may benefit by investing in a new fund specializing in this area. In these cases, investors are willing to accept a lower expected financial return in exchange for the non-monetary benefits that the investment may provide. Along similar lines, many first-time funds have found that individual investors, particularly those with backgrounds in hedge funds or investment banking, have a greater appetite for risk than institutional investors and a higher tolerance for the variable returns that often come with first-time funds.

- *Strategy #3:* Establish an alliance with an existing institution such as an investment bank or another venture capital group. In many of these arrangements, the first-time fund and its strategic partner jointly own the management company that runs the new venture group. The strategic partner may also play an important role in the governance of the fund, perhaps even having the right to review and approve all investment decisions.

    There is a caveat: While such an alliance may impart credibility to a fledgling venture group, it also comes with some real costs. Other investors in the fund may fear that the strategic partner will distort investment decisions (for instance, blocking investments that might compete with its long-standing clients). They may also fear that, with a substantial flow of carried interest toward the institution, the venture capital investors won't have as strong an incentive to succeed. The good news is that many venture capital groups that have used this part-nering strategy have gone on to establish stellar track records. Over time, they've realized that they no longer need these institutional ties to raise money and gradually ended the relationships. (The bad news is that unraveling such ties can prove costly and time-consuming.)

- *Strategy #4:* Recruit a lead investor (often known as a special limited partner) to contribute a significant percentage (often 20 percent to 50 percent) of the capital of the fund. This lead investor may also provide general partners with some "seed funding" before the fund closes, so as to cover the often substantial costs incurred in marketing a new fund.

    Michael Cronin and Michael Lazarus, for instance, used the fourth strategy when raising their first fund. They recruited Mercury Asset Management, the British equity manager, to serve as a lead investor. In this role, the British fund contributed $25 million in cap-ital and defrayed some organizational expenses. In exchange, Mercury benefited in three ways. First, because it contributed one-third of the fund's initial capitalization, it received one-third of the payouts to the limited partners. Because limited partners typically receive 80 percent of the capital gains of a first-time fund, this translated into about 27 percent of the overall profits from the fund. In addition, special limited partners often receive a share of the fund's carried interest. In this case, Mercury gained one-third of the carried interest, or another 6 percent of the fund's overall profits. Finally, Mercury paid lower management fees than the other limited partners.

Though involving a special limited partner has benefits, it may also incur costs for the general partners. Payments to the lead investor directly reduce the general partners' returns. These venture capitalists may also have to cede some control over the governance of the fund; for instance, the special limited partner may dominate a powerful advisory board that monitors the fund's activities. Finally, these concessions can alienate potential new investors. To illustrate, Cronin and Lazarus found that other investors interested in Weston Presidio demanded lead-investor concessions for themselves, even though they hadn't demonstrated the same confidence in the team.

Established Funds

Compared to first-time funds, established funds have a much easier time raising capital. Clearly, the information problems that afflict younger funds are greatly reduced here. In the most established groups, funds can be raised with just a few phone calls to existing limited partners.

At the same time, fund-raising can pose a number of dilemmas for even the most established venture fund:

- *How much money should be raised?* In recent times, successful venture groups have found it possible to raise sums that would have been unthinkable just a few years before. The main limitation to the amount raised was in many cases internal; the general partners had to decide how much money they could deploy while still earning high returns. In many instances, the groups also worried about antagonizing long-standing limited partners, who might worry if the group grew too quickly. While others doubtless could replace these investors, would the new investors be as likely to reinvest with the venture group if market conditions turned stormy?

- *From what type of investors should the funds be raised?* At least since
  the late 1970s, venture capital organizations have turned to pension
  funds and other institutions for the bulk of their capital. But over time,
  the general partners of established funds have amassed significant
  wealth. These partners have been deciding to contribute far more
  than the traditional 1 percent to their fund's capital. Eventually, such
  investments can crowd out other investors.[24] For instance, Benchmark
  Capital raised $1 billion in its fourth fund in late 1999. Fully 35
  percent of the capital was contributed not by institutional investors,
  but by the general partners themselves and by the founders of companies they had previously funded (which included many successful
  e-commerce concerns). The partners undertook this allocation despite the many institutional investors clamoring for access to the fund.

- *Who should be in the general partnership?* Many venture groups have
  sought to grow by recruiting more staff. But it is not easy to rapidly
  scale an organization by recruiting more partners and associates. In
  many cases, the groups have found the acculturation of new staff challenging, and the need to build new organizational structures daunting.
  A related challenge has been succession within the partnership.[25] In
  some cases, newly wealthy senior partners have sought to retire too
  soon, leaving a leadership vacuum as the younger partners struggle
  for direction. In others, the opposite problem has occurred: senior
  partners have refused to relinquish control (and their substantial share
  of the carried interest) for too long. In these instances, impatient
  junior partners are likely to defect to rival groups or start groups of
  their own.

How Venture Groups Are Managed

We've looked at how venture organizations have evolved over the years,
how they respond to their investors' concerns, and how they raise capital.
But once the funds are gathered, how are these groups managed?

There is tremendous diversity in management styles. For instance,
successful venture groups use very different approaches for assessing
opportunities. In some cases, all the partners must agree before the group
completes a transaction. In other instances, the objections of at least two
or three partners are required to scuttle a transaction. In yet others, a

formal review process requires one partner to actively present the case for a particular investment, while another argues against the deal.

To a certain extent, these differences reflect the varied nature of the investments that these groups are making. For example, it's unlikely that a venture company specializing in early-stage investments in highly competitive Silicon Valley could survive if it demanded an exhaustive evaluation of every *possible* investment. But the diversity of management styles also reflects the simple fact that there's no best avenue to venture capital success.

Still, there appear to be three hallmarks of effective venture organizations, and all three transcend particular investment approaches. These hallmarks are:

- Speed of approach

- Systemization

- Intergenerational management

The Need for Speed

Speed lies at the very heart of the venture capital process. Venture-backed firms rarely succeed if they don't move quickly in response to competitors' behavior and shifts in the market. Granted, these firms may be sharply focused on their target markets. But the challenges of competing with large corporations are so daunting that firms must continue to quickly take advantage of new opportunities.

Similarly, these firms' investors face a major challenge: responding rapidly to new opportunities while avoiding "black holes," or costly investments that yield no returns. There's no question that rapid decision making on the part of venture-fund managers is essential.

Sequoia Capital's May 2000 decision to invest in the Internet content-delivery firm Bang Networks illustrates how important speed is to venture capital success.[26] Sequoia had learned about Bang Networks on a Wednesday in May 2000 and became instantly interested. Bang Networks' management team had plans to meet with another leading West Coast venture organization on the following Monday (the day when venture partners traditionally gather to review their investments' progress and weigh new opportunities) to discuss a possible financing. Hearing this, Sequoia assembled a special meeting of partners on the next day, Thursday. After a brief meeting following Bang's presentation, the venture group offered the young firm a term sheet, which Bang accepted that weekend. By moving quickly, Sequoia grabbed what promised to be an attractive opportunity—and prevented another venture group from investing.

The Benefits of Systemization

The systemization of processes and routines may sound quite antithetical to fast decision making. Many venture organizations do begin their lives with a very informal approach to just about every aspect of their business. Indeed, the very nature of the venture capital process—investors continually searching for technologies that established players have neglected—might seem to defy rigid systemization.

But a systematic approach to evaluating investment opportunities and then monitoring investees' progress is critical if a venture firm wants not only to survive but also to thrive. For example, successful firms methodically manage the risk of their overall portfolio. Senior partners frequently monitor the mixture of investments in the portfolio in terms of industry focus, investee stage of development, and size of holdings to minimize the impact of external events. This isn't to say that these firms never make exceptional "bets" in particular areas. But without sharply defining their investment and oversight process, venture groups risk falling victim to utter chaos.

Pittsburgh-based Adams Capital Management exemplifies this kind of systemization.[27] As a late venture-industry entrant based in a city not known for its investment activity, the fund's founder, Joel Adams, knew he needed to make his investment approach crystal clear. He developed a process that he termed "structured navigation." Through this process, he and his partners identified investment opportunities by calling on outside experts to periodically review a wide variety of industries and identify possible sources of attractive opportunities. Adams created a similarly disciplined process for nurturing individual investments, including five criteria (for example, the establishment of strategic alliances) defined in advance.

The Intergenerational Dilemma

A critical success factor in a venture capital fund is the venture team itself. But in many cases, venture groups haven't bothered to develop a strategy for cultivating and retaining talented team members and investors. Some have paid a high price in the defection of key investors and even the dissolution of the group itself.

One roadblock to the retention of talent is controversy over the distribution of carried interest. Often, junior partners clamor for a larger share of the profits, arguing that they are responsible for the bulk of the day-to-day work in the fund. Senior partners might counter these claims by pointing out that they're the ones who created the "franchise value." Without that value, the senior partners add, the younger folks would find it much harder to reel in attractive opportunities. Moreover, the senior partners often have strong ties to the key limited partners, and can provide guidance based on decades of experience. In groups that have weathered a number of transitions between generations, often a shared consensus emerges: that senior partners should gradually disengage from the day-to-day management of the partnership and, accordingly, reduce their share of the carried interest.

These kinds of disputes have sometimes led to the dissolution of well-known venture firms. For instance, after sixteen years of successful investing in such firms as Broderbund Software, Chiron Corporation, Continental Cablevision, and Powersoft Corporation, Burr, Egan, Deleage and Co. decided in 1995 not to raise another fund.[28] The firm had been struggling for several years to come up with a formula to properly reward younger partners while at the same time recognizing the contributions of the founders. The process proved increasingly contentious, and many of the younger investment professionals left to join other established venture groups or begin funds of their own. Ultimately, the group decided that the only solution was for the partners to go their separate ways.

These challenges are not unique to venture capital. Firms specializing in law, accounting, and other professional services struggle with them as well. But the modest size of venture groups and their intense reliance on key personnel intensify the pressures in the venture capital environment—all the more reason for a thoughtful approach to these issues.

Venture Capitalists: A Class of Innovators in Themselves

A diverse array of organizations have undertaken venture capital investments over the years, using a broad range of management styles and practices. By trial and error, venture capitalists have developed partnership, compensation, and contractual structures that specifically address the severe information gaps and other problems plaguing investor relations. And the best among them have honed their processes and operations. All of these strategies have helped venture professionals better tackle their primary challenges—selecting and nurturing portfolio firms—and weather the ups and downs of the venture capital market.

Sandwiched between the expectations and opportunities of both their own investors and the promising young firms that they fund, venture capitalists face a sobering set of challenges. And while the partnership model has been a remarkably powerful one, venture firms have by no means cleared all these hurdles. In the next chapter, we'll look up close at boom-and-bust cycles and the challenges they continue to pose for venture capitalists. In chapter 10, we'll consider the quite dramatic ways in which the partnership model is likely to evolve over the next decade.

6

---

*Boom and Bust
in the
Venture Industry*

■

The overshooting in the venture capital market in 1999–2000 is an all-too-familiar pattern.

The general partners at Mayfield Fund, an old-line Silicon Valley venture organization, have experienced one of the swings in funding that characterize the venture capital industry.[1] In the early days, the group practically had to sweat blood to raise its first funds. For example, in 1969 it managed to scrape up a meager $3.7 million. Five years later, the partners did little better—raising just $7.5 million despite their initial fund's considerable success.

Flash forward to 1999—a year when venture capitalists enjoyed a robust investment market. That year, Mayfield closed on a $450 million fund, which was nearly twice as large as the fund it had raised just two years before. Ten months later, Mayfield's partners were back in the market yet again, this time closing on a $1 *billion* fund.

In chapter 5, we mentioned a key dynamic within the venture capital industry: the ebb and flow of fund-raising and investing. The pattern of "feast or famine" that Mayfield and so many other venture organizations experience is more than just an item of intellectual curiosity to venture groups. Historically, a direct relationship has emerged between fund-raising and investment performance. Often, periods of accelerated fund-raising activity have preceded an alarming downturn in returns. Figure 6-1 depicts this relationship.

Perhaps not surprisingly, this pattern has spawned a deep pessimism among many venture capitalists. The industry, they lament, is inherently cyclical; all the players can do is ride out the waves. Each boom in fund-raising sparks too-rapid growth and tempts investors to take extreme risks.

Figure 6-1   Venture Capital Fund-raising and Returns

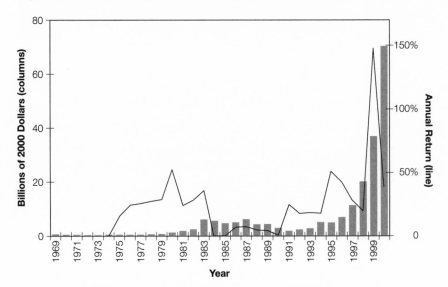

Source: Based on information published in the *Venture Capital Journal* and *Private Equity Analyst,* as well as
unpublished databases compiled by Venture Economics and Asset Alternatives.

Note: Returns were slightly negative in 1974 and 1984.

Eventually, returns suffer, which in turn triggers a decline in funds raised. Then the cycle begins all over again.

But just how accurate are these assumptions? Do boom times *have* to lead inevitably to busts? And do venture capitalists *have* to resign themselves to the nature of the fund-raising cycle? Not necessarily. By looking at the venture capital process through the lens of supply and demand, we can see that although shifts in either aspect of the industry can indeed pose challenges for everyone involved, the boom-and-bust cycle is *not* inevitable.

Specifically, we need to consider

▪ the differences between short-term and long-term developments in the venture industry,

▪ the forces behind "overshooting," or a jump in available venture capital that outstrips actual demand, and

▪ whether the boom in venture capital that hit in 1997–2000 represents the all-too-familiar feast-or-famine pattern—or a fundamental shift in the industry.

For an institutional investor, a venture capital group, a promising entrepreneurial firm, or an investment bank, these perspectives can illustrate—
and suggest a response to—the ebb and flow of money into the venture
capital industry.

The Dynamics Behind the Boom-and-Bust Cycle

Since the early 1960s, the business press has commented on the venture
capital market. Searching for clues as to the state of the market, analysts
have focused their attention on changes in capital raised, deals forged and
liquidated, and valuations assigned to firms. But to really understand the
forces behind these phenomena, we need to step back and consider what's
driving the fundamental pattern.[2]

Let's start by looking at a core part of the industry: the amount of venture capital raised. To do this, we'll use two tools from basic economics: a
demand curve and a supply curve. Just as shifts in supply and demand
shape the markets for commodities such as oil and semiconductors, these
same kinds of changes influence the amount of capital that venture funds
can raise.

But what determines the *supply* of venture capital? Simple: the willingness of investors to provide money to venture firms. This willingness in
turn hinges on the kinds of returns these investors expect to receive from
their venture activity compared with what they think they can earn from
other investments. Figure 6-2 captures this fundamental dynamic. As the
returns investors expect to earn from their venture funds increase—that
is, as we go up the vertical axis—these investors are willing to supply more
and more capital (we move to the right along the horizontal axis).

Now let's turn to the *demand* side of the picture. The desire of entrepreneurial firms for venture capital drives demand. But, like supply,
demand also varies with expected returns. How? As investors insist on
higher returns—for example, when a bout of inflation leads investors to
revise their investment benchmarks upward—fewer entrepreneurial
firms can come through with those returns. (After all, when you keep raising the bar, fewer can clear it.) As figure 6-3 shows, demand typically
declines when investors' expectations rise.

Together, supply and demand determine the amount of venture capi-
tal available for investing, as well as the returns that investors receive.
Superimposing figures 6-2 on figure 6-3, we get the results in figure 6-4.
In the figure, we can discern the amount of available venture capital (Q)

Figure 6-2   Supply Curve for Venture Capital

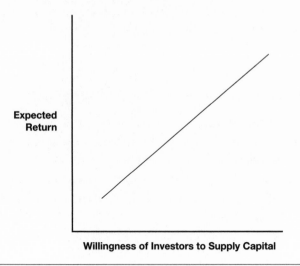

Willingness of Investors to Supply Capital

Figure 6-3   Demand Curve for Venture Capital

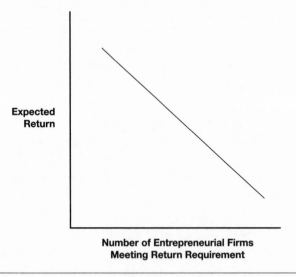

**Number of Entrepreneurial Firms
Meeting Return Requirement**

and the average return that it expects to earn (R) by drawing a straight line to the point at which supply (S) and demand (D) cross.

So far, the figures we've looked at depict changes in supply and demand as straight lines. But in the real world, these changes don't always unfold with such consistency. For instance, think back to the U.S. Labor

Figure 6-4   Steady-State Level of Venture Capital

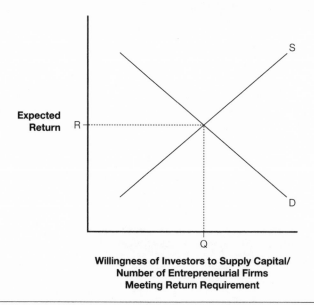

Willingness of Investors to Supply Capital/
Number of Entrepreneurial Firms
Meeting Return Requirement

Department's 1979 clarification of the "prudent man" rule of the Employee Retirement Income Security Act, which we discussed in chapter 5. Before 1979, investors' willingness to provide capital looked like the supply curve shown in figure 6-5. The part of the curve that angles up and to the right reflects investors other than pension funds. As before, the higher the expected return, the more they were willing to invest in venture capital. The abruptly vertical segment of the curve represents the fact that, before 1979, the supply of venture capital was, in essence, fixed at a certain level. That's because pension funds—which controlled a considerable portion of the economy's long-term savings—could not invest in venture capital. Thus, no matter what kinds of returns investors expected and how willing they were to provide capital, the *actual* supply of capital was limited by pension funds' inability to participate.

Four Pivotal Events

Obviously, these graphs are oversimplified and can't capture all the complex institutional realities that affect venture capital fund-raising. Still, they *can* help us understand large trends in the venture industry. Let's use them to look at four pivotal events that have occurred over the past four

Figure 6-5   Supply of Venture Capital Prior to 1979 ERISA Policy Shift

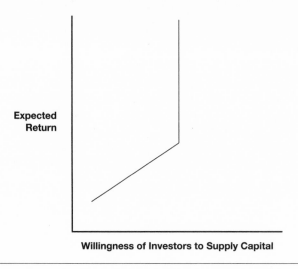

Expected
Return

Willingness of Investors to Supply Capital

decades. With each turning point, we'll identify whether the event represented a shift in the supply of or demand for venture capital, and we'll explore the event's implications for fund-raising and returns. These interpretations, to be sure, simplify a messy reality. At the same time, they clearly demonstrate that the pessimistic view discussed above—that more venture capital fund-raising must inevitably lead to a decline in returns—is unwarranted.

1995–1998: Demand Shock

In the mid-1990s, more and more people gained access to the Internet, and the use of the World Wide Web exploded. The new technologies' ability to transfer graphics and text quickly and interactively provided businesspeople everywhere with a new, powerful tool. Indeed, this technology would transform commerce as well as the internal management of firms in almost every industry.

Not surprisingly, these developments spurred demand for venture capital financing, as shown in figure 6-6. In the figure, the demand curve shifts to the right, from D_1 to D_2, as more and more firms seek venture financing. Thus, no matter how high the return demanded by any given investor, there are considerably more firms that could meet these expectations. In turn, this shift triggered an increase in available venture capi-

Figure 6-6   Impact of Demand Shock

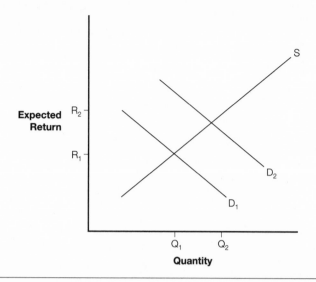

tal, from Q_1 to Q_2, as institutional investors and venture firms jumped into the action. These results belie practitioners' claim that every boost in venture activity must inevitably lead to a decline in returns. Far from declining, the rate of return actually rose, from R_1 to R_2.

1979: Supply Shock

When the U.S. Department of Labor lifted the curbs on pension-fund investments in venture capital, fund-raising in this sector boomed. But rather than increasing entrepreneurs' demand for venture capital, the easing of restrictions on pension funds boosted investors' (pension funds') willingness to supply capital. Thus this pivotal event created a supply, rather than demand, shock. Figure 6-7 shows how this played out.

After the ERISA policy shift, the supply curve moved from S_1 to S_2, as shown in the figure. Pension funds, which had previously been prohibited from venture capital investing, now could participate. Moreover, because these funds were tax exempt, they required a lower expected rate of return on venture investments than taxable investors did.

With pension plans' new freedom to jump into the venture market, the amount of venture capital raised ballooned (from Q_1 to Q_2). But this shift did *not* spur a corresponding rise in returns. Rather, returns eroded

Figure 6-7 Impact of a Supply Shock

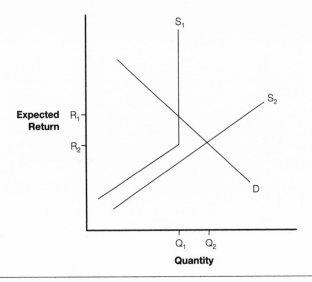

from the extraordinary level witnessed in the mid-1970s (R_1) to a more modest level (R_2). Why? Primarily because demand for venture capital stayed constant, while the supply increased sharply.

1974: Demand Shock with a Twist

Shifts in supply and demand don't inevitably lead to big changes in the amount of venture capital raised. Instead, these changes may affect only returns. This possibility came to light in 1974. Around that year, technological advances made computers faster—and cheaper—than ever. Armed with this speedier and more affordable computing power, companies could introduce a much wider—and more affordable—array of software applications for businesses.

We might think that this accelerated application of technology would stimulate the amount of venture capital fund-raising. After all, as we saw in chapter 3, these funds target high-tech companies that consist mostly of intangible assets and operate in a climate of great uncertainty and rapid change. But in fact, the level of venture financing changed little after the computer boom of 1974.

The reason? The pre-1979 regulatory curbs on pension funds constrained the supply of venture capital available in the economy. Figure 6-8 shows what the picture looked like at this time. While the demand for financing increased, note that available venture financing increased only

Figure 6-8   Impact of a Demand Shock with Restricted Supply

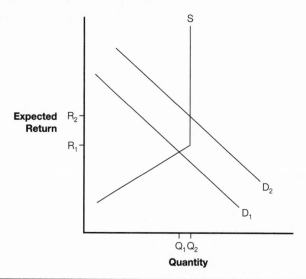

marginally (Q_1 to Q_2). Returns, however, improved substantially (R_1 to R_2). Because the supply of capital could not increase (due to the regulatory restrictions), only the most profitable of the many attractive transactions got funded.

1957: A Double Whammy—Supply and Demand Shock

In 1957, both supply *and* demand rose—but not because of any internal workings of the U.S. economy. Instead, an external event—the Soviet Union's launch of *Sputnik*—sent U.S. political leaders scurrying to catch up in a technological race that it felt it could not afford to lose. As one result, the government's actions stimulated both the supply of and demand for venture capital financing:

▪ The Small Business Investment Company program, as we saw in chapter 5, sought to release a wave of funding for early-stage technology companies by providing guarantees for investors in venture funds. Because the program eliminated most of the downside, *expected* returns increased. This, of course, made investors more willing to commit their capital to venture funds.

▪ The government's ramp-up of defense and aerospace spending also fueled demand for venture capital. Manufacturers of scientific instruments—one of the best-financed sectors at the time—could count on

Figure 6-9   Impact of a Supply and Demand Shock

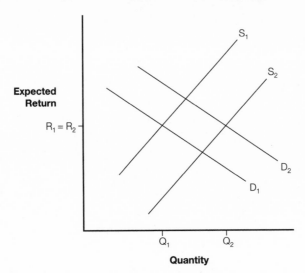

strong sales of their products to defense contractors. Thus, more and more companies could provide the kinds of returns investors expected.

Figure 6-9 shows how these developments affected the venture capital demand-and-supply picture. As the two parts of the diagram reveal, the quantity of venture capital raised rose noticeably. But the impact on actual returns was quite modest. While the increase in demand for venture capital would normally trigger rising returns, the supply of funds shifted at the same time. As a result, the impact on venture capital returns was minimal.

Short Term versus Long Term: Why Venture Capital Isn't Like Snack Food

Each figure represents just a snapshot of what available venture capital and returns might look like at a single point in time. In particular, these figures imply that venture capital and investment returns respond instantly to regulatory, market, or other events. In reality, the adjustment process can take a long time.

To see how this works, let's compare and contrast the venture capital market to the market for snack food. As we might well imagine, companies like Frito-Lay and Nabisco closely monitor demand for their products. They do this primarily by getting daily purchasing updates from supermarket scanners. They send the stores additional inventory every few days, adjusting their product offerings in response to changing consumer tastes. If imbalances occur the manufacturer can quickly adjust by providing coupons or special offers (which boost demand) or by trimming production and delivery (which decreases supply).

The quantity of venture capital in the market, however, can't shift nearly as rapidly as the amount of snack food on store shelves, due to the ways in which venture partnerships are structured and the lengthy information lags.

The Venture Partnership Structure

When individual investors want to put money into public equities or bonds, they can do it quickly, cheaply, and easily. These public markets are liquid markets, where purchases and sales can be readily executed. Venture capital markets are very different, largely due to the nature of the venture partnerships themselves.

First, venture funds raise capital only every two or three years, for periods of a decade or more. Thus venture capitalists cannot readily accept or return money to their limited partners. (While limited partners can sell their partnership interests to others, the market for such interests is very inefficient, and the partnerships frequently trade at a steep discount to their asset value.)

Moreover, venture funds may not accept as much capital as an individual or institution might want to commit. Often this is due to the limited number of *experienced* venture capitalists. Most venture capitalists don't learn their trade through formal education; rather, they develop their knowledge and skill through a process of apprenticeship. Furthermore, it's no small task to add partners in a venture firm, as we discussed in chapter 5. Thus, many of the best venture groups have resisted expanding too rapidly, even if investor demand gets so great that these firms could easily raise many billions of dollars doing so. Consequently, at any given time, there aren't many experienced venture capitalists in the market willing to accept an institution's capital.

These realities can lead to substantial lags—often of several years— between the time that an investor decides to boost its allocation to venture capital and the time that it actually makes the needed commitments to venture funds. Even then, the actual deployment of the funds is likely to take several additional years: venture groups typically draw down the capital committed to a given fund as it is needed, over a number of years.

The same logic works in reverse. If an investor decides to scale back their commitments in the venture market, this process can take years. The U.S. economy experienced this "stickiness" firsthand after the stock-market correction of 1987.[3] Many investors, alarmed by the equity market's volatility and the poor performance of small, high-tech stocks, rushed to exit the venture capital market. But despite the correction, flows into venture capital funds continued to rise because of earlier commitments that had not yet been drawn down by venture capital groups. In fact, this influx didn't reach its peak until the last quarter of 1989.

The self-liquidating nature of venture funds only increases this stickiness. When venture funds exit investments, they return the capital to their investors rather than reinvesting the proceeds. These distributions typically either take the form of stock in firms that have recently gone public, or cash. The pace of distributions varies with the rate at which venture capitalists are liquidating their holdings. Thus, during "hot" periods—times when there are a lot of IPOs and acquisitions and hence a lot of investor interest in venture opportunities—limited partners receive substantial distributions from venture funds. To maintain the *same* percentage allocation to venture funds during these peak periods, institutional and individual investors must accelerate their rate of investment—which, as we've seen, is difficult because of the limited number of funds in the market at any given time and the intense competition among investors for slots in the most desirable funds.

Conversely, during "cold" periods, when many investors want to reduce their venture allocations, they receive few distributions. A number of large institutions found themselves in this position in early 2001.[4] These institutions realized they had overcommitted to venture capital because the value of the public securities in their portfolios had declined abruptly. Reducing their exposure to venture capital was difficult because the distribution of stock and cash from the funds had slowed to a trickle. (The difficult public market conditions precluded taking even the most promising firms public). While these institutions could cease making new commitments to new funds, their exposure to venture capital would remain high until their partnership holdings were liquidated or market values changed again.

Thus, during periods of rapid change in the market, investors find it difficult to quickly bring their level of investment in the venture industry in line with their *desired* level.

Information Lags

Whereas mutual and hedge funds holding public securities see "marked-to-market" prices on a daily basis, it can take much longer for the various players in the venture industry to become aware of and respond to changing market conditions. For instance, investments in Internet-related securities in the mid-1990s yielded extremely high returns, yet most institutional investors didn't recognize the magnitude of this opportunity for several years. Similarly, when the investment environment soured, as it did during the spring of 2000, investors often continued to plow money into venture funds because the returns reported by the funds continued to appear attractive. (Limited partners continued to receive distributions of shares that had previously been taken public by the venture groups for many months after April 2000.)

Some of these delays stem from aspects of entrepreneurial firms themselves—particularly the substantial uncertainty and information gaps surrounding these entities that make it hard for investors to assess the health of the private companies in a venture capitalist's portfolio. But the way in which the performance of a fund is reported can also exacerbate these information problems.[5]

First, venture firms often value their portfolio companies conservatively, especially before they go public or get acquired. This conservatism is intended to protect investors in a fund from being misled by overstated fund performance. But it also delays the flow of feedback to investors about the state of the market. Specifically, it prohibits the limited partners from discovering in a timely manner which venture funds specializing in a particular segment are doing well, and which ones are in real trouble.

Moreover, relatively few entrepreneurial firms go public during "cold" markets, whereas many do during "hot" ones. Because venture capitalists usually value companies conservatively before they go public, we tend to see more dramatic valuation write-ups when public markets are active. But the *actual value-creation process* in venture investments unfolds with a very different rhythm. In many cases, the value of a portfolio firm increases gradually over time, even as the venture capitalist is holding the investment at cost. Thus, the low returns during periods with cold public markets understate that progress, just as the high returns during peak periods overstate portfolio firms' success during those years. In short, the basic "scorecard" that limited partners use to track the performance of their funds is riddled with inaccuracies.

When we pull all of these dynamics together, we can see that investors receive market information that is not only delayed but also incomplete and even misleading. Certainly, grocery store shelves would offer shoppers odd mixtures of products if the same process were used!

Depicting Stickiness in the Venture Market

Because it takes time for the supply to respond to market signals—whether from investors or firms—imbalances between supply and demand can grow from small discrepancies to yawning chasms. Thus, in trying to understand how venture capital supply and demand work, we need to consider both the short and the long run rather than look only at one point in time. Figure 6-10 gives an example of how we might depict this. In the short run (line SS), the supply of venture capital may be essentially fixed, if investors can't or won't adjust their allocations to venture funds. Over the long run, however, the supply (line SL) may increase or decrease, depending on the nature of the demand in the market.

Figure 6-11 provides additional insight. As we have seen, the discovery of a new scientific approach, such as genetic engineering, or the diffusion of a new technology, such as the transistor or the Internet, can utterly reshape the venture capital landscape. As large, not-so-agile businesses struggle to adjust to these new technologies, numerous fast-moving, small companies rush to exploit the new discovery or technology (D_1 to D_2). As a result, for any given level of return demanded by investors, there are many attractive investment candidates.

In the long run (line SL), the quantity of venture capital provided by investors will adjust upward from Q_1 to Q_2 as supply eventually meets demand. Actual returns will also ultimately increase, from R_1 to R_2, because there are now more attractive investment opportunities.

In the short run, however—the immediate months or even years after the demand shock—the amount of venture capital available may remain essentially fixed due to the nature of the fund structure. Instead of a rise

Figure 6-10   Short- and Long-Run Supply Curves

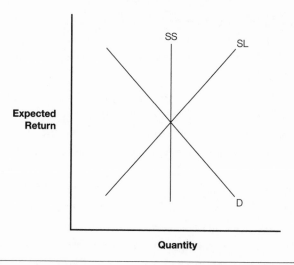

Figure 6-11   Long-Term Impact of a Demand Shock

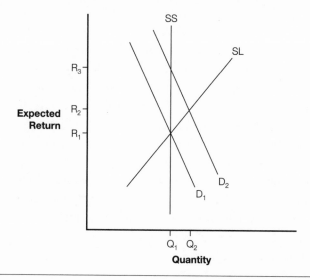

in the number of companies receiving venture funding, investment return rates may climb dramatically (R_3), as only the highest quality deals get funded. Only with time will returns gradually subside as the supply of venture capital adjusts upward in response to the enhanced demand.

Overshooting

As noted, the supply of venture capital ultimately rises to meet any increase in demand. However, when there's a long lag between a shortage and an attempt to fill that shortage, supply may "overshoot" demand. That is, the amount eventually provided may be far more than is actually needed to fix the imbalance. This can spawn even more problems, as venture firms end up funding too many opportunities. As just one example, between late 1998 and 1999 alone, *nine* online pet stores received venture funding.

Overshooting can also cause excessively high valuations: When the number of attractive deals is limited, venture capitalists may compete on price, offering progressively higher valuations for portfolio firms. Higher valuations at the time of investment are likely to lead to lower returns.

The "overshooting" can occur in reverse. A relatively modest drop in demand for venture capital can trigger a wholesale withdrawal by institutional investors, shrinking the supply of available capital. Returns shoot up as a result, because there is little capital to fund the many attractive deals. The supply will ultimately recover, but in the meantime, promising companies may miss out on funding.

Figure 6-12 depicts this dynamic. Consider a case where demand rises from D_1 to D_2. Initially, supply shows no response: As we saw earlier, the short-term supply curve (SS_1) is fixed. Eventually supply (SS_2) will respond to the new opportunities. However, because of information problems, supply may first overshoot demand (SS_3), leading to overfunding and disappointing returns (R_3). Though the market will ultimately return to equilibrium, the ensuing disruption exacts a heavy toll on investors, entrepreneurs, and venture capitalists alike.

Figure 6-12 illustrates *what* happens during a period of overshooting, but it doesn't fully explain *why* overshooting occurs. Let's explore two possible forces behind this phenomenon: (1) misleading information from public markets, and (2) venture capitalists' underestimation of the cost of beefing up their investment activity.

Misinterpreting Market Signals

Institutional investors and venture capitalists alike sometimes misinterpret the admittedly confusing signals coming from the market. Examples abound where venture capitalists have made substantial investments in new sectors, at least in part because of inflated public market valuations

Figure 6-12   Overshooting in Venture Capital

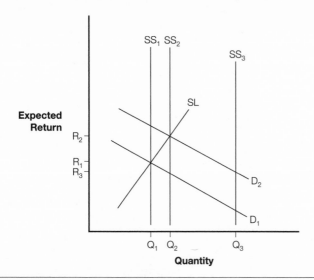

of these industries. Even if they are skeptical about the reasonableness of the valuations in a certain sector, venture capitalists may be drawn into investing anyway. For instance, in 1999 and early 2000, many senior venture capitalists harbored grave doubts about the viability of many the B2C and B2B Internet business plans being considered by their firms.[6] Nonetheless, most groups made such investments. In many cases, the senior partners bowed to the pressure from limited partners and their junior colleagues, who asked why their funds did not include such investments, when so many other groups were making vast sums by "flipping" (investing in and then rapidly taking public) such firms.

Assessing all the forces behind the periodic misvaluation of public securities is beyond the scope of this book. One explanation may be that some public investors fail to account for the impact of competitors: They assign value to a promising firm in a new industry as if it were the sole company active in a sector, failing to include numerous competitors' influence on revenues and profit margins in their calculations.

Thus, investors sometimes overestimate the number and quality of new investment opportunities. Excited by an enticing market, limited partners (with the acquiescence of the general partners) bump up the supply of venture capital to meet that perceived demand. Figure 6-13 shows what this situation would look like using our supply and demand

Figure 6-13   Misleading Public Market Signals

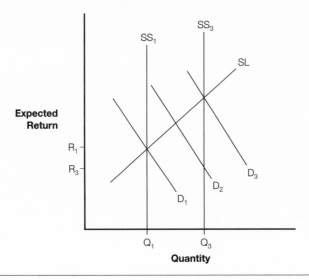

curves. Actual demand for venture capital rises (D_1 to D_2), perhaps owing to a technological breakthrough. However, limited and general partners, as a result of misleading signals from the market, mistakenly believe that the curve has shifted out to D_3—and raise extra amounts of capital to satisfy the demand. The short-run supply curve thus shifts from SS_1 to SS_3, leaving excessive investment—and thus disappointing returns—in its wake.

Whatever the causes of these misvaluations, historical examples abound: The recent disappointments surrounding B2B and B2C Internet companies are far from unique. During the early 1980s, for instance, nineteen disk-drive companies received venture capital financing.[7] Two-thirds of these investments came in 1982 and 1983, as the valuation of publicly traded computer-hardware firms soared. Many disk-drive companies also went public during this period. Though industry growth exploded during these years (sales soared from $27 million in 1978 to $1.3 *billion* in 1983), industry analysts questioned whether the scale of investment really made sense, given the fierce price competition that almost inevitably would result. Indeed, between October 1983 and December 1984, the average public disk-drive firm lost a whopping 68 percent of its value. Worse, numerous disk-drive manufacturers that had yet to go public went out of business. Venture capitalists, suffering from poor returns, abandoned the industry.

The peak period of biotechnology investing in the early 1990s provides another vivid example of the destruction that overshooting can cause.[8] Though the biotechnology industry promised to lessen human disease, the valuations of both public and private firms struck many observers as hard to justify. For instance, between May and December 1992, the average valuation of privately held biotechnology firms financed by venture capitalists reached $70 million. (This figure represents the "pre-money" valuation, which doesn't include any capital put into the company during financing.) Reality struck in early 1993, when biotechnology valuations sank after the well-publicized Centoxin drug was rejected by the U.S. Food and Drug Administration. By December 1993, only 42 of 262 *publicly traded* biotechnology firms had a valuation over $70 million. Most of the biotechnology firms financed during the second half of 1992 ultimately yielded disappointing returns.

Swings in the public markets may also lead to over- and underinvestment in venture capital as a whole. Specifically, when public equity values climb, institutional investors tend to want to allocate more of their portfolio to venture capital in order to keep the percentage allocated to venture capital consistent. If the high valuations subsequently prove to have no basis in reality, the amount of venture capital in the economy overall will have once again overshot its target.

Underestimating the Cost of Change

Venture capitalists themselves sometimes don't understand the true costs associated with expanding their investment activity. The very act of growing the pool of venture capital under management introduces disruption and tension in any venture firm.

Figure 6-14 shows how these stresses and strains affect venture capital supply and demand. Consider a case where the long-run demand curve shifts out from D_1 to D_2. General partners, noting this shift as more attractive firms emerge and seek venture financing, raise more capital from investors by seeking larger and more frequent funds. The supply of venture capital thus moves from SS_1 to SS_2. But while D_2 may accurately represent the long-run opportunities in the industry, the *short-run* opportunities may be better represented by D_3. As long as the quantity of venture capital raised does not change *too* dramatically, D_2 and D_3 do not differ much: In other words, investors can exploit almost all the new opportunities. But if there is a *major* shift in the quantity of venture

Figure 6-14　Adjustment Costs

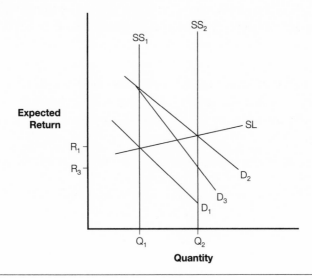

capital available, then venture capitalists will find it difficult to success-fully fund more than a fraction of these opportunities. If they do try to fund all the new transactions, returns are likely to fall to R_3.

Where do these adjustment costs (the gap between D_2 and D_3) come from? One possibility is that growth frequently imposes pressures on the venture investment process—which can ultimately eat away at returns. For example, rather than making more investments, rapidly growing ven-ture organizations often try to increase their average investment size. In this way, the same venture firms can manage a larger amount of capital without increasing the number of portfolio companies a partner needs to scrutinize. (We touched on the problems associated with the latter course in chapter 5.) This shift to larger investments can prompt venture part-ners to make bigger capital commitments to firms up front. Thus the ven-ture firm loses some of the control over investees that it previously gained through staged financing. Furthermore, when companies do get into trou-ble, the losses borne by the venture fund are more substantial.

Similarly, rapidly expanding venture firms syndicate less than their more stable peers do, in order to put more of their own fund's money to work while keeping the number of companies the firm is responsible for down to a reasonable level. But once again, this strategy has costs as well as benefits. Specifically, without the protections that come with syndication—for instance, the benefit of having a second set of eyes assess and monitor a firm—venture firms risk making expensive investing mistakes.

Growth also puts a strain on the venture organization itself. Decisions take longer as the partners struggle to manage the myriad demands of their larger investment portfolios. Also, if the income from management fees grows dramatically, the alignment between the investors' and venture firm's interests may break down: The venture capitalists may be generating so much income from fees that the "carrot" of the carried interest may no longer be compelling. Thus the ties that make the partnership a cohesive whole start to unravel.

The experience of Schroder Ventures helps us understand how this can play out.[9] Schroder's private-equity effort began in 1985 with funds focused on British venture capital and buyout investments. Over time, however, the firm added funds focusing on other markets (such as France and Germany) and technologies (such as the life sciences) in which the venture capitalists—and the institutional investors backing them—had identified tempting opportunities.

But as the company grew, the partners began encountering problems. In particular, the firm found it increasingly difficult to monitor the investment activities of each investment group. This posed a real concern, for the parent organization served as the general partner of each fund, and thus was ultimately liable for any losses. Each group saw itself as an autonomous entity. In some especially troubling cases, one group resisted cooperating (and sharing capital gains) with other groups. Though the organization eventually restructured itself so as to raise a single fund covering all of Europe, the process proved slow, painful, and costly.

These tensions can surface in any large venture organization, not just international ones. In some instances, one group in a venture organization has become convinced that the other is getting a disproportionate share of the organization's rewards in light of their relative investment performances. In others, the groups have encountered problems coordinating and overseeing their many disparate activities.

These kinds of conflicts can do more than just slow down decision making and ruffle partners' feathers. They can actually force a group apart. For instance, in August 1999, Institutional Venture Partners and Brentwood Venture Capital—which had each invested about $1 billion over several decades—announced their intention to restructure.[10] The information-technology and life-sciences venture capitalists from the two firms indicated that they would join with each other to form two new firms. The first new firm, Pallidium Venture Capital, would pursue only health care opportunities, while the second firm, Redpoint Ventures, would focus on Internet- and broadband-infrastructure investments. Press accounts suggested that the decision stemmed largely from the dissatisfaction of several information technology partners at the original firms, who felt that their stellar performance had garnered insufficient recognition and compensation.

In other cases, a key partner—often dissatisfied with his role or compensation—has left a venture group—an event that can powerfully disrupt any organization. For instance, Ernest Jacquet departed Summit Partners to form Parthenon Ventures shortly after Summit closed on a $1 billion buyout fund.[11] While limited partners rarely ask for their funds to be returned when a key partner departs, it can happen. In one such case, Foster Capital Management returned $200 million to its limited partners after several junior partners defected in 1998.[12]

Even in groups that stay together, the pressures that come with rapid growth can consume huge amounts of the partners' time and mental energy. It's relatively easy to identify investment opportunities; but expanding wisely and efficiently so as to exploit those opportunities is a challenge.

Can the Venture Capital Boom Continue?

How will the venture capital industry evolve over the next decade? Given the spectacular recent growth in this sector, it's natural to ask whether the industry overall can sustain this success. Will fund-raising fall precipitously? Is the industry destined to experience relentless boom and bust cycles?

These are fair questions. As we saw above, some boom periods in the past have led to disappointing returns for investors. And the trends that have emerged in recent years—larger fund sizes, more substantial investments in portfolio firms, increasing valuations of those firms, and organizational disruption—suggest that the players in this industry will face another round of disappointment. In particular, the events of 1998 through 2000 suggest that the overshooting that accompanied past booms has occurred. We may well anticipate that in reaction to poor returns a period of "undershooting" will follow, in which limited partners will trim their commitments to venture funds excessively.

Keep in mind, though, the distinction between this short-term view and the *long-term* picture that we have emphasized in this chapter. The long-run demand for venture capital is shaped by forces such as the pace of technological innovation and regulatory change, the presence of liquid and competitive markets (whether for stock offerings or acquisitions) through which investors can exit their investments, the treatment of capital gains in the tax code, and the willingness of highly skilled managers and engineers to work in entrepreneurial environments.

When we consider these forces, we can detect some substantial changes for the better—changes that first began in the 1990s. Two particularly dramatic trends are the acceleration of the rate of technological innovation and the decreasing "transaction costs" associated with venture investments.

The clearest indicator of an increase in innovation is trends in patenting. Patent applications by U.S. inventors, after hovering between 40,000 and 80,000 annually over the first eighty-five years of the twentieth century, surged to almost 150,000 per year by the end of the 1990s.[13] This proliferation does not appear to reflect changes in domestic patent policy, shifts in the success rate of applications, or a variety of alternative explanations. Rather, it suggests a fundamental shift in the rate of innovation. The breadth of technology appears wider today than ever. And as we've seen, the acceleration of innovation provides fertile ground for future investments, especially by venture capitalists.

The efficiency of the venture capital process has also improved tremendously with the emergence of intermediaries familiar with its workings. The expertise of lawyers, accountants, managers, and others—even real estate brokers—specializing in working with venture-backed firms has slashed the transaction costs associated with forming and financing new firms. In addition, more and more professionals and managers are now accustomed to the employment arrangements offered by venture-backed firms. Increasing familiarity with the venture capital process has made the long-term prospects for investment more attractive than ever before.

These kinds of advances have set a virtuous circle in motion: Venture capitalists have funded innovative firms, which have in turn created opportunities for new venture investments. All of this leads to more capital formation—and thus additional financing of innovation.

In some respects, it seems that this virtuous circle has only just begun gaining momentum.[14] The fact is, today's venture capital pool is still relatively small. At the end of 2000, for every $1 of U.S. venture capital in an investment portfolio, there were about $160 in publicly traded equities. Thus the share of value in small, privately held start-ups probably is well under 1 percent. At the same time, the size of the foreign venture capital pool remains far below that of the United States. In 1998, the ratio of the venture capital pool to the larger economy was just under fourteen times higher in the United States than in Asia, and almost nine times higher in the United States than in continental Europe. These disparities suggest tremendous possibilities for future growth in the global venture industry.

Implications

As this chapter draws to a close, let's emphasize the implications for the limited and general partners of venture funds. While there is little that a single investor or venture capitalist can do to stem the tide of venture fund-raising, several actions will help make the most of these shifts:

- *Carefully consider the drivers of shifts in fund-raising activity.* As we have seen, many venture capitalists mistakenly assume that increasing flows of venture capital into the industry is automatically "bad news." Limited and general partners considering their investment strategies should seek to carefully understand what is behind these changes. Is this a case where demand for such funding is growing, which is likely to signal higher returns? Or rather, is there a change in the willingness of investors to supply capital underway, which may have less benign consequences?

- *Be skeptical of the public markets as a signal of venture opportunities.* In numerous instances, inflated public market valuations have led to the overshooting of investments in certain segments, of which the B2C and B2B sectors are only the most recent examples. At the time, skeptical observers suggested reasons why the public market valuations were almost impossible to reconcile with economic fundamentals. While resisting the tidal wave of public enthusiasm may be difficult, it is far sounder to base investment decisions on sober assessments of market and technological potential than on these alluring but frequently misleading signals.

- *Don't underestimate the costs of growth.* Scaling a venture capital firm is by no means easy. A number of cases of overshooting seem to have stemmed from excessive optimism on the part of venture firms about the readiness with which such changes could be accomplished. Believing they could rapidly grow to take advantage of the new opportunities, they found themselves encumbered with too much capital and suffered unattractive returns.

■ *Limited partners should press for increased "transparency" in the venture market.* As we have emphasized in this chapter, the manner in which general partners reveal how their portfolio companies are doing leaves much to be desired. The lack of transparency contributes both to the stickiness of the market—the failure of the supply of venture capital to adjust rapidly to new opportunities—and to the overshooting that often results once the supply does adjust. By providing more timely and meaningful information to their limited partners, venture capitalists could do much to ease these problems.

A Dynamic Industry

The turbulence of venture capital fund-raising and investing has defined this industry over the past six decades. And as history reveals, the relationship between venture fund-raising and returns is far from constant. Though some boom times have led to falling returns, others have boosted returns. In this chapter, we have provided a framework to understand the complex forces that come together to sculpt the venture capital landscape.

While the next years are likely to be troublesome for the industry, over the longer horizon, the industry's prospects seem quite bright.

We will revisit the future of the venture capital industry in chapter 10. Before we do so, however, we will consider ongoing efforts to transplant the venture capital markets into three seemingly hostile environments: large corporations, publicly funded research institutions, and international markets.

PART

The Emulator's Challenge

■

The venture industry has spurred unprecedented growth in innovation, as businesses capture promising new ideas and profit from them. And by driving innovation, venture capital also creates jobs and expands the overall economy. Not surprisingly, these achievements have excited the imaginations of more than just venture capital firms. Corporations, research institutions, and universities, both in the United States and elsewhere, want to put innovation to work in their organizations and so have sought to adopt a venture mind-set when making internal and external investments. Government agencies in many countries around the world have also encouraged venture capital activity.

These "emulators" have accomplished some important results—but they also face daunting challenges. For example, melding the corporate model with the venture capital approach creates a union of opposites due to the very different ways of evaluating investment decisions and rewarding success. Though these efforts can work, the players must challenge old (and sometimes intractable) assumptions and traditional ways of doing business—a shift in perspective that is daunting to many organizations. Academic and government-sponsored programs have it even harder. Within these organizations, the clash of cultures that comes with combining tried-and-true approaches with venture capital methods can just about cripple the effort. Some of these attempts *have* succeeded, however, in many cases owing to a special combination of circumstances. What are those circumstances? And how can aspiring, venture-minded organizations duplicate them so as to ensure their own success? The next three chapters suggest some possible answers.

7

The Corporate Venturing Experience

■

The typical corporate venture capital program has been terminated within four years of being launched.

Corporations have good reason to explore new ways of stimulating innovation. All too often, their investments in traditional R&D laboratories have generated paltry returns, as researchers have focused on incremental product advances or on academic ideas with little relevance to the corporation. Even when these corporate laboratories manage to come up with truly innovative ideas, other organizations—especially venture-backed start-ups—have sometimes seized the opportunity to commercialize them.

Corporate venturing—whereby companies stimulate innovation within their own walls or in outside organizations—has had a long track record. Perhaps not surprisingly, interest in this activity has exploded in recent years, both in the United States and elsewhere. Table 7-1 shows the fifteen largest corporate venture capital programs in 2000 and their capital under management. Managers everywhere have recognized venture capital's impact on innovation and growth and have set out to apply features of the industry to their own objectives.

To find out how corporations can best benefit from the venturing approach, we can draw lessons from

- the history of corporate venturing,

- the admittedly daunting challenges and surprising successes that characterize these efforts,

- the program features that seem to ensure the most success, and

- the particularly thorny concerns that frequently surface when corporations design and implement a venture program.

Table 7-1　Corporate Venture Capital Funds

Corporate Sponsor	Capital Under Management
Electronic Data Systems	$1,500
General Electric	1,500
Andersen Consulting	1,000
Comdisco	500
Time Warner	500
Times Mirror	500
Visa International	500
Intel Corporation	450[a]
AT&T	348
Hikari Tsushin	332
News Corporation	300
ValueVision International	300
Comcast	250
PECO Energy	225
Siemens	210

Source: Adapted from *The Corporate Venturing Directory and Yearbook* (Wellesley, MA: Asset Alternatives, 2000).
[a] Includes only some of its venture investments.

Note: If the corporation organizes multiple programs, these are consolidated. Some corporations do not make formal commitments in advance to their venture programs, or do not disclose the size of these commitments. These firms are not included on the list. Among the largest corporate venture capital programs falling into these categories are those of Cisco, Dell, Johnson & Johnson, and Microsoft.

The History of Corporate Venturing Investments

The first corporate venture funds emerged in the mid-1960s—about two decades after the initial institutional venture capital funds were formed.[1] In the decades that followed, these corporate efforts experienced three transformations—and met with some major obstacles.

The First Wave

As traditional venture capital funds fueled the success of giants such as Digital Equipment Corporation, Memorex, Raychem, and Scientific Data Systems, other large companies took notice. Excited by what they saw happening, they began establishing divisions that emulated venture capitalists. During the late 1960s and early 1970s, more than 25 percent of Fortune 500 firms set up such programs.

To tap into this activity, some large corporations financed new firms that were already receiving venture capital from the more traditional venture sources. Most of these efforts, such as General Electric's Business Development Services, Inc., invested directly in start-ups. This strategy let managers tailor their firm's portfolio to its particular technological or business needs. In other cases, the corporations simply provided funds to a venture capitalist firm, which in turn invested the money in high-potential entrepreneurial organizations.

At the other end of the spectrum, projects such as DuPont Corporation's Development Department and Ralston Purina's New Venture Division sought to capture the entrepreneurial spirit already thriving within their organizations. These programs encouraged the company's own product engineers and scientists to forge ahead with their innovations, and provided financial, legal, and marketing support. In some cases, these units were separate legal entities, which at times also had outside equity investors. More typically, however, the corporate parent retained ownership of the program.

In 1973, the market for new public offerings—the primary avenue through which venture capitalists exit successful investments—dried up as small technology stocks experienced very poor returns. Returns of venture funds shrank, and partnerships struggled to raise new funds. Corporations, alarmed by the reversal, began scaling back their own venturing initiatives. The typical corporate venture program begun in the late 1960s was dissolved after just four years.

The Second Wave

The venture industry's prospects brightened again in the late 1970s and early 1980s, mainly because of the revised "prudent-man" rule governing pension-fund investing, the lowering of capital-gains taxes, and the recovery of the IPO market. The flow of funding into the industry swelled, and active venture organizations proliferated once more.

Corporate venturing also revived—so much so that in 1986 corporate funds managed $2 billion, or nearly 12 percent of the total pool of venture capital. Whereas the earlier wave of corporate venturing had taken aim at a broad range of investment opportunities, now high-tech and pharmaceutical companies—such as Control Data, EG&G, Eli Lilly, and Monsanto—led the charge.

Yet these happy times would prove all too brief. In 1987, the stock market crashed and the market for new public offerings again deflated. Returns and fund-raising by independent partnerships shrank as well. This time, corporations scaled back their commitment to venture investing even more dramatically. By 1992, the number of corporate venture programs had fallen by one-third, and their capital under management represented only 5 percent of the venture pool.

The Third Wave

The late 1990s saw yet another revival of venture investment by corporations, as the business press published provocative stories about successful venture investments in Internet companies such as eBay, Netscape, and Yahoo! But this revitalization reflected more than just the envy and enthusiasm that glowing press accounts generated. It showed that many corporations had begun looking at the innovation process in a new way. For much of the century, large corporations had typically relied on central R&D laboratories to crank out new product ideas. Now, these organizations began exploring other ways to access new ideas—including joint ventures, acquisitions, and university-based collaborations. Corporate venture programs offered an attractive route to these ends.

What made venture programs so inviting? For one thing, corporations extracted only a fraction of the value that centralized R&D facilities generated, because many of the best ideas languished, unused, whether because of internal resistance (e.g., from managers of operating divisions who didn't want to see a product launched that competed with one of their offerings) or an inability to execute on the initial insight. In other cases, defecting employees started new firms that turned those ideas into blockbuster commercial successes. The achievements of fast-growing technology firms such as Cisco Systems—many of whom relied on acquisitions rather than internal R&D for the bulk of their new ideas—also made conventional approaches to innovation look lackluster by comparison. Against this backdrop, top-level executives again expressed increasing interest in corporate venturing.

The rapid diffusion of the Internet and its power to enhance or cannibalize bricks-and-mortar businesses intensified this interest. Corporations everywhere realized that e-commerce presented both an opportunity and a threat. They knew they had to act fast to exploit the 'Net and stave off its more troublesome impacts. However, many organizations lacked the internal resources to explore this new frontier. Corporate venturing provided a solution. For example, the Tribune Company, the Sony Corporation, and United Parcel Service all instituted efforts to invest in online businesses.

Finally, numerous venture capital groups, looking for strategic partnering opportunities, expressed interest in collaborating with corporations. In earlier years, traditional venture investors had approached corporate investors with a mix of caution and skepticism. The waxing and waning of corporate interest—which historically had fluctuated more wildly than cycles in the venture industry—made many venture capitalists nervous.

But as the venture capital arena grew increasingly crowded in the late 1990s, the venture community adopted a different attitude. Venture professionals increasingly viewed relationships with corporations as a source of competitive advantage. And a new focus on revolutionary business strategies—such as customer-relationship management—woke venture groups up to their own limitations. A corporate partner, some venture firms surmised, just might be able to provide the knowledge and experience that venture organizations needed to improve their own skills and professionalism. Such firms forged partnerships with corporations, not only accepting money from them as investors but also structuring unique collaborations that sought to draw upon the expertise of the larger organization.

Corporate Venturing Today

Exactly how many corporate venturing programs exist today? Because most corporate programs don't answer to external investors, there is little reporting on these programs. Thus, precise numbers are hard to come by. But figure 7-1 and table 7-2 present some estimates.

Figure 7-1 depicts the number of U.S. Fortune 100 corporations that established corporate venture programs in any given year. The three historical "waves" show up prominently in the graph. Though not all corporations established venturing programs during these decades, those that did often set up more than one. In addition, a single company might abandon and revive a series of such programs.

Table 7-2 compiles the number and (in latter years) the size of venture investments made directly by corporations. These numbers do not include cases where companies committed capital to independent venture groups, who then invested the funds. Nor do they reflect instances where a financial services organization or a subsidiary of an operating corporation (for instance, Goldman Sachs or GE Capital) made an investment. (In these instances, we can assume that financial, not strategic,

Figure 7-1 Number of Fortune 100 Venturing Programs Announced

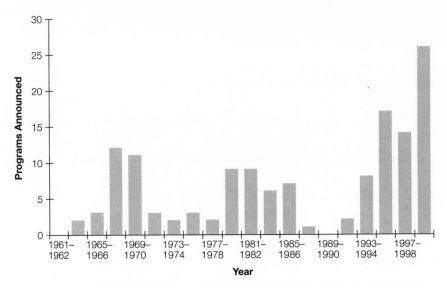

Source: Adapted from Robert E. Gee, "Finding and Commercializing New Businesses," *Research/Technology Management* 37 (January/February 1994): 49–56, as updated by the authors using press accounts in the *Corporate Venturing Report* and elsewhere.

goals drove the investment.) There's no denying the evidence: Corporate
venture investments have not only played a significant role in the venture
environment, they've also skyrocketed in recent years.

Risky Business: The Challenge of Corporate Venturing

Despite profitable collaborations between venture groups and corporations, many independent venture capitalists still express skepticism
toward the very idea of corporate venture capital. Citing the historical
stop-and-start pattern in corporate-venturing activity, these professionals
question whether a corporate decision-making style—characterized by
detailed analyses and hierarchical reviews—can truly work within the
quick-moving venture capital market.

Such skepticism may have merit. After all, the ups and downs of corporate venturing that we saw in the brief history above suggest a faddish
approach to these programs, with investment fluctuations even more
dramatic than those in the independent sector. Many times corporate

Table 7-2 Number of Corporate Venture Capital Investments

Year	Number of Rounds	Dollar Volume of Rounds (in millions of 2000 dollars)
1983	53	—
1984	91	—
1985	139	—
1986	129	—
1987	152	—
1988	179	—
1989	202	—
1990	233	—
1991	249	—
1992	214	—
1993	198	—
1994	193	—
1995	65	193
1996	101	369
1997	229	708
1998	391	1,449
1999	936	7,968

Source: Based on the authors' tabulations of unpublished Venture Economics and VentureOne databases.

Note: The series reporting number of investments before 1995 and in and after 1995 may not be strictly compara-ble. For 1995 and after, the dollar volume of these investments is also reported.

investors are so eager to experience the benefits of these programs that they fail to consider the risks—and corporate venture investing comes with some serious ones. Here are just a few:

- *It can generate disappointing returns.* Many corporations, new to the industry, enter it expecting to gain spectacular returns immediately. However, even the most successful venture groups traditionally earn disappointing returns on *50–75 percent* of their investments.[2] Some of the most seasoned venture groups have lost tens of millions of dollars on a single investment.

- *Returns can fluctuate wildly.* As we saw in the previous chapter, the sudden expansion of capital under management has sometimes been followed by a sharp deterioration of returns. Yet corporations often choose such peak periods to jump into venture investing.

- *New entrants can't always "get a seat at the table."* In competitive markets, beginner players don't always have the opportunity to par-ticipate in the hottest opportunities. Groups that have been in the industry for many years tend to share attractive financings with each other, assuming that their established peers will reciprocate with hot deals of their own. As a result, many corporate venture groups have found the process of building an attractive investment portfolio surprisingly difficult. Moreover, wily venture capital groups sometimes offer them opportunities (such as later-round investments in troubled firms) that the venture groups themselves find unattractive.

- *Corporate venture efforts can distract managers' attention away from other equally important responsibilities.* Some companies have concluded that venturing efforts drain away too much of their managers' time and attention. Indeed, some managers have gotten so immersed in their company's venture capital efforts that they find working with young firms far more enjoyable than their day-to-day responsibilities. In other cases, senior managers tire of mediating disputes over the allocation of venture resources, selection of investments, and compensation.

- *Investments can expose a corporation to embarrassing publicity or litigation.* Young entrepreneurial firms welcome corporate investors in part because these partners provide a stamp of approval that burnishes the firms' image. But this certification has its dark side for the corporate partner: A start-up's troubles—for example, product liability problems—can reflect poorly on the parent corporation. This is particularly true in image-sensitive industries. Perhaps more troubling, if a start-up runs into financial or other difficulties, the corporate investor may become a target for litigation. Even if the corporate investor has done nothing wrong, aggrieved parties may try to plunder its deep pockets.

- *Start-ups can cannibalize corporations' existing product lines.* In the early 1990s, Xerox transferred much of its online document-management software to a start-up, Documentum, in which its corporate venture capital unit had invested.[3] At the time, Xerox saw this technology as tangential to its core strength: physical document preparation. But just a few years later, with the emergence of online publishing, Xerox decided to develop electronic document-preparation products after all. The company found itself competing directly with Documentum— now a publicly traded company with a $1 billion market capitalization.

So Why Take the Risk?

Given all these risks, why do corporations even consider launching venturing programs? And if these risks become reality, why do companies give venturing second—and third—chances?

A cynic might attribute these programs' persistence to greed or naïveté on the part of executives. For instance, a senior executive nearing retirement may announce a venturing program amid much fanfare in the hopes that the market will assign her firm a higher valuation. If the ploy succeeds (that is, the company's stockholders don't catch on until after the executive retires and sells her equity in the firm), she stands to make a large profit. Or, some senior executives simply may believe that *their* company's venturing efforts will be easy to implement and will stand a good chance of succeeding.

But more than an initial flush of enthusiasm keeps corporations coming back for new rounds of venturing adventures even after some of them sour. These corporate venture programs have unique strengths that can be seen by looking at the results they generate.

The Corporate Venturing Track Record

Despite all the dangers described above, corporate venture programs have scored some impressive successes. We can see this by comparing what happened to investments made by corporate venture programs to those made by independent venture groups. Keep in mind, though, that this approach may actually *understate* the success of the corporate programs because these initiatives have complex objectives. Traditional groups, which seek only to maximize their financial returns, aren't likely to benefit much from an investment that gets liquidated or sold at a low valuation. However, for corporate investors, even failed endeavors may bring the firm substantial strategic advantages.

For instance, consider the experience of Massachusetts-based semiconductor manufacturer Analog Devices.[4] This company ran a corporate venture program in 1979 through 1985 that seemed disastrous by any financial standard: Only one of its thirteen portfolio companies went public, and it did so after so many financing rounds that Analog's stake proved modest. The corporation wrote off more than half the amount it originally invested.

But looking more deeply into Analog's situation, we see that this program was successful. The company specialized in developing silicon-based, or CMOS, semiconductors, which dominated the industry at the time. During the early 1980s, some players in the industry searched for alternative technologies—such as Gallium Arsenide (GaAs) and bipolar semiconductors—to go head-to-head with CMOS technology. Through its corporate program, Analog Devices invested in these competing technologies. Over time, these technological threats proved far less formidable than initially believed. Accordingly, the valuations assigned to CMOS-based manufacturers spiked: Analog's value, for example, increased sevenfold during these years.

For Analog, the failure of the competing firms in its portfolio was good news indeed. In a sense, Analog had purchased an insurance policy. Granted, the policy didn't pay out any monetary benefits—but that's because nothing bad happened!

Even though these complex motives—and benefits—make it hard to compare the success of corporate versus independent venturing, a pattern does emerge if we examine the data.[5] In making our comparison, we looked only at corporate venture investments made between 1983 and 1994, to ensure that those efforts had time to mature. The evidence is striking: In more than 30,000 investments into entrepreneurial firms by venture capital organizations of all types, corporate efforts appear to be as successful as those backed by independent venture organizations (using such criteria as the probability of a portfolio firm's going public). As table 7-3 shows, 35 percent of the investments by corporate funds went to companies that had gone public by the end of the sample period, as opposed to 31 percent for independent funds. The differences persist when we use different criteria for success, such as tracking firms that were acquired at a valuation of at least three times the original investment.

It might be thought that these results are just consequences of the fact that corporate groups often invest in later financing rounds, when uncertainties about the firm's development have cleared up and prospects have brightened. But when we control for a portfolio firm's age and profitability at the time of the original investment, we uncover the same results. But as the final column of the table reveals, the success of a venturing effort varies with the tightness of fit between the corporation and the portfolio firm—that is, whether there is a direct, strategic overlap between corporate parent and investee.

Table 7-3   Status of Corporate and Independent Venture Investments

Status at End of Analysis	Entire Sample (%)	Corporate Venture Capital Only (%)	Independent Venture Capital Only (%)	Corporate Venture Capital and Strategic Fit (%)
Initial Public Offering Completed	31.1	35.1	30.6	39.3
Registration Statement Filed	0.7	0.2	0.7	0.3
Acquired	29.0	29.0	30.3	27.5
Still Privately Held	20.6	21.1	19.7	18.3
Liquidated	18.7	14.6	18.7	14.7

Source: Paul A. Gompers and Josh Lerner, "The Determinants of Corporate Venture Success," in *Concentrated Corporate Ownership,* ed. Randall Morck (Chicago: University of Chicago Press for the National Bureau of Economic Research, 2000).

Note: The sample consists of 32,364 investments in privately held venture-backed firms between 1983 and 1994.

Similar patterns emerge when we look at the duration of the programs themselves. The evidence suggests that corporate programs without a close strategic fit with their investments are much less stable than those of independent funds. Many unfocused corporate funds cease operations after only a few investments, with most funds surviving for less than one-quarter the lifetime of the average independent fund. Meanwhile, corporate funds with a strong fit with their investments live almost as long as independent funds do.

How can we reconcile these findings with the anecdotal accounts of poor planning and naïve expectations? Corporate managers bring important expertise and knowledge to the table when they launch these programs. With solid experience in product markets, many of them make sophisticated, wise investors. And though they may not have as much investing experience as traditional venture capitalists, they can bring their corporation's resources to bear in managing their portfolios. The powerful combination of a corporation's knowledge and resources can outweigh some of the risks associated with pursuing venture capital in an uncertain, inhospitable environment.

Many successful corporate venturing efforts survive and thrive when the corporate investors, for whatever reason, manage to score a few successes early in the life of the venture program. Through these initial achievements, the company starts building a reputation as a skilled investor—and begins attracting more and more high-potential business plans. For instance, soon after its founding in March 1999, Dell Ventures made successful investments in such firms as Lante Corporation, Navi-Site, NeoForma.com, and WebMethods.[6] These achievements—and the favorable publicity they generated—resulted in a steady stream of investment opportunities directed toward Dell from entrepreneurs and other venture groups.

Internal Cohesion and External Relationship-Building: Two Essential Components of Successful Corporate Venturing

In addition to strategic fit, market knowledge, and resources, the way a corporation approaches its venture program influences its chances of success. In companies whose venture programs *don't* succeed, managers have made two fatal mistakes:

- They never created consensus *inside* the organization about the program's objectives and its potential benefits to the company.

- They failed to build relationships and establish credibility *outside* the corporation, assuming, in many instances, that the corporation's name alone would ensure success.

Let's see how these two errors can affect a corporate venture program's success.

Solidifying Internal Cohesion

Many corporations plunge into corporate venturing without devoting much time to the program's design. Without proper design, conflict can arise over the program's objectives—and can even force the dissolution of the effort. Departments that feel threatened by or otherwise uncomfortable with the program might push to have it terminated. Or the venture unit's interests and the corporation's goals may be out of alignment.

Exxon Enterprises, whose venture capital effort ranks among the most spectacular failures in the field, suffered the consequences of internal dissension.[7] The oil giant (called Esso at the time), seeking to diversify its product line, had launched its venture program back in 1964. The program began with a mandate to exploit technology developed in Exxon's corporate laboratories, such as the opportunity to make building materials out of petroleum derivatives.

In the late 1960s, however, the fund managers decided to make minority investments in a wide variety of industries, from advanced materials to air-pollution-control equipment to medical devices. In the late 1970s, the fund's strategy changed yet again—now focusing solely on systems for office use. Finally, in 1985, Exxon abandoned the venture effort entirely. Each shift in corporate strategy had brought waves of costly write-downs. The information-systems effort alone generated an estimated $2 billion in losses for the corporation.

What explains this disaster? In part, the corporate venture team came to the project with scant investment experience and made numerous poor decisions. But equally important, senior managers at Exxon couldn't agree on the program's overarching purpose, and so provided no strategic direction. This lack of oversight paved the way for internal dissension over the management and structure of the program. Various divisions at Exxon insisted on detailed reviews of the program, which consumed the fund managers' time and attention, to the detriment of the selection and oversight of investments. Also, various organizations within the corporation were allowed to tinker with the program's structure. For instance, Exxon's human resources staff complained that the venture firms' compensation schemes did not mirror those of the overall corporation. In the late 1970s, the HR department succeeded in replacing the venture staff's separate stock-option schemes with a standard salary-plus-bonus plan. An exodus of fund managers soon followed.

Internal consensus is particularly important in venture programs with strong strategic objectives. The $100 million Java fund, launched in 1996 by Kleiner Perkins Caufield & Byers, is one example of a fund that gave a number of corporations a chance to invest primarily for strategic reasons.[8] The fund specifically invested in companies that used Java, a programming language developed by Sun Microsystems that ran on a wide variety of operating systems and challenged Microsoft Windows. In addition to raising capital from traditional limited partners (such as the Harvard, Stanford, and Yale University endowments), the fund also tapped firms such as Cisco, IBM, Netscape, Oracle, and—of course—Sun. Even though these firms competed intensely with each other, they all wanted to see this programming language take root because it would "level the playing field" with their formidable competitor Microsoft.

Cultivating External Relationships

Good relationships with independent venture firms are also essential to the success of corporate programs. Why? The venture capital business is highly competitive. Identifying and gaining access to attractive opportunities can be difficult for new players. Investors have to make decisions quickly, often with scant information about an opportunity. Close ties between corporate venture efforts and traditional venture firms can

- Bring promising opportunities to the corporate fund's attention

- Bring early-stage transactions—which often have lower valuations and more strategic potential—to the corporate fund's attention

- Ensure that venture capitalists deal with corporate capitalists professionally and respectfully

- Let corporate groups tap into independent groups' knowledge

Despite all these potential benefits, relations between corporate and independent venture groups continue to suffer from strain. The venture capital community is close-knit; many leading firms have syndicated transactions with each other for decades. Though these firms' skepticism about corporate venture funds has abated somewhat, a residual distrust remains. Furthermore, corporate programs are wary of unscrupulous venture groups that have been known to exploit naïve corporate investors.

To make relationship building even more difficult, it takes time for corporations to build credibility in the eyes of independent venture capitalists. As we've seen, many corporations launch venture programs assuming that their names alone will earn them instant respect. They then discover that their venture program isn't going anywhere without "road shows" with venture groups, conference presentations, and press releases to publicize the company's activities.

Can corporations hope to speed up this relationship-building process? The answer is yes—though this, too, takes work. Here are some strategies:

- Form an appropriately sized fund. Too small a fund suggests a limited commitment by the corporation to the program; too substantial an effort leads to speculation that the corporation does not understand the dangers associated with growing too quickly.

- Recruit one or more of the fund's investment professionals from the venture capital community.

- Articulate a clear investment strategy.

- Simultaneously invest in venture capital partnerships specializing in similar technologies.

- Consider joint ventures with: (1) a specific venture capital firm (for instance, Softbank and Kmart formed a collaboration called Blue-Light[9]); (2) several other corporations and a venture capitalist firm (such as Kleiner Perkins's Java Fund); or (3) a number of venture capital firms (for instance, Sutter Hill Ventures, Technology Crossover Ventures, and buyout fund Bain Capital joined in mid-2000 with the consulting firm eLoyalty to establish the eLoyalty Ventures Fund[10]).

Designing and Implementing a Successful Corporate Venture Program

With the above caveats about internal cohesion and external relationship building in mind, how can corporations design and implement venture programs to maximize their chances of success? They need to pay close attention to four facets of the process:

- Fund structure

- Partner compensation

- The fund partners' degree of autonomy

- The management of investments

It's probably no surprise that these four aspects of corporate venturing also have the most potential to create internal controversy.

Structuring the Fund

In launching corporate funds, some companies have emulated the limited partnership structure found in traditional venture funds, with the corporation acting as a hands-off limited partner of the venture group. This is particularly true of funds that independent venture groups organize for corporations—for example, Advent International and Hambrecht & Quist's venture fund (now known as Granite Associates).

In arrangements like these, the limited partnership structure is a familiar and comfortable one. Equally important, it signals that the corporate partner won't interfere with the fund's operations, thus demonstrating its commitment to outside venture groups, prospective fund employees, and entrepreneurs.

Intel Corporation is a case in point.[11] In late 1998, the company's venture unit, Intel Capital, sought to establish a fund that would help diffuse its next-generation semiconductor chip into the market. By investing in firms that were developing hardware and software designed to capitalize on the new chip's power, the fund managers believed they could accelerate the launch of the chip and thereby enhance Intel's profits. (The bulk of the profits from new chips comes from sales during the earliest months and years after the product launch, before rivals can introduce competing offerings.) Intel also hunted around for strategic coinvestors—particularly the company's key manufacturers and chief information officers of Fortune 500 corporations. By linking these partners' returns to those of the new chip fund, Intel believed it could intensify interest in the new technology. The only practical way to implement such a plan, Intel discovered, was to set up the fund as a separate partnership. Without this structure, investors would have worried that Intel might focus on investments that offered strategic promise but little financial return.

In Intel's case, following the independent model aligned the various players' interests and let Intel put its strategic plans into action. But many companies have deviated from the independent model, instead linking the venture unit closely to the corporation. Many companies don't even set aside a dedicated pool of funds for the venture group to invest. The venture capitalists have to appeal to the corporation for each investment. As top executives in these corporations see it, this approach lets them direct the venture effort into areas of greatest strategic benefit for the firm.

Numerous corporations also retain the right to dissolve the fund at any time. As they (rightly) argue, the venture capital market is highly volatile. The supply of start-ups—and the opportunity and threat that they represent to existing companies—may dwindle in a heartbeat. These companies want to ensure that they don't get locked into a costly venture capital effort. All companies that deviate from the traditional limited partnership structure have a similar rationale: They want substantial input into and control over the fund, especially if its purpose is to yield strategic benefits.

Clearly, venturing corporations face a tough trade-off when deciding how to structure their programs: They want tight control over the venture effort, but they also need the external credibility that comes with agreeing to the traditional limited partnership structure. The best of these efforts have sought to maintain the independence of the venture effort, while ensuring clear information flow to the corporation.

For instance, Xerox anchored its Technology Ventures (XTV) program in a corporate division but let XTV establish a partnership agreement between the fund managers and the corporation.[12] The arrangement resembled the traditional limited partnership structure, as it carefully delineated each side's responsibilities and prerogatives. For example, the document stipulated that the fund report to a small oversight committee, and provided profit-sharing and governance rules. When the venture managers discussed the fund with outsiders and potential investees, they made sure to mention the agreement—which eased outsiders' concerns about the fund's staying power.

But the balancing act is a tricky one! These kinds of compromises may provide a partial answer to the dilemma of fund structure, but they can't stave off all problems. In the case of the Xerox effort, for example, the corporation eventually grew unhappy with the program, despite the fact that it had achieved spectacular success. (A conservative calculation puts the proceeds to Xerox from the $30 million fund at $175 million. This figure implies a net internal rate of return for Xerox of at least 56 percent— far above that of the typical independent venture capital fund launched in the same year.)

What made Xerox so dissatisfied with a seemingly stellar venture effort? Much of the unhappiness appeared to stem from the corporation's perception that the companies that had been taken public by the venture fund presented more and more of a competitive threat to the corporate parent, despite an investment review process that the corporation engaged in to avert this kind of situation.

In 1996, tensions came to a head. Xerox decided to terminate XTV, well before the end of the program's agreed-upon ten-year life span. A new venture program—one that did not involve Xerox relinquishing control of firms and downplayed the involvement of outside venture investors—replaced XTV.

Dell also tried to preserve the independence of its venture group while ensuring clear communication. The corporation wanted to establish a fund that was flexible and quick to move but that would also collaborate with Dell's various business units. To address this problem, the company adopted an innovative hub-and-spoke system. At the hub sits Dell Ventures itself—a collection of principals, associates, and analysts who evaluate opportunities and make investment transactions. This hub is in turn surrounded by spokes—liaisons in each of Dell's business units. These liaisons meet frequently with the investment professionals, communicating the divisions' perceptions of the market environment as well as their emerging technological needs. During these sessions, the liaisons also learn about various prospective investments and the challenges facing the investors. While the ultimate success of this young program remains uncertain, theirs is an ingenious solution that other corporations would do well to consider seriously.

Compensating Corporate Venture Staff

As we've seen, in most independent venture firms, the partners' compensation consists mostly of carried interest. This profit-sharing arrangement pays around 20 percent of the earnings directly to the investment principals. This carried interest arrangement helps these firms attract and retain talented professionals—and motivates these professionals to create value. It also helps address the fact that the investors have relatively limited control over the fund's activities.

Nevertheless, many corporations have rejected these kinds of incentive schemes, fearing that the substantial rewards that these structures generate might raise internal tensions and generate questions from shareholders. Indeed, many senior executives cringe at the image of their venture staff pulling in millions—or tens of millions—of dollars.

The traditional incentive scheme poses another potential problem for corporations: If the company ends up acquiring a firm in its portfolio, the traditional incentive structure will create a conflict of interest for the venture group. Specifically, the more the corporation pays to acquire the firm, the more the venture capitalists will get paid for their services. For example, Xerox committed to pay XTV 20 percent of all capital gains from its investments.[13] When Xerox acquired Advanced Workstation Products, one of ATV's portfolio firms, for $15 million, XTV received nearly $2 million in compensation.

Though these concerns are understandable, companies that have rejected the carried interest scheme have paid a high price. Here are just a few results:

- Companies are unable to recruit from the venture industry because experienced venture capitalists, who are used to earning industry-standard compensation, turn up their noses at opportunities to join the corporate venture staff.

- Independent venture firms conclude that the corporate venture staff are either unskilled or about to defect.

- Key principals, frustrated at not receiving an acceptable share of the profits, leave the organization. (One large industrial corporation, for example, established three successful corporate venture units between 1968 and 1995. In each case, the company had to abandon the effort after key personnel, upset over insufficient compensation, defected and began their own funds.)

Given this backdrop, corporations have three choices in designing venture compensation schemes:

- *Provide no carried interest at all.* This strategy can work in corporations that focus on passive investments—that is, when company representatives do not sit on investees' boards or form strategic relationships with portfolio companies. Though these groups may experience considerable attrition, they require limited venture-investment skills and thus can easily replace defectors. Similarly, if the corporation already has a strong entrepreneurial culture, with extensive employee equity holdings, explicit incentives for fund managers may not matter as much: Employees may be motivated to work hard just through their substantial holdings of the parent firm's equity.

- *Follow the 20 percent profit-sharing rule.* Corporations that want to cultivate strong external relationships and structure complex transactions with portfolio firms need sophisticated and experienced individuals to manage the fund. To attract and retain these individuals, the corporation will likely have to follow the 20 percent profit-sharing rule that's so prevalent in the venture industry. Such compensation is especially likely to be needed when the success of a corporate venture program hinges tightly on investors' ability to add real value—whether by skillfully screening transactions or sustaining profitable ties with portfolio firms after they make an investment. To deprive these professionals of reasonable, industry-standard profit sharing that reflects their expertise and contribution will almost certainly spell disaster.

- *Adjust the profit-sharing percentage.* Some corporations have worried that the 20 percent rule will push investors to maximize financial returns at the expense of strategic benefits to the corporate parent. To guard against this danger, some companies have successfully employed hybrid approaches. A remarkably stable venture program, SmithKline Beecham's S.R. One, operated under a single head, Peter Sears, from 1985 to 1999.[14] The fund achieved impressive successes, investing in medical technology firms like Amgen, Cephalon, and Sepracor, and coinvesting with major venture firms such as Kleiner Perkins and New Enterprise Associates. Its compensation scheme played a large role in this success. During most of this period, the corporate venture capitalists received 15 percent of the profits they generated. In addition, they received a bonus based on less tangible benefits to the corporation which could run as high as another 5 percent of the fund's capital gains. This approach kept SmithKline's venture investors sensitive to both its financial objectives and the parent company's strategic needs. Such reward schemes are, of course, inherently subjective—unlike the other alternatives—and hence more challenging to administer.

The experience of Intel demonstrates the costs and benefits of the first approach. Recently, Intel's corporate venturing program achieved extraordinary results. In the second quarter of 2000 alone, the fund reported capital gains of $2.3 *billion.* But instead of paying out a 20 percent share of these gains to its investment staff, the fund enhanced staff members' salary and stock options. However generous these packages were, though, they couldn't possibly rival the size of the payouts that the 20 percent rule would have generated. To be sure, this move meant lower compensation costs for Intel, and hence greater profits for its shareholders. But it also caused the investment staff to leave in droves to join independent private equity organizations, launch start-ups, and participate in other corporate venture programs. Only time will reveal the full impact of these defections on Intel's corporate venturing effort.

There's no one right approach to compensation. Corporations should structure their incentive schemes to reflect the strategic objectives of the program and the circumstances of the firm.

Defining the Autonomy of Corporate Venture Groups

Traditional limited partnership agreements provide relatively few restrictions on venture capitalists' autonomy, allowing these professionals a great deal of discretion in choosing and overseeing investments. Corporations, on the other hand, usually insist on more oversight of their venture-unit professionals. And whereas most institutional investors in venture funds care only that the funds create financial value, corporations care deeply about where their venture units invest. The reason is simple: If an investment isn't likely to yield strategic benefits for the parent company—or, worse, if it unwittingly gives an adversary an advantage—heads may roll. Corporations also face regulatory pressures, as well as legal liability for soured investments. Many corporations thus insist on reviewing potential additions to their internal funds' portfolios.

Yet in order to perform well, a venture group—whether independent or corporate—needs flexibility and freedom. A corporation that completely stifles this autonomy may suffer. In some cases, a detailed review procedure keeps venture capital professionals from moving fast enough to seize the best opportunities. For instance, before IBM's Fireworks Partners (established in 1993) could make an investment, it had to get signed approvals from numerous divisional vice presidents.[15] When IBM abandoned the program just two years later, the fund's initial proposed investments were still tied up in internal review, and the venture groups that had originally notified IBM of these opportunities had long since funded the investments themselves. These kinds of delays not only frustrate corporate venture professionals, they also send a poor signal about the group's effectiveness to outsiders.

So how can corporations strike a balance between their need for control and the benefits that come from giving their venture professionals a long lead? Again, the options are limited, and each has its advantages and costs:

- Corporations can restrict venture professionals' investments to those that benefit the parent company strategically. For instance, the company can insist that senior managers and division heads sign off on all investments.

- The company can let the venture group pursue a broad range of opportunities. This policy may help the corporation retain talented venture staff—professionals who rightly feel that they can make wise investment decisions. Moreover, few corporate managers can predict which investments will have strategical importance two or three years down the road. By allowing bright people to invest in interesting companies, the parent company might, in the process, serve its own long-term interests.

Probably the wisest course here is to emulate the more restrictive independent venture partnership agreements. For instance, an oversight board may approve each investment (at least above a certain size) but delegate day-to-day operations to the venture group. In addition, the board could commit to a rapid response—say, no longer than seven days—in reviewing proposed transactions.

Managing Portfolio Companies

When independent venture firms invest in young companies, they insist on numerous terms and conditions—including service on the companies' boards. On average, venture investors receive just under three board seats, representing a majority of the board, at the time of investment. This arrangement lets them protect their investment by stepping in if events take a troubling turn.

In many cases, corporate investors seek the same kind of board representation. Board service not only lets them protect their investments but also may have additional special benefits. For example, it can help close the substantial information gaps that exist. While any investor can look over the minutes of these meetings and review financial statements, physically attending the sessions can provide vital insights into industry trends and strengthen relationships among directors.

At the same time, board service carries substantial costs. First, many entrepreneurs fear—with good reason in some cases—that a corporate investor or strategic partner will try to appropriate their ideas. Moreover, they may perceive an inherent conflict between a corporate executive discharging his responsibilities to his employer and the fiduciary responsibilities expected of a director. Thus, the aggressive pursuit of board seats by corporations may turn off entrepreneurs who prefer to keep these players at arm's length. Furthermore, most venture capital funds negotiate board composition at the time of the initial financing. A corporate investor who insists on a board seat in every case may well be excluded from a number of attractive investment opportunities.

Second, board service can expose a corporation to litigation. Though class-action litigation against directors of public companies has attracted the most publicity, directors of private firms also get sued. Aggrieved parties—dissatisfied customers, terminated entrepreneurs, and minority shareholders—often target corporate directors in such suits. The plaintiffs know that many corporations faced with this situation will settle out of court rather than exposing themselves to damaging publicity and risking much more by going to trial.

Thus, however desirable having a board seat might be, compromise here might be the wisest course for corporate venture groups. For example, a corporate unit might initially ask to serve as a board observer, who attends meetings, but does not vote or assume fiduciary responsibilities. This role lets the corporate venture team become familiar with the key issues facing the portfolio company, learn about industry dynamics, and build relationships with the venture capital community without triggering entrepreneurs' fears or exposing the corporate parent to the same degree of litigation risk. As the corporation's venturing team develops experience and builds visibility, it can gradually play a more active role by serving as a director on portfolio firms' boards.

Which corporate representative serves as a board director or observer matters as well. Entrepreneurs become especially worried when a general corporate officer sits on their firm's board. These fears can be well founded. General corporate officers often have little time to devote to their roles as board directors. At the same time, they tend to find it difficult to distance themselves from the perspective of the corporate parent. Most entrepreneurs believe that corporate venture fund representatives fit in better with the other venture directors. At the same time, some companies have found that placing operating managers on portfolio companies' boards can deepen the corporation's understanding of these companies' potential and thus help both parties work together more effectively.

Regardless of who serves on the board, however, it is important that there be clear communication about what is being learned. Cambridge Technology Partners (CTP) provides a disturbing illustration of what can happen when this communication fails.[16] This Boston-based information-technology consulting firm set up a fund, Cambridge Technology Capital, as a freestanding partnership in 1997. The fund was located in California and run by a successful entrepreneur who had not previously worked for CTP. The fund scored some substantial hits in the years that followed, with investments in such firms has E.piphany, Silknet, and WebLogic. Indeed, the rate of return on the fund reached 237 percent through May 2000, with much of the fund's success deriving from its Internet-related commitments.

Meanwhile, the parent company stumbled, primarily because it failed to anticipate a major shift in its large corporate customers' needs. Specifically, customers who used to want traditional client-server/systems integration services now wanted e-commerce consulting. Unable to respond quickly enough to this new demand, CTP saw its stock price lose more than 90 percent of its value between the time of the independent fund's inception and October 2000. The situation presented a sad irony for CTP: The exact same shift had crippled the corporation—but had made its own investment fund wealthy. The insights about technological change that had been apparent to the corporate venture capitalists never were incorporated into the operating strategy of the parent.

The Pressure to Innovate

Corporations today face mounting pressure to rethink their approach to innovation. The enormous surge in venture financing and the success of these firms in creating market value have added to those pressures. Many high-tech corporations—even AT&T and IBM, which historically have strongly funded internal research laboratories—are rethinking the value of internal R&D.[17] Some high-tech giants have turned to acquisitions and strategic investments to stimulate and exploit product and process innovations. More and more, corporate venture capital programs provide yet another innovation tool for major corporations around the world.

But assembling a venture capital team and sending it forth into the venture arena isn't enough. Corporations must invest in industries that they know well—industries in which they can select the best possible portfolio firms and add value to the capitalization process. Fund design and implementation—from basic legal structure and compensation schemes to investor autonomy and management policy—can literally make or break the team's future.

Because the independent venture capital model has stood the test of time, corporations might well begin their venturing efforts by adopting the best features of that model. While some compromises will be necessary, the proven model should be the baseline. After all, why reinvent the wheel if one doesn't have to!

We'll now turn to looking at emulating the venture capital model in a different setting: government-backed research institutions, such as universities and national laboratories. While many of the same issues appear, these special environments also pose unexpected challenges.

8

Designing
a Successful Public
Venturing Effort

■

Despite the resources devoted to public venture capital, success remains elusive.

In the United States, the federal government has played an active role in financing new firms, particularly in high-technology industries. This began after the Soviet Union's launch of *Sputnik* in 1957 and has gathered momentum since then, as the government has increasingly recognized the power of venture financing to stimulate innovation and economic health. In recent years, European and Asian nations—as well as many U.S. state governments—have adopted similar initiatives. A majority of these programs are designed to stimulate entrepreneurial firms, particularly in high-technology industries. Others have focused on encouraging the commercialization of technology developed in government-funded research institutions.

To be sure, the sums of money involved are modest compared with public expenditures on defense or retiree benefits. However, when we compare these programs to contemporaneous private investments in new firms, we get a quite different picture, as the following examples suggest:

- Between 1958 and 1969, the United States' Small Business Investment Company (SBIC) program directed $3 billion to young firms—more than *three times* the total private venture capital invested during these years.[1]

- In 1995, public small-business financing programs in the United States provided $2.4 billion in equity financing—more than 60 percent of the amount disbursed by traditional venture funds in that year.

And the bulk of these funds went to early-stage firms, which in the past decade had accounted for only about 30 percent of disbursements by independent venture funds.[2]

- Some of the United States's most dynamic technology companies—including Apple Computer, Chiron, Compaq, and Intel—received support from the SBIC and Small Business Innovation Research (SBIR) programs before they went public.[3]

In the United States, government venturing programs have taken many different forms, with unique complexities associated with each. Collectively, however, we can term these programs "public venture capital" initiatives, though some of them provide funds through a contract or as an outright grant, rather than as equity investments. These programs are also quite diverse in terms of where the funds come from: some expend tax revenues directly, while others are financed through loan guarantees.

Why Public Venturing?

Public venture programs can not only help fledgling economies construct the commercial and financial infrastructures needed to stimulate innovation; they can also make a positive difference in economies that already have well-developed venture sectors. For example, these programs may boost an investment's chances of success by providing a stamp of approval for struggling portfolio firms. Less directly, public venturing can help nurture an environment where start-ups can thrive, whether funded by the government or the private sector. As we'll see, however, serving these functions introduces some complexities, especially in economies that already have a strong venture capital component.

Creating Infrastructure

The United States' Small Business Investment Company program provides an ideal example of how public venture programs can help a nation create a venture-investing infrastructure.[4] To be sure, after the launch of the program in 1958, SBICs drew criticism for the low financial returns generated and the fraud and waste associated with some funds. Viewed with hindsight, however, the program takes on a different appearance. Though few of today's significant funds began as a part of the SBIC program, the program did stimulate the proliferation of many venture-minded institutions in Silicon Valley and Route 128—the nation's two major breeding grounds of venture capital. These institutions included law firms, accounting groups, and services providers geared specifically to the needs of entrepreneurial firms. For example, Venture Economics, which originated as the SBIC Reporting Service in 1961, gradually expanded its scope to become the major source of returns data on the entire venture industry.

Boosting the Chances of Investment Success

Now that the United States has an active venture sector, public programs must shift their focus from building infrastructure to two new functions: assessing a company's potential and providing appropriately sized funding. If these conditions can be satisfied, public programs can complement the private venture capital industry.

Assessing Potential. In the United States, private venture capitalists specialize in assessing the potential of new ideas and financing the firms that generate them. Thus they strengthen the reputation of the entrepreneurial organizations in their portfolios. Why should the government compete with independent venture capitalists in this regard?

It's simple: Venture capitalists back only a tiny fraction of the technology-oriented businesses that crop up each year. In 2000, a record year for venture disbursements, just over 2,200 U.S. companies received venture financing for the first time.[5] Yet the Small Business Administration estimates that in recent years about 1 million new businesses have started up annually. Furthermore, private venture funds have concentrated on a few industries: For instance, in 2000, 92 percent of venture funding went to firms specializing in information technology and health care, and more specifically, 46 percent of venture funding went to Internet-related companies. Thus, many promising firms in other industries are *not* attracting venture capitalists' notice. If government programs can identify and support firms in these neglected industries, they might provide the credibility these high-potential, underfunded firms need to succeed.

Granted, the patterns of concentration that have emerged in the private venture industry may offer unique advantages that public programs can't match. Clustering in a particular industry, for example, lets local firms share knowledge, specialized labor markets, and critical suppliers. Despite the benefits of such concentration, however, the extreme unevenness of venture funding across industries suggests that public funds can play a valuable role.

Providing Appropriately Sized Funding. If public venturing programs are to complement private venture investing, they must also provide the right amount of financing.

Too small a program is unlikely to make much of a difference. For instance, some public programs have invested only a few million dollars. Such an effort is very unlikely to make an impact in an economy as large and diverse as the United States. Few venture capitalists or other investors will learn about the program, and the possibility that such funding will serve as a signal to others will be remote.

On the other hand, if public programs become too large, they can crowd out, or discourage, venture capitalists from investing in a given market, because all attractive opportunities have been already funded by the public funds.

The experience of the Canadian Labor Fund Program provides a good illustration of this danger.[6] The Canadian government, seeking to encourage venture capital, established in 1993 a series of labor funds with total capital of over CAD$3 billion —more than the entire independent sector. Investors received exceedingly generous tax credits for investing in these funds, which were managed by labor unions and other organizations that were quite unfamiliar with the venture process and had compensation schemes very different from traditional independent partnerships.

While the program sought to encourage the Canadian venture industry, the effect was quite the opposite. The relatively few independent Canadian venture funds found themselves competing against uninformed investors, who were in many cases willing to commit capital at huge valuations. Many of the independent groups, convinced that they could not generate profitable returns in the Canadian market, shifted to investing in the United States instead.

Encouraging R&D "Spillovers"

As an innovation picks up momentum, a phenomenon known as a spillover can occur when the knowledge or technology flows from one organization to another or to society as a whole. An innovation may stimulate some companies to develop complementary products. For instance, the development of the personal computer led to the formation of many software developers geared to this market. The sale of complementary software proved to be far more profitable than PC manufacturing itself. Consumers also benefit from spillovers when the price of new goods drops rapidly.

It's hard to compute the exact returns that innovators on the one hand and other firms and society on the other enjoy from new innovations. Nevertheless, most estimates suggest that the different parties receive markedly different benefits because of these spillovers: Society reportedly benefits 50–100 percent more than innovators and their investors do.[7] The consequences are clear: Other parties benefit more than the company who originally created and invested in the new idea. The original innovator bears all the costs associated with the research and development—but captures only a fraction of the benefits. These inequities can create particularly severe problems for small firms that lack the resources to defend their intellectual property or extract adequate profit from a commercially successful innovation. As a result, firms may hesitate to undertake innovation.

These problems suggest a third rationale for public venturing programs. To address the spillover problem, the government can subsidize some of the cost of developing new products or processes by young firms. Even entrepreneurial firms that are not viable as businesses may constitute attractive investments from the perspective of a government that wants to encourage innovation across the entire economy. For instance, a biotechnology firm developing a new reagent may never form a very profitable business, but if the chemical compound accelerates the work of researchers in industry and academia, the benefits to society may be great.

When Government Programs Go Wrong

Public venturing programs have the potential to play a very positive role. But government subsidies often have a negative side. For example, powerful, avaricious interest groups may try to direct subsidies into their own coffers. Similarly, politicians may use subsidies to reward loyal constituents or campaign donors. Unfortunately, opportunities for corruption and graft abound. In addition, a public-program official may select portfolio firms based on their likely success, and fund them regardless of whether the firms really need government backing. The official can then claim credit for the firms' ultimate success—and then use that success to justify the renewal, or even the expansion, of the venture program (a sure-fire way for said official to keep her job).

Distortions at Work: The SBIR Program

The largest public venture program in the United States, the Small Business Innovation Research (SBIR) program, sets aside 2.5 percent of all federal external R&D expenditures (the research not directly undertaken by government scientists) to fund small, high-tech businesses.[8] In recent years, the program has invested about $1.1 billion each year. We can see the effect of this policy by comparing the performance of program recipients with that of matching firms. Table 8-1 shows that the awardees grew considerably faster than companies in the same locations and industries that did not receive awards.

Sounds like a happy situation, right? Unfortunately, beneath these positive results lie some intense political pressures and conflicting interests. For one thing, congressmen and their staffers have pressured program managers to award funding to companies in their states. Reflecting these pressures, in almost every recent fiscal year, all 50 states have received at least one SBIR award.

Table 8-1 also highlights the consequences of such political pressures. In particular, it contrasts what happened to the workforce size of SBIR awardees located in regions characterized by considerable high-tech activity (that is, in zip codes where at least one independent venture capital financing round occurred in the three years before the SBIR award) and those elsewhere.

The story? In the ten years after receipt of SBIR funding, the workforce of the average award recipient located in a high-tech region grew by forty-seven, basically doubling in size. The workforces of other awardees—those located in regions not characterized by high-tech activity—grew by only thirteen employees. Though recipients of SBIR awards grew considerably faster than those in a sample of matched firms, the superior performance, as measured by growth in employment (as well as sales and other measures), was confined to awardees in areas that already had private venture activity. In the name of geographic diversity, the program funded firms with inferior prospects.

Table 8-1   Growth of SBIR Awardees and Matching Firms

	Change in employment for . . .	
	SBIR Awardees	**Matching Firms**
Entire sample	+26	+6
Firms in zip code with venture capital activity	+47	+3
Firms in zip code without venture capital activity	+13	+7

Source: Based on Josh Lerner, "The Government as Venture Capitalist: The Long-Run Effects of the SBIR Program," *Journal of Business* 72 (1999): 285–318.

Note: This table presents the growth in employment between 1985 and 1995 of 541 firms that received Phase II awards between 1983 and 1985 as part of the Small Business Innovation Research program, as well as that of 894 firms that did not receive awards but were selected to match these firms as closely as possible. The tabulation is presented for all awardees, and for firms that were or were not located in a zip code with at least one early-stage venture financing between 1983 and 1985.

In addition to the geographic pressures, particular companies have managed to capture a disproportionate number of awards. These "SBIR mills" often have staffs in Washington that focus only on identifying opportunities for subsidy applications. This problem has proven difficult to eliminate, as mill staffers tend to be active lobbyists. Moreover, these firms commercialize far fewer projects than those firms that receive just one SBIR grant. Though a *single* SBIR grant does seem to encourage performance in awardee firms, the program clearly still has some work to do in eradicating waste and distortions.

Minimizing Public-Venture Problems: Structure as Solution

For better or worse, public venturing is a major presence in the U.S. economy today. And as with corporate venturing, the way in which these programs are structured influences their success. Three aspects of program structure stand out as especially important: (1) complementing independent venture capital firms, (2) flexibility, and (3) due diligence.

Complementing—Not Competing with— the Private Venture Industry

As a key first step, government officials must understand when it's time to ramp up public venturing—and when it's time to slow down. Private venture organizations move far more quickly and effectively than government efforts. Thus, while the SBIC effort played a key role in jump-starting the venture industry in the early 1960s, by the 1980s and the 1990s it had far less relevance. This was due to the success, not the failure, of the SBIC—it had accomplished its goal. Unfortunately, far too many public programs continue operating with their initial focus long after they've served their purpose. Such programs should consider shifting the program's focus to one that better reflects changing economic times—or, better yet, shutting it down entirely.

Public venture officials must also make investments with an eye to what the private venture industry is doing. The key? To complement—not compete with—the private arena. Independent venture firms tend to focus their efforts on a few areas of technology that they believe have high potential. As we discussed in chapter 6, during periods when private venture fund-raising is increasing, intense competition for opportunities within a particular set of technologies is likely to erupt. If public venture fund administrators put additional funds into these hot industries, the effect will be akin to splashing gasoline on an already burning fire. Moreover, by the time public investors get active in a hot sector, the best prospects have often already received venture funding, leaving the government stuck with lukewarm opportunities that yield less-than-stellar financial—or social—returns.

Instead, public venture administrators should adopt two potent strategies:

- Focus on technologies that *aren't* currently popular among private venture investors. As noted above, venture funding is typically very concentrated in a few areas and many promising technologies in other sectors see very little financing.

- Provide follow-on capital to firms already funded by private venture capitalists during periods when the stream of private funding has rapidly lessened. As we discussed in chapter 6, both "overshooting" and "undershooting" characterize the venture market. During periods when institutions dramatically withdraw venture funds, many promising companies may not be able to obtain refinancing, creating another opportunity for public venture administrators.

To see what can happen when public programs do not follow these strategies, let's look at the experience of the Advanced Technology Program (ATP), founded in 1990 and run by the U.S. Department of Commerce.[9] Since its inception, the program has awarded over $1 billion in research and development funding to over 300 high-tech projects conducted by U.S. companies and industry-led joint ventures. During the program's first eight years, 36 percent of ATP funding went to small businesses, with an additional 10 percent directed to joint ventures led by small businesses.

In choosing from among the many available investment opportunities, ATP often selects industries that are already well funded by the venture capital community, such as Internet tools and genomic sequencing. ATP administrators continue to eagerly pursue opportunities in venture-saturated industries—allowing the program's reports to Congress to brim with "success stories" about the progress of these firms. While such publicity may enhance the likelihood that the program is renewed, the value of funding more companies in such well-financed sectors is almost certainly very low.

Making Room for Flexibility

Private venture capitalists back young firms under conditions of tremendous technological, product-market, and management uncertainty. Rather than trying to eradicate all the uncertainty in advance, these capitalists remain actively involved after each investment. They use their contractually specified control rights to guide the firm in response to changes in product-market strategy, the management team, and so forth—changes that arise naturally during the investment process.

Indeed, the entire entrepreneurial process is fraught with unpredictability. Very few entrepreneurs, whether in high- or low-tech settings, commercialize a new product or service in the time frame they originally imagined. Rather, successful entrepreneurs gather signals from the marketplace in response to their initial efforts, and then adjust their plans accordingly. Once they identify an opportunity, they move quickly to take advantage of it before major corporations can beat them to it.

All too often, government administrators view these shifts not as natural aspects of the innovation process but as troubling indications that investees are deviating from the plan. The problem only worsens when federal agencies, worried about being accused of just "picking winners," push entrepreneurs to focus purely on precommercial research. But by doing so, the firms risk missing out on an essential source of information:

customer feedback. Even more dangerous, some publicly backed companies become afraid to chase after an attractive commercial opportunity because the companies' managers fear jeopardizing their public funds. Though well intentioned, restrictive investment policies may thus unwittingly punish success.

For instance, as we alluded to in chapter 2, one ATP awardee, Torrent Systems, completed preproduct R&D ahead of schedule. ATP rules forced Torrent to decide between giving up the unused money or expanding R&D into nonessential areas. Ultimately, Torrent decided to pursue a rapid-commercialization strategy despite these concerns, including an alliance with IBM—while sticking to the terms of its agreement. ATP promptly impounded the remaining funds. Torrent wasn't anticipating another round of venture financing for a number of months, so its executives now had to scramble to replace the lost financing. All of these events—along with threats from ATP to shut down the company and subject it to an exhaustive audit—consumed immense amounts of Torrent's decidedly limited time and money. As a result of government officials' lack of flexibility, Torrent paid a heavy penalty for its success.

Doing Due Diligence

The investment portfolios of many public venture capital programs today contain far too many underachieving firms. How can these managers learn to avoid a bad bet? By conducting due diligence effectively. One red flag is a company that has received numerous research grants from different government sources but has few, if any, tangible results to show for these R&D dollars. By attributing their lack of results to the high-risk nature of technology development, these firms can avoid accountability indefinitely. Indeed, government-backed research organizations often drift from one federal contract to the next, feeling little motivation to satisfy the program's objectives or to generate respectable returns.

Worse, companies with substantial government-grant experience have several advantages over other firms when they apply for future public awards. Past grants, regardless of project outcomes, enhance a company's reputation in a particular area of research. These grants also help the company acquire the equipment and personnel it needs to do future work. In addition, some public officials try to "piggyback" on other government programs, hoping to leverage their grant dollars. Finally, companies grow increasingly savvy about the grant-application process with each proposal they submit. Armed with all these advantages, these firms have a much greater chance of winning future government grants than other firms do. The result? Streams of government funding flowing into companies that consistently underachieve.

To weed out underachieving firms, public venture capital programs should scrutinize the amount of funding a company has already received from government sources. They should also conduct a comprehensive evaluation of a company's past performance and assess the firm's *tangible* progress—such as products developed or commercialized—attributable to each government grant the firm has received. In imitation of independent venture capitalists, it makes sense for public officials to conduct "reference checks," whether with other industry executives or with their peers in government who have previously funded the firm.

Public programs should also keep an eye out for troubles that undermine a company's ability to complete and commercialize government-funded technology. For example, pending lawsuits can divert human and financial resources away from R&D projects or force cataclysmic changes in the company's size and structure.

Similarly, too many auxiliary research projects can undermine performance. For instance, one company that had been developing software for supercomputers got involved in an e-commerce project that was only distantly related to the company's core (and ATP-funded) technology. Although the firm didn't use its ATP grant to fund this auxiliary project, it diverted a substantial amount of time, energy, and capital toward the tangential research, slowing the development of its core technology. In this case the problem stemmed in part from lack of corporate discipline. If a venture capital firm had invested in this company, it would have provided this discipline by closely monitoring the company and limiting its R&D activities to areas that had direct links to its core technology.

Lack of experience among managers can also constitute a red flag, especially in early-stage companies. Although some managers may have strong backgrounds as consultants or as members of large organizations, operating a new, small firm demands a different set of skills. Thus when venture capitalists sink substantial funds into a company, they often handpick the top manager—typically an individual who has already successfully managed an early-stage company in a similar industry.

The lesson? Government officials must ask themselves whether a particular company will serve as a viable vehicle for accomplishing the venture program's goals. This process entails far more than simply assessing feasibility of a business plan. Most of these documents say nothing about the worrisome characteristics we've just discussed. Regardless of how promising a new idea or technology is, or how well a business plan is constructed, a company burdened with legal troubles, distracting side projects, or mediocre management makes a risky investment indeed. Detailed reviews of applications, reference checking, and in-person visits to the companies will limit these problems.

All this requires public programs to perform a delicate balancing act. On the one hand, these programs should target industries not already saturated by the flood of private venture capital. As we have emphasized above, it's a mistake for government venture efforts to compete head-to-head with independent funds. On the other hand, much like private venture capitalists, public fund managers have to work hard to spot and address flaws in the companies that they do back and take an active role in monitoring them after the investment has been made.

Transferring Technology from the Laboratory to the Marketplace: The Promise and Challenge of Public Venturing

Given our discussion above, we might understandably conclude that all public venture capital efforts aim to stimulate entrepreneurship in the economy as a whole. In fact, many such programs have had a more sharply focused goal: to use venture capital to transfer *federally funded* technology into the commercial marketplace, and thus to generate financial returns for the institution and the government and to benefit society.

Despite their seemingly modest goal, such efforts might have a major economic impact. The U.S. government is by far the single largest performer *and* funder of research and development in the world. Between 1941 and 2000, it spent $2.7 trillion (in 2000 dollars) on R&D—just under one-half of the total amount of R&D undertaken in the United States.[10] (See figure 8-1.) And in recent years, the U.S. government's R&D expenditures represented about 15 percent of the total funding of R&D in major industrialized countries around the world.

These efforts pose special management challenges. In most public venturing efforts, such as the ATP and SBIR programs, fund managers distribute the capital to a wide variety of companies, in the hopes of fertilizing at least a few ventures. Efforts that seek to commercialize technology from a particular facility face a more daunting challenge: shaping

Figure 8-1   U.S. R&D Expenditures

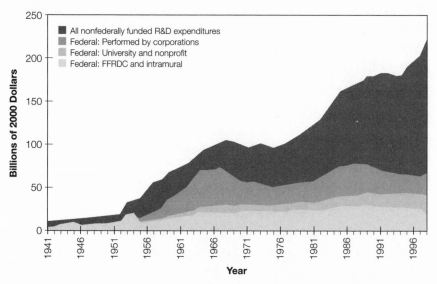

Source: Data on federal and total R&D between 1960 and 1998 are from National Science Board, *Science and Technology Indicators—2000* (Washington: Government Printing Office, 2000), and earlier years. Federal R&D data between 1955 and 1959 are from U.S. National Science Foundation, *Federal Funds for Research and Development* (Washington: U.S. Government Printing Office, various years), and are obligations (not actual spending, as elsewhere in the figure) for each fiscal year (instead of calendar years). Federal R&D for 1953 and 1954 and total R&D between 1953 and 1959 are from U.S. Department of Commerce, Bureau of the Census, *Historical Statistics of the United States* (Washington: Government Printing Office, 1975). All data before 1953 are from National Academy of Sciences, *Applied Research in the United States* (Washington: National Academy Press, 1952). Data from 1953 and before is less precise than in later years. FFRDC stands for "federally funded R&D centers" (e.g., national laboratories).

successful companies from a much smaller pool of promising projects. Moreover, the projects in many cases are at much earlier stages of development, and require intensive assistance from the public-fund managers.

The Challenges

Venture capitalists have long involved themselves in the commercialization of federally funded research. Indeed, the first modern venture capital firm, American Research and Development, set out to commercialize military technologies developed at the Massachusetts Institute of Technology and elsewhere during World War II. As founder Georges Doriot noted:

> Scientific intelligence does not always bring business modesty. Success would be attained more often if good idea men would entrust their ideas to good operating men. The discovery of the beauty of an expense account does not always suggest good controllership.[11]

Despite the long history between venture funds and research institutions, the relationship changed in the 1990s. Governments and universities, eager to improve their financial standing, became increasingly interested in venture capital–backed spin-offs as a mechanism for commercializing early-stage technologies and producing high returns. Indeed, the director of Yale's Office of Cooperative Research recently stated:

> It is . . . instructive to look at Yale intellectual assets that could have matured into new ventures . . . like Human Genomic Sciences [HGS] or Incyte Pharmaceuticals. Each has a market capitalization in excess of 500 million dollars. Though Yale had the ideas, technology, and personnel to form such a company a year or two in advance of HGS or Incyte, it did not happen because our development strategies were limited to licensing.[12]

As a result, these institutions have shored up their infrastructure to help support venture capital–backed spin-offs. In particular, they added staff members whose sole responsibility is to collaborate with researchers to establish new firms. Similarly, the federal government and universities have earmarked funds for investment in the new firms spawned by these institutions. Table 8-2 summarizes these new initiatives.

However laudable these efforts may be, they present several grounds for concern. For example, consider the experience of Boston University.[13] The school's venture capital subsidiary invested in a privately held biotechnology company, Seragen, founded in 1979 by a number of scientists affiliated with the institution. As part of its initial investment in 1987, the school bought out the stakes of a number of independent venture capital investors, who had apparently concluded after a number of financing rounds that the firm's prospects were unattractive. Between 1987 and 1992, the school, investing alongside university officials and trustees, poured at least $90 million into the private firm. (By way of comparison, the school's entire endowment at the fiscal year in which it initiated this investment was $142 million.) Though the company successfully completed an initial public offering, it encountered a series of disappointments in developing its products. Ultimately, it was sold to a San Diego–based biotechnology concern for only a few million dollars.

Venture funds focused on publicly funded research face three major hurdles:

- *Political interference can doom the effort.* Programs entailing the commercialization of federally funded research always risk hearing cries of "Unfair!" from competitors. For instance, Martin Marietta,

Table 8-2   Academic-Affiliated Venture Capital Funds

Name	Location	Year Begun
Enterprise Development Fund	MIT	1972
Community Technology Fund	Boston University	1974
British Technology Group Venture Capital Fund	Various British universities	1981
Center for Biotechnology Research	Stanford University and University of California	1982
BCM Technologies	Baylor College of Medicine	1983
Tennessee Innovation Center	Oak Ridge National Laboratory	1984
Dallas Biomedical Corporation	University of Texas/Southwestern Medical Center	1985
A/W Company	Washington University in St. Louis	1987
Triad Investors	Johns Hopkins University	1988
Medical Science Partners	Harvard University	1989
ARCH Venture Partners	University of Chicago and Argonne National Laboratory	1989
Technology Ventures Corp.	Sandia National Laboratory	1993
Northwestern University Investment Partners (Evanston Business Investment Corp.)	Northwestern University	1993
Thermo Technology Ventures	Three U.S. national laboratories	1994
JAFCO	Two Japanese universities	1997
Southwest One	Virginia Polytechnic Institute and State University	1998
Centennial Venture Partners	North Carolina State University	1999
Chancellor Fund	Vanderbilt University	1999
Two venture funds	Hebrew University	2000
Illinois Advanced Technology Fund	Illinois public universities	2000
Biomedical Innovation and Commercial Innovation	University of Minnesota	2001

Source: Based on a review of a wide variety of press accounts.

Note: In some cases, these funds were abandoned before any investments were made; in others, the fund focus ultimately shifted to include other institutions or types of investments.

the contractor that operated Oak Ridge National Laboratory, drew fire from the U.S. General Accounting Office and Representative John Dingell of Michigan for its venture capital initiative at the laboratory.[14] Martin Marietta had established a venture capital subsidiary, the Tennessee Innovation Center, which sought to establish new businesses around Oak Ridge. Martin Marietta had also invested in a business that later received an exclusive license to develop an Oak Ridge technology. As a result of the congressional criticism, the contractor restructured the relationship with its affiliate in a financially unattractive way. Soon after, Martin Marietta abandoned the effort.

- *Regulations can severely restrict researchers' involvement with a start-up firm.* In extreme cases, all formal relationships with outside start-ups are prohibited. More frequently, university or laboratory policies let publicly funded researchers serve as directors of and consultants to spin-off companies, but forbid them from holding equity in these enterprises. Though officially these researchers may be slated to receive a share of all profits generated by the institutions, in many cases deductions to reflect their share of overhead have absorbed almost all the proceeds. These same institutions often make it difficult for employees to take leaves to work with these companies. These regulations may be in place to prevent abuses, but they also stifle efforts to commercialize technologies.

- *Public programs may fail to recruit and retain the best talent.* This failure often stems from the limited compensation and autonomy that these programs offer investors. Forced to recruit less experienced managers, these funds suffer when the managers make unwise decisions: for instance, funding firms with limited commercial potential or exhausting the institution's resources on seed investments that they can't support with follow-on financing.

To see how these challenges can affect results, let's take a closer look at the experience of one early fund, ARCH Venture Partners, set up in 1989.[15] As we saw in chapter 5, this fund had a mandate to commercialize technologies from Argonne National Laboratory and the University of Chicago. (The university had operated Argonne for the U.S. Department of Energy and for its predecessor organization, the U.S. Atomic Energy Commission, since 1946.)

The university had pioneered a variety of commercially important discoveries, including the first sustained nuclear reaction, the isolation of proinsulin, and the invention of the scanning-transmission electron microscope. However, its record in profiting from these inventions was poor. Among its most conspicuous failures, the university had been the first to isolate the hormone erythropoietin—but didn't manage to patent it. The drug based on this hormone ultimately generated annual revenues of $2 billion for Amgen, which it marketed as Epogen. (Johnson & Johnson also sold erythropoietin.) The university received neither royalties from these sales nor equity in Amgen or Johnson & Johnson. Clearly, something had to change.

In 1986, the university recruited Steve Lazarus to found ARCH. With an extensive career in the U.S. Navy, and experience gained from work in the federal government and at the medical-product manufacturer Baxter International, Lazarus had a broad mandate to generate more licensing revenues from the university's technology and promulgate spin-off companies. As his first step, Lazarus publicized the ARCH effort to researchers and administrators in an effort to overcome their suspicions about the venture. Yet he also realized that to maximize returns to the university, he would have to develop new businesses in addition to simply licensing technologies to existing firms. That's when he raised the actual funding—$9 million—for ARCH Venture Partners, which was a wholly owned subsidiary of the university. In the five years that followed, the companies launched by ARCH encompassed a broad range of technologies. Though ARCH encountered challenges associated with its mandate, it achieved some real successes in funding firms and attracting coinvestments from top-tier private venture groups.

But soon the relationship between ARCH and the University of Chicago was restructured. Other academic institutions had begun contacting ARCH officials and urging them to get involved in technology transfer at their own organizations—activities outside the scope of ARCH's mandate. Furthermore, tensions mounted over the design of the first fund, including the fact that neither Lazarus nor his two partners received a share of the fund's capital gains. The university received all the capital gains, while the three partners received a salary comparable to that of other university officials.

In 1993, Lazarus and his partners managed to renegotiate their relationship with the university, which gave them permission to raise a second, more substantial, venture fund. As part of the revised agreement, the venture capitalists retained sole responsibility for ARCH Venture Partners. However, they relinquished their direct role in the licensing of university technology and ceased to be employees of the university. The university endowment invested in the second fund as well, alongside the various other institutional and individual investors that the fund had attracted. This time, the three ARCH venture capitalists shared the carried interest in the new fund.

The ARCH fund itself expanded quickly after raising its second fund, adding a vice president, three postgraduate fellows, and a number of consultants. It began operations at other national laboratories and universities based in Massachusetts, New Mexico, New York, and Washington State. These new locations generated a stream of fresh investment opportunities, and ARCH began to do less and less business with the University of Chicago and Argonne. Only a little more than a year after the closing of ARCH Venture Partners II, the partners began seeking a third fund with a broad mandate to pursue early-stage technology investments. In 1997, they succeeded in raising $107 million, primarily from institutional investors and corporations.

The experience of ARCH Venture Partners illustrates the variety of challenges facing university-affiliated funds. With ARCH, many things went right: The University of Chicago hired a talented fund manager; the fund and university administrators overcame regulatory barriers designed to forestall conflicts of interest and informal organizational concerns; and ARCH's investments proved reasonably successful. Nonetheless, the original program structure itself didn't last, and the overall project delivered few long-lasting benefits to the university.

Ingredients for Success

Can public venture programs devoted to technology transfer ever work? Having looked at a variety of successful efforts, we can detect three specific principles for success in addition to the more general guidelines outlined above.

1. A degree of distance between research institutions and public venture organizations can provide the venture capitalists with some protection against political interference and other distractions. Academic institutions, like many others, have conflicting agendas. Unless the venture capital team has some independence from the rest of the organization, unhealthy pressures can distort the group's work. For instance, a brilliant scientist with a stellar publication record may not have the best idea for a start-up, despite his own beliefs to the contrary!

2. The programs must provide not only financial capital but also assistance in entrepreneurial skill building for awardees. When venture groups fund projects being spun out of research institutions, they

don't have the luxury of working with fully formed, seasoned teams. By building these research managers' capabilities before the venture starts, a public program improves its chances of succeeding.

3. The incentives of all parties must be aligned. Most critically, the founding teams must be able to obtain substantial equity stakes. Research institutions must develop creative ways to address conflict-of-interest problems and preserve the academic culture without making equity ownership impossible. Similarly, without the promise of wealth creation, talented people won't be attracted to managing venture programs at academic institutions.

An Illustration: The Idaho National Engineering and Environmental Laboratory

Shortly after World War II, the U.S. government decided to find an isolated location to test nuclear reactors. It established the predecessor to the Idaho National Engineering and Environmental Laboratory (INEEL)—the National Reactor Testing Station—in 1949 on an 890-square-mile site in the southeastern Idaho desert. During the war, the military had used that same area as a practice bombing range.[16]

Over the years, the laboratory initiated major research programs that aimed to develop and test prototypes of nuclear-reactor-carrying naval vessels and (until 1961) airplanes. INEEL also reprocessed the large amounts of uranium generated by these reactors. As time passed, the laboratory was managed by a series of contractors, including Aerojet Nuclear (a subsidiary of General Tire) and a consortium made up of EG&G and Westinghouse Electric.

As one of these contracts neared its end date in 1994, the U.S. government realized that the next contractor would need to demonstrate a commitment to technology transfer activities. What prompted this shift in focus? INEEL was a major employer in Idaho. Local politicians had pushed the laboratory to soften the blows of employment and funding cutbacks at INEEL by creating spin-off firms that would hopefully provide employment and revenues for former INEEL workers and allow the region to remain economically healthy.

Clearly, INEEL needed to improve its technology transfer record: In 1992, the laboratory had generated no spin-offs and just $7,000 in licensing revenues. Though INEEL's current contractor stepped up its signing of cooperative and licensing agreements in response to these pressures, the government awarded the new contract to a consortium led by a subsidiary of the Lockheed Corporation (now Lockheed Martin). This consortium also included Thermo Electron Corporation, a Massachusetts company with a history of spinning out new technology businesses into publicly traded entities.

The new contract included a variety of features to help ensure that the new contractor would take technology transfer seriously. For example, the contractors promised to provide entrepreneurial training to INEEL researchers who might later lead spin-off firms. In addition, Thermo Electron agreed to establish a $10 million venture capital fund that would finance new businesses generated by the laboratory.

Perhaps most important, Lockheed signed a contract linking its compensation to its technology transfer success. In particular, Lockheed agreed to forgo several millions of dollars from its annual fee for managing the laboratory. In return, it would receive a share of fees and royalties generated over the course of the five-year contract. Until Lockheed received its first $1 million of licensing payments, it would get 20 percent of the revenue from these arrangements. (The remainder would be divided between the scientists and the federal government.) For the next $1 million in licensing fees generated, Lockheed would receive 30 percent of revenues; thereafter, it would receive 35 percent.

To implement this contract, the new consortium changed the structure of the technology licensing office as well. Lockheed recruited individuals who had held senior business-development positions with companies such as General Motors and IBM, as well as licensing account executives with private-sector sales and marketing experience. In addition, the company organized industry-focus teams and charged them with establishing relationships with companies in specific industries and marketing INEEL capabilities and technologies to those companies.

The result? Licensing and spin-off activity skyrocketed. Between 1995 and 1998, the laboratory achieved twenty-seven spin-offs. In 1997 alone, INEEL created seven out of the nineteen spin-offs generated by the entire set of national laboratories owned by the Department of Energy—including the much larger Los Alamos, Oak Ridge, and Lawrence Livermore facilities.

These achievements didn't come easily, however. In just one example, laboratory researchers trying to obtain an exclusive license to a technology they had worked on faced an exhaustive, slow-moving review process.

Though Lockheed's senior managers and the entrepreneurs all had powerful incentives to commercialize technologies, the middle managers at INEEL did not. These officials threw up one barrier after another, leaving technology transfer agreements in tangles. Even if an entrepreneur managed to overcome concerns about fairness and conflict-of-interest, in many cases the middle managers demanded excessive payments and royalties in light of the early stage of the technologies.

In addition, entrepreneurs at INEEL struggled to raise additional capital once they had exhausted the seed funds that the small Thermo Electron fund and other local investors had provided. And despite the considerable success of the INEEL effort, the Department of Energy decided in September 1998 not to renew Lockheed's contract. Though the department rated Lockheed's technology transfer effort highly, it voiced concerns about the contractor's worker-safety record and its failure to undertake an environmental clean-up project at INEEL for an agreed-upon price. Only time will reveal whether the next contractor can spin out as much technology as Lockheed and Thermo Electron did—and whether it will surmount the problems that plagued its predecessors.

The INEEL initiative had the ingredients for success—the commitment of the government and the contractors to technology transfer, the willingness of the contractors and government to offer scientists "high-powered" incentives, and the presence of an experienced technology transfer team from Thermo Electron and Lockheed Martin. Nonetheless, INEEL's success proved incomplete and temporary. Is that simply the fate of public venture efforts linked to research institutions? Or can these public programs devise a new, more effective approach to venturing? No one yet seems to have the answers.

A Rocky Relationship

When the public sector takes on the venture capital process, both parties can expect to face difficulties. A process that has its origins in small partnerships with well-defined objectives suffers strain when it gets translated into large organizations with complex objectives. Problems inherent in government—political conflicts, bureaucracy, and inflexibility—only make matters worse. As we've seen, the difficulties increase when a public venturing effort's goal is not to merely stimulate entrepreneurship but to transfer technologies from a research facility to the commercial marketplace.

Are government venture initiatives even worth the effort? They can be. But rather than encouraging the *supply* of venture financing in a region, policymakers often would be much better served thinking about the *demand* side. Are there steps—for instance, technology transfer programs or entrepreneurial education initiatives—that can boost the number or quality of firms seeking venture funding? All too often, as we have seen in this chapter, the "quick fix"—providing public venture capital—is ineffective, or even self-defeating.

In this chapter, we've focused on the experience in North America. In the next chapter, we'll consider the challenges associated with stimulating venture capital overseas, whether by public or independent funds.

9

Engineering
International Venture
Capital Success

■

Between 1989 and 1999, venture capital activity outside of North America grew by more than 300 percent.

During the 1990s, public venture capital programs proliferated around the globe. Numerous governments, attracted by the technological innovation and job growth that venture capital has spurred in the United States, strove to stimulate similar development in their own countries.

These programs have experimented with a variety of structures. Venture funds (and their investors) have received direct capital investments, loan guarantees, and targeted tax breaks from their home governments. The vast majority of these public programs, however, are intended to directly expand available capital for young, growing companies.

At the same time, conditions have ripened for venture capital to flourish in countries and regions around the world. The same underlying technological innovations and business management practices driving the U.S. venture capital revolution have unleashed similar results elsewhere. Countries with relatively dismal track records of financing fresh ideas are now experiencing the first stirrings of entrepreneurial revolution. All this points to an optimistic future for venture capital markets outside the United States.

Yet despite all this, the international venturing experience has received little attention from researchers or the press. This may stem in part from the difficulties inherent in measuring entrepreneurial activity in many countries. Most governments haven't invested in the data-collection technologies needed to gather useful feedback on their policy initiatives. In addition, some nations haven't yet built the business, legal, and economic foundations necessary to promote a healthy entrepreneurial environment.

To deepen our understanding of international venture capital, we'll look closely at the forces of supply and demand that are influencing entrepreneurship and venture capital in Europe, Asia, and Latin America. On the supply side of venturing, tax policies and attitudes of large institutional investors play a prominent role in the availability of venture funding. On the demand side, legal, regulatory, and cultural forces alike determine whether people with creative ideas will be motivated to seek the financial backing they need to commercialize their innovations. As we might well imagine, these supply- and demand-side forces differ markedly from country to country.

Venturing Around the Globe

On the international stage, private investment takes a variety of forms. We can think of these forms collectively as private equity—an investment class that includes not only venture capital, but also the following:

- *Investments in buyouts*—the purchase of mature, public companies

- *Consolidations*—the purchase of multiple companies in the same industry with the express purpose of combining their operations to gain efficiencies

- *Distressed turnarounds*—the purchase of a failing company in the hopes of returning it to profitability by intervening in the company's business

- *Mezzanine securities*—the purchase of equity in private companies immediately before they go public

U.S. investors make a clear distinction between private equity and venture capital with venture capital defined as investment in early-stage, growth companies. However, to people in most other regions of the world, the term *venture capital* encompasses *all* private equity investments. Though we'll try to keep the distinction clear, the lack of sufficient data on venture capital and private equity investments outside the United States can cloud the picture.

Figure 9-1   Venture Capital and Private Equity Fund-raising Around the World

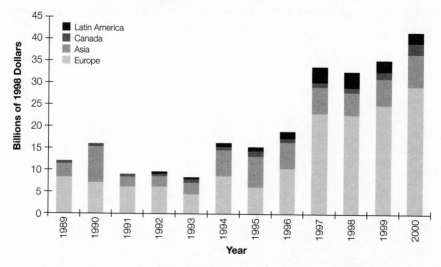

Source: Compiled from a wide variety of sources published by Asset Alternatives, European Venture Capital Association, and *Asian Venture Capital Journal*.

A Cyclical Pattern

As in the United States, international private equity activity shows a cyclical pattern. Figure 9-1 depicts commitments declining substantially from 1989 to 1991. Many of these early funds had disappointing returns, mirroring the U.S. experience in those same years. Between 1991 and 2000, however, international private equity commitments increased nearly fourfold. Let's consider separately the experience in Europe, Asia, and Latin America.

The Venture Capital Scene in Europe

European private equity funds invested about $32.3 billion during 2000, making Europe the second most developed private equity market after the United States. (See table 9-1.) Still, not all European nations enjoy the same degree of private equity action. Figure 9-2 shows the growth in various European markets between 1992 and 1999. The largest and most developed private equity market in Europe is the United Kingdom, followed by Germany, France, Italy, and the Netherlands. Not surprisingly, these markets also undertook the greatest efforts to encourage and promote entrepreneurial activity.

Table 9-1 European Private Equity Fund-raising

	Venture Capital (billions of euros)	Venture Capital Fraction of Private Equity (%)	Buyouts and Other Private Equity (billions of euros)	Total (billions of euros)
1984	0.15	29.4	0.36	0.51
1985	0.35	25.5	1.02	1.37
1986	0.33	23.6	1.07	1.40
1987	0.34	12.0	2.50	2.84
1988	0.43	12.5	3.02	3.45
1989	0.42	9.8	3.85	4.27
1990	0.35	8.5	3.77	4.12
1991	0.32	6.9	4.31	4.63
1992	0.28	6.0	4.42	4.70
1993	0.20	4.9	3.92	4.12
1994	0.31	5.7	5.13	5.44
1995	0.32	5.8	5.23	5.55
1996	0.44	6.5	6.35	6.79
1997	0.71	7.4	8.94	9.65
1998	1.62	11.2	12.84	14.46
1999	3.13	12.5	21.88	25.12
2000	6.64	19.0	28.32	34.96

Source: *European Venture Capital Association 2000 Yearbook* (Zaventum, Belgium: European Venture Capital Association, 2000), and <http://www.evca.com> (accessed in July 2001).

Figure 9-2 European Private Equity Fund-raising

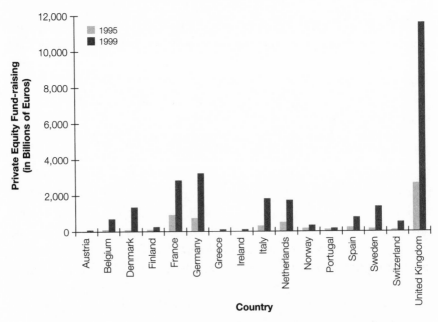

Source: *European Venture Capital Association 2000 Yearbook* (Zaventum, Belgium: European Venture Capital Association, 2000).

Boom and Bust

European private equity has endured a roller-coaster ride similar to that in the United States, with a boom in the late 1980s followed by a bust in the early 1990s. The closing years of the 1990s saw an extraordinary recovery. Fund-raising—fueled by U.S. institutional investors' heightened interest in European opportunities—far surpassed earlier milestones.

The source of all this attention? In the late 1990s, European funds had delivered attractive returns to investors—with the average fund showing a 24.9 percent annual return.[1] In addition, competition for venture capital investments had stiffened in the U.S. market because of the rapid growth in capital, causing institutions to look abroad to gain returns.

Some observers caution that the booming venture capital and buyout market may herald another bust in some European countries. Indeed, investors have seen deal prices escalate and bidding wars break out—all signs that too much money may be chasing too few deals.

Venture Capital Overtakes Private Equity

The European venture capital market has experienced the same changes as the larger private equity market. In its earliest years, the European private equity industry contained a considerable portion of venture capital investments. Over time, however, that portion dwindled owing to these funds' poor performance. For instance, between 1980 and 1994, mature, *large* buyout funds in Great Britain boasted a net return of 23.1 percent, and the average *midsized* buyout fund earned 14.7 percent. Meanwhile, the typical venture fund had a net return of just 4 percent over this same period. As a result, most venture capital specialists failed to raise new funds, and generalist investors (such as Apax and 3i) began targeting buyouts instead.

This situation began reversing itself around 1997, in part because of new attention from U.S. venture groups—particularly East Coast–based organizations such as General Atlantic and Warburg Pincus. Attracted by the modest valuations of European technology and biotechnology start-ups relative to their U.S. counterparts, general partners from these firms began traveling to Europe to invest in portfolio companies. This trend accelerated at the end of the decade, as U.S. groups such as Benchmark Capital and Draper Fisher Jurvetson began targeting large amounts of capital—sometimes in dedicated funds—for investment in Europe. The superior performance of these investments in the last years of the decade also helped revive the market. In fact, by the end of 1999, the ten-year track record of venture capital funds in Europe (17.2 percent) was almost indistinguishable from that of buyout transactions (17.5 percent).

Meanwhile, European-based funds also made more venture capital investments. Historically, over 90 percent of European private equity funds were allocated to buyouts or other late-stage investments. However, between 1995 and 1999, early-stage funds—*true* venture capital commitments—grew more than tenfold in Germany—from €89 million to more than €1 *billion* in 1999. Similarly, venture capital commitments in France grew from only €26 million in 1995 to €519 million in 1999. Groups that had been active for a number of years, such as Atlas Ventures, now were able to raise large funds, thanks to some visible successes in technology investing in Europe and investors' increased willingness to invest in European venture funds. New entrants—many of them modeled after U.S. groups—also ramped up their involvement in this investment arena. (Examples include Amadeus in the United Kingdom and Early Bird in Germany.) Finally, generalist funds increased their allocation to venture capital again.

In the past, national boundaries have compartmentalized the key sources of capital for European venture investing. Venture firms would raise funds from banks, insurance companies, and governmental bodies within their own country, with little involvement from outside investors. The one exception has been the United Kingdom, where fund-raising has long had a strong international flavor—particularly heavy involvement from U.S. institutional investors. These barriers are now breaking down, however (see figure 9-3). The reason? Institutional investors—particularly in the United States—are now investing more in European funds, as are international venture capital firms.

As one consequence of these changes, investment advisors, sometimes called gatekeepers, have multiplied. These firms advise investors, primarily large institutions, about their private equity investments or directly manage their holdings. Several large U.S. gatekeepers have headed for Europe, excited by pension reforms there as well as European *and* U.S. institutional investors' new involvement in that region's venture industry. Local advisors have also established successful concerns.

European versus U.S. Venturing

Unlike their U.S. counterparts, many European venture capitalists have financial or consulting, rather than operating, backgrounds. Perhaps as a

Figure 9-3 Geographical Sources of Private Equity Fund-raising in Europe

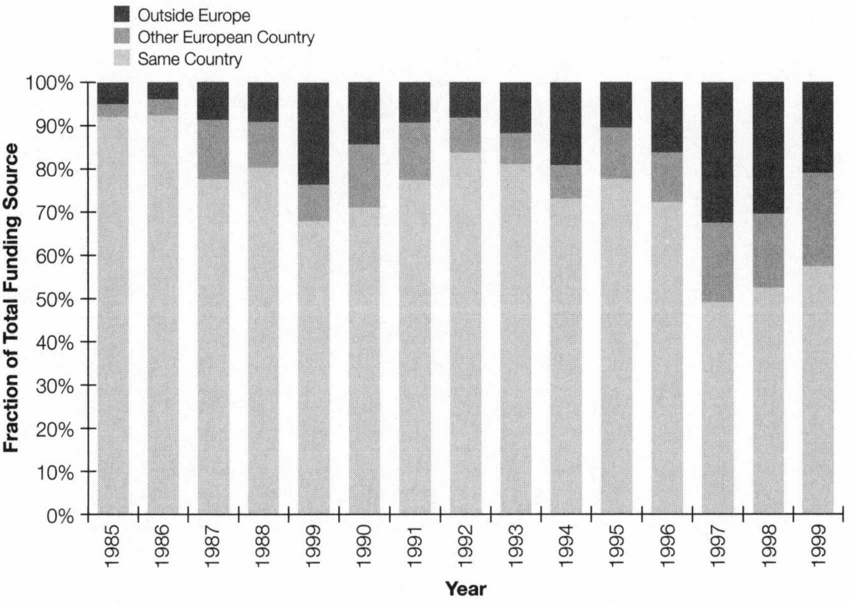

■ Outside Europe
▨ Other European Country
▨ Same Country

Source: *European Venture Capital Association 2000 Yearbook* (Zaventum, Belgium: European Venture Capital Association, 2000).

result, Europeans venture capitalists tend to employ a hands-off management policy. Instead, they focus more on assessing those firms' financial performance. They prefer to invest in companies with complete management teams and spend less time overseeing the investment. However, the U.S. model has attracted new adherents in Europe.

Another difference is that European venture firms tend to invest in the same country where the fund is located. This preference reflects traditional legal and regulatory restrictions (which have since eased) and the distinct business cultures that characterize the various European nations. Figure 9-4 shows that this pattern is gradually changing. However, localization of investment still strongly defines the "European way."

Finally, whereas the size of U.S. venture capital transactions has ballooned in recent years, European transactions have not followed suit. As a result, some European start-ups find it difficult to compete in the "winner-take-all" contests that characterize the high-tech industry. In time, however, the differences between European and U.S. investors will likely ease.

Figure 9-4 Geographical Sources of Private Equity Investment in Europe

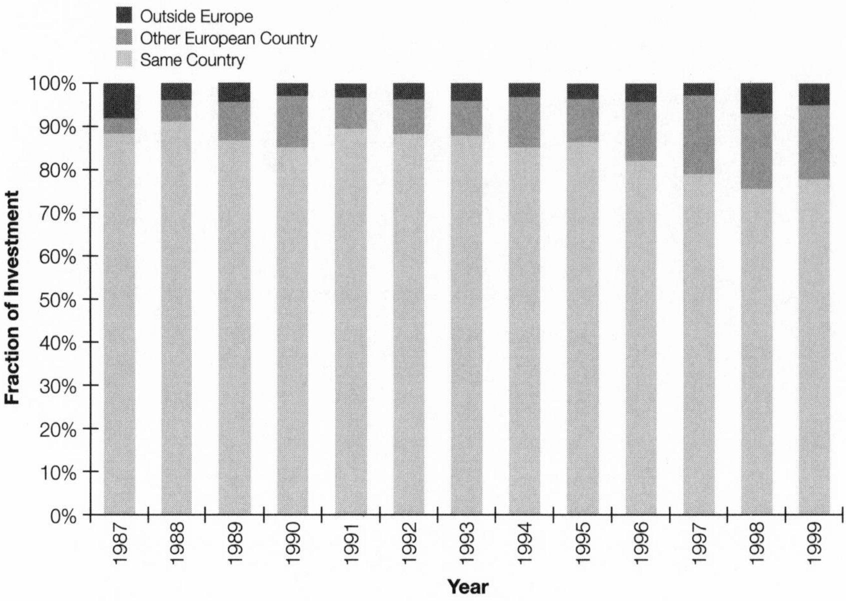

Source: *European Venture Capital Association 2000 Yearbook* (Zaventum, Belgium: European Venture Capital
    Association, 2000).

Outside Europe and North America

Europe and North America have relatively long histories in venture capital and private equity. In other markets, particularly Asia and Latin America, this unique form of investment has taken root only recently. Let's look at the overall forces that have shaped this pattern.

The mid- to late 1990s witnessed two developments in venture capital activity outside Europe and North America: when activity skyrocketed, then crashed, and when venture capital funds began emphasizing early-stage investments.

Events in the United States have had a hand in these two developments. In the mid-1990s, many U.S.-based institutional investors expected to see their venture returns decrease, owing to greater competition for deals in the United States. As a result, they began to increase investments in non-U.S. venture capital funds. Then, as the decade drew to a close, and returns on U.S. venture capital funds hit triple digits, these investors once again poured capital into North American and European funds.

What about the shift toward early-stage investments? In the late 1990s, some U.S. institutions, prompted by deal prices that were being driven to unsustainable levels, sank capital into more and more venture funds outside North America—particularly funds that targeted early-stage Internet and communications companies. This influx of capital prompted Asian and Latin American funds to expand activity.

This increased investment by U.S. institutions in venture capital funds outside of North America is illustrated by a 1999 survey of 204 of the largest U.S. institutional investors conducted by Goldman Sachs and Frank Russell Capital.[2] It found that international venture capital had increased from representing zero percent of all alternative investments in 1992 to 18.3 percent in 1999. Nearly half the respondents identified international venture capital as the most attractive subclass of private equity in the next three years.

One reason behind institutional investors' interest in early-stage venture capital funds outside the United States and Europe is the similarities these investors perceive between these investment opportunities and U.S. venturing. Like venture capital investing itself, many companies in these other nations operate under conditions of enormous uncertainty, with difficult-to-value assets and yawning information gaps. Thus investors assume that they stand the same chances of getting attractive returns in these environments as they do in investments in the United States.

In addition, many economies outside North America and Europe quickened in these years because of liberalization of their domestic markets and globalization of the overall business environment. With the relaxation of curbs on foreign investments in many of these same nations came an increasing ability to attract competent investment professionals with the right experience to promote venture capital investments.

The Shape of Private Equity Funds

Until recently, private equity funds outside the United States and Europe have been built on three categories of events: (1) privatization, (2) corporate restructuring, and (3) strategic alliances.

- *Privatization.* The World Bank estimates that, in recent years, 80 countries have made privatization a priority in their push to modernize.[3] Through privatization, a government sells its ownership stake in an enterprise to private investors. More than 7,000 large-scale privatizations have occurred since 1980, at an annual rate of $25 billion per year, providing ample opportunity for private equity. Many newly privatized enterprises suffer from lack of sufficient capital and outdated processes and systems. In many cases, the national capital markets haven't matured, and only the largest firms enjoy access to international markets. Consequently, governments and the private sector have increasingly turned to venture capital to fill the investment gap.

- *Corporate restructuring.* Globalization has stiffened competition for many businesses operating in countries outside the United States and Europe. Lower trade barriers and new regulatory dictates have forced companies to become more efficient. Furthermore, the transfer of technologies and business practices from developed to developing nations has created new challenges. These challenges can flummox managers who haven't prepared for them. As a result, many venture capital investments in these regions have focused on either purchasing and improving the operations of established firms or business units, or consolidating smaller businesses to achieve large, more cost-effective enterprises.

- *Strategic alliances.* In many cases, major U.S. and European corporations have made strategic investments (acquisitions, joint ventures, and alliances) in developing countries without understanding the business environment or their new partners' unique needs and priorities. To narrow such information gaps, these corporations have increasingly welcomed venture capital funds as third-party investors who can help monitor and interpret the local partner's decisions and actions.

As we have noted, however, true venture capital investors have recently proliferated in countries outside the United States and Europe. These funds follow a number of strategies. They may provide services that initially emerged in developed nations, such as investments in business-to-business exchanges and online auction sites geared to a particular region. They might also link workers in these nations with labor-starved Western corporations. In India, for example, numerous software firms have received venture backing to provide programming services to U.S. and European corporations. Finally, venture capital transactions can help commercialize technology originating in countries outside Europe or North America and encourage its sale in the global marketplace.

With these larger themes in mind, let's now see what shape venturing takes in specific regions.

Figure 9-5 Venture Capital Fund-raising in Asia, Australia, and New Zealand

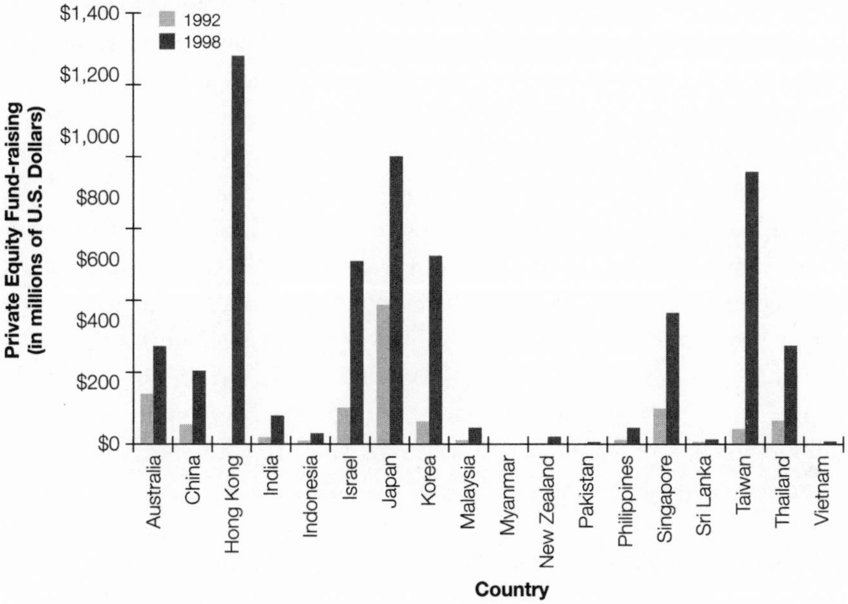

Source: *Guide to Asian Venture Capital 2000* (Hong Kong: *Asian Venture Capital Journal,* 2000).

Asia and Australia

The Asian and Australian venture capital markets flourished during the 1990s. As figure 9-5 demonstrates, fund-raising in these regions grew more than five times between 1992 and 1998 as investors saw an opportunity to earn substantial returns in these newly thriving economies. The Asian economic wobble in 1997, however, prompted a slight downturn in fund-raising as many large investors reevaluated their involvement in the region.

As in Europe, individual countries in these regions have experienced different growth rates. For example, venture fund-raising in Australia only doubled over this seven-year period, while in Taiwan it increased almost twenty times. China, Hong Kong, Israel, and Singapore all enjoyed tremendous growth and dynamic economies during the period, with government support of venture capital helping build their industrial base.

Venture Capital versus Private Equity and Other Investments. In most of these regions, private equity funds went to buyout and later-stage opportunities—already profitable businesses with substantial tangible assets. For example, in Australia, Indonesia, Japan, and Malaysia, only 16 percent or less of total investments was allocated to venture-capital opportunities. By contrast, fund-raising in China and Hong Kong, and especially in India and Israel, was largely directed toward early-stage opportunities. These countries have seen a remarkable metamorphosis in their economies. For instance, venture investing in China has let entre-preneurs develop a host of new markets and technologies. In Israel, the effect has proved even more dramatic. In the late 1980s, the Israeli econ-omy had just begun recovering from hyperinflation. Growth had stalled, and concern over the nation's economic future reached a fever pitch. Over the next decade, however, venture capital reconfigured the entire economic landscape. High-technology office parks sprouted up across the country, and average real wages and opportunities for computer scientists and engineers increased almost fourfold. More than one hundred Israeli high-tech companies are now listed on Nasdaq.

Funding Destinations. Figure 9-6 shows that most Asian funds invest in their local markets. Hong Kong and Singapore firms are the only excep-tion. A mere 9 percent of the venture capital invested by Hong Kong groups stays within Hong Kong; 89 percent gets invested in other Asian countries. This ratio reflects Hong Kong's small technology base and its status as a major financial center in Asia. In this respect, Hong Kong strongly resembles New York.

In addition to investing in domestic markets, the majority of funds raised by Asian countries come from domestic sources. China, Hong Kong, and India vary slightly from this pattern. China's venture industry receives roughly equal contributions from domestic, other Asian, and non-Asian sources. Hong Kong, on the other hand, receives nearly three-quarters of its funds from outside Asia. Similarly, half of the capital going into Indian venture funds derives from non-Asian sources.

Funding Sources. Asian venture capital markets differ markedly from the U.S. version in a major respect: Asian funds contain very little domestic capital from pension funds. Australia and New Zealand are the only two Asian countries that have funded pension programs; thus they alone raise substantial venture capital from these funds. Most workers in Asia don't have access to an employer-sponsored pension program. Those who do are covered by "pay-as-you-go" programs, which pay out retirement income based on the firm's current earnings. So where do Asian venture funds get

Figure 9-6 Venture Capital Investment Focus in Asia, Australia, and New Zealand

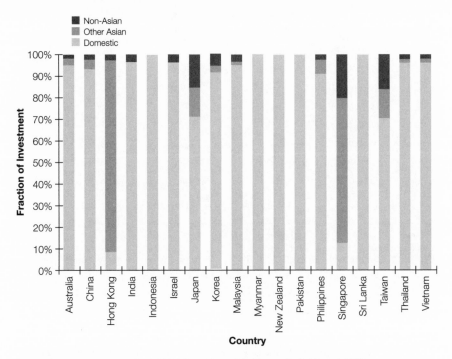

Source: *Guide to Asian Venture Capital 2000* (Hong Kong: *Asian Venture Capital Journal,* 2000).

their capital? The vast majority of money for venture capital investing in Asia comes from corporations. New Zealand and Australia are the only two markets in which negligible funds come from corporations. In India, for example, 61 percent of venture capital comes from corporations. Corporate funding sources can introduce weaknesses into the Asian venture industry, as corporations don't always make the most reliable venture capital source. Their appetite for venturing can vary depending on managers' fancy at the time. As the Asian venture capital market evolves, it must attract more investments from pension funds and other institutions that have consistent interest in venturing and that will stay in the game for the long haul.

Latin America

In Latin America, privatization and improved economic stability have fueled vigorous growth in venture investing. Table 9-2 vividly captures

Table 9-2   Venture Capital and Private Equity Investing in Latin America by Country

	1996–1998 ($ millions)	1999–2000 ($ millions)	Growth (%)
Argentina	2,873.9	4,213.6	47
Brazil	3,765.8	1,740.4	−54
Chile	297.3	0.0	−100
Columbia	297.3	183.2	−38
Mexico	792.8	549.6	−31
Other	891.9	458.0	−49
Regional	991.0	2,015.2	103
Total	9,910.0	9,160.0	−8

Source: *Latin American Private Equity Review and Outlook 2000/2001* (Wellesley, MA: Asset Alternatives, 2000).

this development. The figure shows the amount of money raised by private equity funds based *in* Latin America. (Many non–Latin American funds, primarily from North America, have also invested in the region.) Although the entire region raised only about $100 million of private equity in 1992 and 1993, the economic stability and improved growth prospects that came with global economic growth and local economic reforms soon caught the attention of outside institutional investors. By 1998, Latin American funds had raised over $3.5 billion. Nevertheless, several high-profile crises, along with burgeoning investments in the U.S. market, reversed the situation. Fund-raising in 1999 fell more than 50 percent to $1.7 billion.

National Variety. Argentina and Brazil far outstrip their fellow Latin American countries in size of venture investments. Table 9-2 shows these patterns over two time periods. In both periods, nearly two-thirds of the total investment capital available went to Argentina and Brazil. In the earlier period, Brazil received as much as $3.7 billion of private equity investment—though this number plummeted to $1.7 billion in the later period owing to economic and political instability. Argentina, on the other hand, saw its venture investments jump from $2.8 billion in the earlier period to more than $4.2 billion recently, thanks to a perceived opportunity for attractive investments.

A Changing Investment Mix. The industries targeted by private equity investment in Latin America also shifted during the late 1990s. Table 9-3

Table 9-3   Venture Capital and Private Equity Investing in Latin America by Industry

	1992–1995 ($ millions)	1996–1999 ($ millions)	Growth (%)
Telecommunications	2,081.1	1,557.2	–25
Internet	0.0	1,832.0	NA
Transportation	1,783.8	0.0	–100
Cable TV	1,288.3	732.8	–43
Retail	1,189.2	1,190.8	0
Media	0.0	732.8	NA
Food and Agribusiness	693.7	1,557.2	124
Financial Services	693.7	0.0	–100
Power and Utilities	495.5	0.0	–100
Other	1,684.7	1,557.2	–8

Source: *Latin American Private Equity Review and Outlook 2000/2001* (Wellesley, MA: Asset Alternatives, 2000).

tabulates the total investments for various industries. The earlier time period witnessed intensive investment in basic utilities like telecommunications, transportation, and cable television—not surprising, given that at the start of the decade, many Latin American economies had outdated and substandard industrial infrastructure. As these economies matured, outside investors saw an opportunity to make decent returns by supplying the basic services many developed markets already enjoy. For example, power and utilities received almost $500 million in investments over this time period.

Once Latin American nations had beefed up their utilities infrastructure, attractive investment opportunities emerged in other industries as well—particularly communications and media.

Supply and Demand: Building the Foundation of a Venture-Capital Economy

We've seen what's happening to venture capital globally. How can these various countries—with their wildly different governments, cultures, and economies—nurture the most vibrant venture capital industry possible? Perhaps more important, why *should* they? The answer is simple: With the globalization of business and the dissolving of economic boundaries around the world, the ability to innovate has become crucial for any nation that wants to compete on the international stage. A healthy venture capital

industry can put a developing country on the road to economic maturity—
and boost a mature economy to the top echelon of global players.

For any country interested in building a venture sector or strengthening their existing one, attention to the basics—the fundamental structures
and qualities on which venturing thrives—is essential. In its simplest
sense, this foundation consists of the two core components of venture
capital activity: supply and demand.

The Supply Side: What Draws Investors to a Venture Capital Fund?

The supply of venture capital in any economy depends on three things:

- Investors' belief that a venture fund will yield better returns than any other investment opportunity

- A regulatory climate that favors venture investing

- The number of seasoned venture capitalists actively doing business within that economy

Let's see how these factors can affect the elements of the worldwide venturing effort.

The Problem with Pension Funds. In the United States the easing of
investment restrictions on private pension funds in 1979 opened the
floodgates for a huge supply of new venture capital—contributed by
sophisticated investors in for the long haul. It's hard to imagine this event
occurring in any other country. For one thing, most nations' pension systems have the "pay-as-you-go" policy discussed earlier. Moreover, many
countries explicitly prohibit pension funds from investing in venture capital. Supplies must come from somewhere else.

Government Participation. In the face of pension-fund limitations, many
governments have tried to foster a venture capital sector—and thus innovation—through direct manipulation of the economy. In China, for example, much of the venture capital comes from the government. Similarly,
some governments give capital directly to companies. For example, in the
early 1990s, France's government set up a pool of more than $100 million
to finance biotechnology start-ups.[4] It also instituted programs that gave
researchers affordable lab space and lowered taxes on earnings and
investment gains in this industry.

Japan has also provided direct financial assistance to entrepreneurial firms. Both the Ministry of International Trade and Industry and Japan Development Bank (JDB) have developed programs that offer financial assistance to young, entrepreneurial firms.[5] This assistance has taken a variety of forms, from actual operating facilities (incubators) to equity investments and loans. For instance, JDB established a fund to provide five-year loans at subsidized rates (typically 3.25 percent and less) to young high-tech firms—loans that the bank secured through these firms' patents and other intellectual property. And in late 1996, JDB raised capital from more than 100 corporations and government agencies to make traditional equity investments.

Successful government efforts have often let market forces and independent players drive the supply of venture capital investors. Specifically, these governments ease restrictions on capital flows and investment or provide incentives for experienced venture capitalists—many from the United States and Europe—to come and establish independent funds.

Israel has achieved particular success using this approach. In June 1992, the government established Yozma Venture Capital Ltd. (*yozma* means "initiative" in Hebrew), a $100 million fund wholly owned by the Israeli government.[6] Yozma had three goals:

- To promote the growth of promising high-tech firms in Israel

- To encourage the involvement of major international corporations in the Israeli technology sector

- To stimulate the development of a professionally managed, private-sector venture capital industry in Israel

Underlying all these goals was Israel's desire to bring foreign venture capitalists' investment expertise and contact network to Israel. Accordingly, Yozma discouraged Israeli financiers from participating in its programs.

Yozma shared the risks associated with its venture investments. Yet it also offered its partners an option to buy out Yozma's share of the investment within five years on attractive terms. The risk inherent in the fund's investments would normally have justified a much higher interest rate. Yozma hoped that more favorable terms would catch the eye of experienced international investors.

The legislation that created Yozma capped the amount the firm could contribute to a particular venture capital fund at $8 million and required Yozma to find a venture capitalist to match the $8 million by raising money from investors as limited partners. Therefore, the minimum fund size was $16 million. Thus if one of these funds tripled in value over seven years—net of fees and carried interest—both the limited partners' and Yozma's investment would triple from $8 million to $24 million. The limited partners could then buy out Yozma's $24 million stake for about $10 million, collecting $38 million on the fund's $18 million overall investment. This turned an internal rate of return of 17 percent into one of 25 percent—without taking on more risk. Yozma leveraged the bounty if the fund succeeded, yet shared fully in the losses if it failed. And the venture capitalists could collect management fees and carried interest on the entire fund.

The Yozma program delivered as promised. Venture capital investments in Israel increased fivefold from 1993 to 1998. Many of the original Yozma funds, including Gemini and Walden Ventures, earned spectacular returns and served as precursors to larger, follow-on funds. In recognition of this success, the Israeli government privatized its stake in the fund in 1998, declaring the goals of the program met.

The success of the Irish government's efforts to increase capital flows also illustrates the power of the market approach.[7] In November 1993, the so-called Murray-Walsh report claimed that investments in venture capital funds had yielded attractive returns in both Ireland and the United States, but found that the supply of venture capital in Ireland had fallen in the early 1990s with the economic slowdown. The demand for venture capital, however, would likely mount through the mid-1990s, owing to the general economic recovery and the attractiveness of high-technology investments in Ireland.

Galvanized by these projections, the Irish Association of Pension Funds encouraged its members to invest a proportion of their assets in projects run by venture capital professionals. With little experience with this form of investing, the members had been reluctant to put their investors' savings at risk. But by 1999, thanks to urging from Ireland's pension-fund association, these plans accounted for nearly 27 percent of venture capital contributions, compared to about 4 percent in 1992.

Outside Investors: Help or Hindrance? In most developing countries, venture funds have had to rely on investors from outside their home markets for their supply of capital. Who are these sources? They're largely the same ones who tend to invest in venture capital funds based in the United States: pension plans, corporations, insurance companies, and wealthy individuals. To date, U.S.-based organizations have made up the bulk of these outside investors, though European investors have gradually increased their participation in newly emerging venture industries.

But there are several additional, equally important sources of venture capital supply:

- U.S. foreign-aid organizations such as the U.S. Agency for International Development (USAID)

- Quasi-governmental corporations like the Overseas Private Investment Corporation (OPIC)

- Multinational financial institutions along the lines of the International Finance Corporation (IFC)

These programs often provide financial support through long-term loans or direct grants. They also guarantee private investors' capital.

These public efforts have had mixed results. A recent internal critique at USAID argued that of all the funds the organization had supported over the past two decades, only one—the Latin American Agribusiness Development Corporation (LAAD)—had endured.[8] And this fund had achieved its staying power only because USAID had shifted from equity funding to more conventional agribusiness lending.

What explains this poor performance? Clearly, the difficult investment environment is an important factor. But there are other elements at work as well. In many cases, agency officials have had little or no experience with this form of investing and so often choose the wrong venture capital funds to invest in or guarantee. Additionally, because of government restrictions on the compensation of investors, these funds don't always attract the most talented portfolio managers. Finally, many venture capital funds have narrow mandates. For example, the fund managers may specifically aim to support small businesses, the agricultural sector, women-owned endeavors, and so forth. Though their intentions may be laudable, such restrictions can threaten a fund's sustainability. In other cases, the government bodies conduct such lengthy reviews of investment opportunities that other investors snap up the most attractive deals first.

Retirement Savings: Another Source of Home-grown Capital? Given the scant participation from pension funds in venturing—and the spotty record of outside governments—most nations could benefit from other sources of "home-grown" venture capital. One possibility? Retirement savings in the developing nations themselves. East Asian nations boast particularly impressive savings rates, often as high as 30 percent of gross domestic product. These rates reflect demographic patterns—developing countries have younger populations—as well as cultural differences. Though many people in these nations have invested their savings informally in the privately held businesses of relatives and friends, they've directed scant amounts into institutional venture capital funds.

In time, personal-savings patterns will likely change. For example, Chile has led the way by privatizing much of its retirement savings, which created new pools of capital that seek out long-run, high-return investments. Pension funds have spurred the privatization process; many of these plans have equity positions of between 10 percent and 35 percent in privatized firms. As pension funds have grown, regulators have increasingly widened their investment playing field. In the last couple of years, several pension plans have considered initiating venture capital programs.

Seasoned Venture Capitalists. Talented venture capitalists possess a rare blend of strengths—technical knowledge, operational experience, the ability to strike a smart deal, and an eye for skilled portfolio-firm managers—that have taken many years to develop on a large scale in the United States. By contrast, most venture capitalists in European and Asian markets with backgrounds in investment banking or management consulting have yet to develop this unique mix of skills.

Israel's Yozma program found an ingenious way to attract experienced, outside venture capitalists by making matching funds available only to venture capital firms based outside Israel. This arrangement let Yozma draw on these outside investors' experience, as well as train a cohort of new, Israeli venture capitalists.

This kind of approach can also pose a problem, however. As is always the case when outsiders enter new territory, these sponsoring venture investors—though seasoned—may lack knowledge of local culture and law. This unfamiliarity can lead to missteps in attitude or action that can sabotage the entire project.

Aligning Incentives through Fund Structure. As we've seen, the limited partnership fund structure aligns all parties' incentives more effectively than any other approach can. This alignment in turn mitigates the conflicts of interest that uncertainty and information gaps can create. The result? More venture capital circulating through the economy.

But the limited partnership structure requires a legal system that supports it. Many countries interested in growing a venture sector—Asian countries, for example—don't have laws in place to create limited partnerships. Consequently, venture capital funds in these nations have been structured as corporations. This approach carries a price. Specifically, it provides investors with much less control than they would have as limited partners. That's because corporations lack the forced-liquidation structure of venture funds. With forced liquidation, general partners must obtain additional funds from limited partners after exiting a fund within a specified period of time, allowing the limited partners to better control conflicts of interest. Without this feature, Asian venturing efforts can encounter real difficulty because their incentives diverge from the investors' incentives.

In addition to the limited partnership fund structure, venture capital investors in developed nations use a variety of financing instruments—including preferred stock, debt, and convertible preferred equity, which allow fund managers to stage investments, allocate risk, control the management of portfolio firms, provide incentives to executives, and demarcate ownership—all of which align incentives, create an environment conducive to start-up ventures, and thus help strengthen the supply of venture capital in the overall economy.

By contrast, venture capital investors in many developing countries primarily use plain common stock. Some governments, especially in Asia, don't permit different classes of stock with different voting powers. Thus, investors must find other ways to control portfolio firms. And because most companies that Asian venture capitalists invest in are family owned or run, control generally centers on messy controversies such as succession disputes.

So how do such investors secure some measure of control over their portfolio firms? Affirmative covenants, such as investors' right to have access to a firm's premises and records, provide one option. Negative covenants that limit the actions that entrepreneurs might take, such as selling or buying significant assets of the firm, offer another. Regardless of the nature of these covenants, their enforceability varies by country. In countries with lax enforcement, these covenants may not provide enough reassurance to attract investors.

Tax Policy. A nation's tax policies—especially its capital-gains tax rates—can powerfully influence investors' willingness to supply money to venture capital funds. Here's how it works: The returns on venture investments are taxed at long-term capital-gains rates instead of at ordinary-income rates. In many countries, the tax rates on capital gains have differed dramatically from the tax rates on ordinary income. If a government lowers capital-gains taxes, more investors will become attracted to venture capital opportunities.

Capital-gains tax policies vary widely around the globe. Yet the experience of the U.S. venture industry has prompted many governments to reduce long-run capital-gains taxes. These reductions often stem directly from lobbying by national venture capital organizations.

For example, in 1990 Germany set a tax rate of 35 percent for both ordinary income and capital gains. In the past, the German government had not taxed long-term capital gains at the individual level. In the view of many venture capitalists, the 1990 change would prevent them from attracting investors to new funds. Some professionals in the high-tech community lamented the burden that the new tax rates placed on entrepreneurs who wanted to start their own companies. Political lobbyists eventually persuaded the government to gradually reduce the capital gains tax rate over the period 1999–2004, eventually eliminating it entirely. In Latin America, stiff taxes and complicated tax regimes have put venture capital investments at a huge disadvantage. For example, Mexico taxes all capital gains at 30 percent. While Brazil has a lower rate at 15 percent, Brazilian companies must navigate through a quagmire of more than fifty national and local taxes.

The Demand Side: What Excites Entrepreneurs to Start New Ventures?

The lushest supply of venture capital in the world doesn't mean anything without attractive investment opportunities—that is, entrepreneurial demand for financial backing. In fact, strengthening demand may play a far more important role in development of a robust venture industry than boosting the supply of venture capital can.

Demand hinges on the following conditions:

- A regulatory environment and legal structure that remove hurdles for new firms, are friendly toward debtors, and reward entrepreneurs adequately for their investment of time and money

- Sufficient infrastructure, technology, and human skill to support new firms and markets

- A cultural attraction to the entrepreneurial spirit—particularly risk taking

- A healthy economy, including a robust IPO market

A Favorable Regulatory Environment. When governments tightly control important markets, entrepreneurs shy away from stepping onto the playing field. As it is, all start-ups face managerial, technological, and competitive risks when they decide to raise venture capital. Regulatory risk adds yet another discouraging obstacle.

For example, biotechnology start-ups in France must grapple with significant government intervention. For instance, the government owns major stakes in pharmaceutical companies, controls the drug-approval process, directs funding for research, and sets the prices charged for various new therapies.[9] As a result, many promising technologies have either migrated to the United States or have simply never made it to market.

In Israel, government involvement has had a more positive influence on entrepreneurship. There, the government serves as the primary source of R&D funding—much of it directed toward technologies with defense applications. However, these technologies often find their way into the commercial sector, as their inventors identify civilian applications for them. In fact, most Israeli high-tech start-ups can trace their technology back to the Israeli Defense Force.

Israel spends more on R&D (relative to its size) than any other developed, Westernized country—3 percent of its entire gross domestic product. Of this 3 percent, more than 60 percent goes to the electronics sector, which in Israel includes telecommunications, data communications, medical electronics, defense systems, and software. In 2000, R&D employed 83,000 in Israel, which has the world's highest ratio of scientists per capita and an absolute research population equal to that of Switzerland or Sweden. As a result, Israelis produce over $4 billion of high-tech exports annually.

Eastern European economies provide additional examples of how regulatory policy can shape entrepreneurial activity and the demand for venture capital—though these nations face special difficulties in transitioning from Communist rule. In Hungary, for example, the government introduced reforms starting in 1980 that let individuals open private shops.[10] These reforms also decentralized oversight of industries and eased restrictions on direct foreign trade for domestic companies. The government introduced price and tax reforms, set up commercial banks, established a legal structure for firms and corporations, and generally lifted restrictions on economic activity. By the end of the decade, political parties had emerged. In 1990, Hungary held its first free elections, from which a coalition government formed.

Intrigued by the new possibilities in Hungary, investors flocked to the country. The influx of foreign direct investment (FDI) fueled further economic reform. Starting in the early 1990s, Hungary received more foreign investment than any other Eastern European country—indeed, it garnered over 50 percent of all FDI in the region. Hungary's low inflation, political and social stability, low asset prices, affordable wages, and relatively well-developed institutional infrastructure all intensified investor interest. Many Hungarians had also kept their ties outside the old Soviet bloc, receiving their education outside the country and mastering English and other languages.

Not that investors had it entirely easy, however. After all, they had decided to do business in an economy that had never had a market-based legal regime. Though Hungary had transitioned peacefully from a planned economy to a democratic, market-based one, unrest simmered in other countries in the region. As a result, foreign companies were concerned. Entrepreneurs also found it difficult to take funds out of the country to repay investors or purchase foreign supplies. Although Hungarian law allowed conversion of the local currency to dollars, its frequent changing of legal institutions gave no comfort that the law would not change suddenly.

And although the Hungarian government instituted broad economic reforms that encouraged new business, once entrepreneurs made it through the planning stages, they ran headlong into a weighty bureaucracy. 'Even finding an office location proved virtually impossible—the government owned most commercial property. A tangled web of planning and health authorities—including a "chimney committee," "refrigerator officials," a "toilets authority," and a "music authority"—only worsened matters.

A "Debtor-friendly" Legal System. Legal systems that severely punish debtors who can't pay their obligations will stifle the entrepreneurial spirit faster than just about anything else. Most continental European countries have "debt-unfriendly" legal systems. For example, both France and Switzerland have strong bankruptcy provisions. In France, these laws mete out stiff penalties to managers and directors of firms that go bankrupt—and sometimes hold them personally liable for the company's debts. In Switzerland, managers and directors of companies that go bankrupt get listed in the "Register of Bankrupts." Because the failure rate of start-ups is so high, these regulations pose a real concern for entrepreneurs, researchers, and venture capitalists

By contrast, bankruptcy laws in the United States are far more lenient. Managers of bankrupt firms can file under "Chapter 11," which lets them propose a restructuring plan. Similarly, managers and directors of failed firms are not liable for debts unless they have committed fraud or gross negligence. Such a system allows entrepreneurs and venture capitalists to aggressively develop new businesses.

Infrastructure. It may seem obvious, but entrepreneurship can't flourish in an economy that lacks basic services such as roads and power, as well as a computing and communications infrastructure. Yet some nations have had difficulty developing these services and infrastructure.

India, a market with tremendous human capital and huge entrepreneurial potential, has been stymied by its weak industrial infrastructure. Roads and transportation are poor; electricity, water, and communications unreliable. For example, in Bangalore, India's Silicon Valley, power outages are a common occurrence. Most high-tech companies spend a considerable amount on battery back-ups and generators to keep their computers from crashing and to supply electricity, if necessary, for several weeks. In addition, India also has just one telephone line for every seventy people, a rate far too low to support broad voice or data communications.

A Stable Economy. Low inflation, high growth, and reliable currency and interest rates all boost demand for venture capital. Indeed, the recent surge in venture capital activity in the developing world in part derives from these nations' economic progress during the 1990s—which in turn hinged on capitalist economic reforms. Capitalism has rolled through developing economies at breathtaking speed. Just a dozen years ago, only 1 billion of the world's citizens lived in capitalist economies. Today, that number has tripled.

Other macroeconomic reforms were initiated by the developing nations themselves, though often with the prodding of such international bodies as the International Monetary Fund. One arena for such reforms has been major tax reforms, with many developing countries realizing that one way to fuel the economy is by lowering taxes on

capital gains, thereby encouraging entrepreneurial activity. Lower capital gains tax rates make it relatively more attractive for a manager to start
his own company. Most of a manager's compensation comes in the form
of salary and cash bonuses that are taxed at the ordinary income tax rate.
Most of an entrepreneur's compensation is in the form of capital appre-
ciation on the equity of the company. Reductions in the capital gains tax
increase the demand for venture capital as more people decide to
become entrepreneurs.

Some of these thriving economies, in addition to instituting capitalist
reforms, have relaxed restrictions on foreign investment. Many of these
restrictions had prohibited investments in particular industries, forced
foreign investors to hold a minority stake, or limited the repatriation of
profits (i.e., sending profits made by business within the domestic market
back to the parent company in another country). Finally, several emerging economies have improved their accounting and disclosure standards,
thereby lowering the costs of investing and diminishing information gaps
between local companies and foreign investors.

Economic progress and stability can come from external forces as
well—for example, developed nations' lowering of trade barriers to
imports from developing nations. Both exports and imports by developing
nations increased almost threefold between 1987 and 1999. And thanks to
innovations in information and communication technologies, investors in
developed countries—whether corporations or institutions—can better
monitor their investments. Finally, a substantial decline in inflation-
adjusted transportation costs has also paved the way for trade and investment. These trends have spurred spectacular growth in many developing nations. Though developed economies grew at an inflation-adjusted
annual rate of 1.9 percent between 1990 and 1999, emerging market
economies grew at 5.8 percent during that same period.

The Right Talent and Compensation. The value of a start-up is largely
embodied in the skills and experiences of the firm's employees. Thus venture capitalists must be able to recruit the right talent, fire them if they
don't perform, and compensate them for the risks that they're taking by
joining young, uncertain ventures. Though most people in the U.S. high-
tech industry understand the nature of recruiting, termination, and stock
options, entrepreneurs in other countries with more socialist-leaning governments find labor and compensation regulations onerous at times.
These regulations can hamstring the venture capital industry.

Many countries outside the United States have restrictive labor laws that make it difficult for start-ups to acquire the workers they need to grow and succeed. In France, for example, it's very difficult for firms to fire workers once a company reaches a certain size, and the government mandates generous benefits and vacation time for employees at large companies. The result? Talented people tend to gravitate toward the bigger firms—leaving start-ups hungry for good workers. Similarly, because few scientists have pursued careers in business, the French workforce has few individuals who possess both a deep understanding of technology and real management skills—the two qualities that start-ups need most. Numerous nations also restrict or prohibit the use of stock options. In many restrictive nations, the government taxes any gain in stock-option value at the ordinary-income rate even before the employee exercises the options and sells the shares. For example, in the United Kingdom, many managers sell shares to pay the hefty tax liabilities that accrue from rising share prices. Though the government makes exemptions for certain option programs, these programs limit the size of options grants to £30,000 (approximately $48,000). Even then, employees must hold the options for at least three years before they can sell the shares and receive tax relief. These tax restrictions make compensating—and thus attracting—skilled employees difficult and expensive. To bear the risk of joining a start-up, talented employees must believe that the firm has major upside potential.

Cultural Attitudes. Clearly, a highly trained workforce isn't enough to spark innovation; the people who make up that workforce must also have an inclination toward entrepreneurship. If a nation's citizens do not embrace risk-taking and individualism, then few entrepreneurs will want to venture out on their own to start new companies. And without a steady stream of enthusiastic entrepreneurs, a true venture capital market can't thrive.

Japan is perhaps the most apt example of a culture that historically has not rewarded individualism and entrepreneurship. In the United States, many business people see failure as valuable experience that helps an individual learn and grow. In Japan, people tend to judge failure harshly and consider it a personal stigma. Until recently, the brightest Japanese students would go work for the largest corporations in hopes of gradually climbing the corporate hierarchy. In this kind of an environment, venture capitalists aren't likely to find many early-stage, high-tech investment opportunities. Even if they did find such a company, they would probably hesitate to invest in it—if the company failed, the disaster would reflect poorly on the venture capitalist's judgment.

Many French businesspeople are also risk averse. Even the French word for venture capital (translated as "risk capital") reveals a cautious attitude toward new investment arenas. This risk aversion in turn makes it difficult for technology-based start-ups to attract talented researchers and managers.

France's bankruptcy laws have only worsened the situation. As noted, until recently French managers and board members could be held personally responsible for the debts of a firm in bankruptcy if the management was found negligent. Few venture capitalists were involved in firm management under these conditions. In addition, French managers often felt uncomfortable with the idea of letting investors run their firm. They preferred to maintain their authority and did not want to have to answer to investors or to have to ask them for additional equity infusions.

Eastern Europe, with its Communist legacy, has other kinds of cultural hurdles to overcome. Because most managers grew up and received their training in a system that forbade financial profits, many resorted to siphoning resources out of the system for their own personal gain. Theft and bribery ran rampant during the Communist era. After the liberalization of these markets, widespread corruption made it difficult for Eastern European nations to enforce laws. Thus many "entrepreneurs" seized opportunities to extract rather than create value. Unfortunately, bribery and corruption continue to mar everyday business dealings in this region. Venture capital will have a hard time flourishing under these conditions.

The general cultural attitudes toward risk-taking and opportunity are at the center of the entrepreneurial revolution sweeping many regions of the globe. Many of the attitudes that discouraged entrepreneurship in the past are changing rapidly. Successful entrepreneurs are now seen as figures who should be admired. An active, profitable venture capital sector can only exist in markets where such activities are rewarded and valued.

A Robust IPO Market. During the 1980s and early 1990s, the European Venture Capital Association and European Commission turned their attention to developing a public market for small-capitalization stocks. Their rationale? European venture groups had in their possession a huge pool of private investment that they hadn't been able to take public. If the association and commission could create a low-cost mechanism for exiting investments, the venture capital sector would have the opportunity to prosper.[11]

In the United Kingdom and on the European continent, venture capitalists historically have exited investments by selling portfolio firms to a corporate acquirer—a transaction known as a trade sale. For a long time, the United Kingdom had an advantage over other European countries in these exits because it boasted a well-developed capital market. Thus, venture capitalists could realistically point to a possible IPO as an exit. Even when a venture capital group sells a company to a corporate acquirer, having the option to take the firm public helps ensure an attractive sale price.

On the continent, the lack of a developed capital market had posed a longtime challenge to small, venture-backed companies. In the early 1980s, many European nations pushed to develop new public markets for emerging companies. These aimed to provide a more hospitable environment for smaller firms than the primary exchanges in those countries, which often had rigorous listing requirements (such as high levels of capitalization or extended records of profitability). At the same time, these governments sought to retain many of the regulatory safeguards for investors that characterized the major exchanges. These new markets let venture capitalists unwind their positions by selling shares to the public. Their success, in turn, generated new demand for venture capital during the 1980s.

Yet in October 1987, things took a decidedly troublesome turn. World equity prices declined dramatically that month. IPO activity in Europe and the United States dried up. The United States managed to recover with a hot IPO market in 1991, but Europe did not. In 1992–1993, the Nasdaq boasted 432 IPOs; Europe's secondary markets (with 30 percent of the region's listed firms) had just 31. Individual countries fared even worse. For example, Germany's two secondary stock markets listed only five companies in 1992 and 1993; Denmark's listed none between 1989 and 1993.

The markets stumbling, European venture capital investors couldn't arrange IPOs for their portfolio firms. They thus exited those investments by selling the companies to third parties—usually large corporations—often at meager valuations. Trading volume in European markets for small-capitalization firms also lagged. The ratio of total transaction volume to end-of-year market capitalization was just 21 percent in European secondary markets in 1992; for the Nasdaq, 138 percent. While U.S. venture capital investors—pointing to their successful exits—succeeded in raising substantial new capital, European venture fund-raising remained depressed during this period.

Frustrated by these dilemmas, the European Venture Capital Association envisioned a new pan-European public market for growing companies with international operations.[12] In November 1996, the association's vision became reality. Easdaq, designed after the liquid Nasdaq market in the United States, sought to provide a financing route for those companies that could not afford (or that simply wanted to avoid) their nation's primary markets. (See table 9-4 for a description of the various European stock exchanges dedicated to young, high-growth companies.)

By 2001, Easdaq had achieved relatively limited success. Only 203 firms had listed on the new exchange, and many of them cross-listed on Nasdaq or another established exchange. Moreover, the bulk of the trading took place in the developed market, where transaction costs proved considerably lower, and not on Easdaq. Easdaq had also attracted competition. Many national exchanges reestablished or upgraded their second-tier markets. Great Britain created the London Stock Exchange's Alternative Investment Market (AIM). In light of these challenges, Nasdaq announced intentions in March 2001 to acquire Easdaq.

The most successful of these challengers was Euro.NM, a coalition of five new equity markets. In 2000, the number of technology firms listed on that exchange doubled, and their capitalization grew to €127 billion. Neuer Markt, the German small-capitalization exchange, tops these markets in terms of the number of firms that trade and the liquidity of those shares. Why did Euro.NM succeed where Easdaq didn't? One possible explanation is its strict disclosure and listing standards, which equal or exceed those seen in the Nasdaq market. This contrasts sharply with the British small-capitalization Alternative Investment Market and many other European second-tier markets.

Overall, however, the European experiment with new public markets for young technology companies has yet to prove itself. Many of the stocks that trade on these markets suffer from illiquidity, making it difficult to sell large quantities of the stock without dramatically depressing its price. Similarly, few European investment banks have enough experienced analysts to cover these companies. As such, these markets still need time to mature.

Venture capitalists in developing countries have the hardest time, because they can rarely rely on public offerings. Even in hot markets,

Table 9-4   European Public Markets for High-Technology Firms

Market	Founding Date	Companies	Market Capitalization (Spring 2001, in billions)
AIM	June 1995	550	£13.0
Easdaq	November 1996	203	€18.9
Euro.NM	March 1996	575	€127.4
Le Nouveau Marche	March 1996	166	€17.6
Neuer Markt	March 1997	340	€87.5
Nieuwe Market	March 1997	15	€0.6
Euro.NM Belgium	April 1997	12	€0.2
Nuovo Mercato	June 1999	42	€21.5

Source: Various exchange Web sites.

when foreign capital flows heavily into the country, institutional investors usually concentrate their capital in a few large corporations.

India offers a good example of this phenomenon. Between January 1991 and April 1995, the Indian public market saw more than two thousand IPOs. Yet the market still doesn't provide an attractive avenue for exiting venture capital investments. The reason? Individual investors buy up the bulk of these offerings, often at huge discounts. (The typical share trades on the day of its offering at 106 percent above its offering price.) After the offering, trading thins out for most newly public firms. For instance, 18 percent of the offerings do not trade on the day immediately after the IPO (and most of these apparently never trade again). A venture capital investor would face a horrendous task in trying to liquidate a substantial stake in a young firm through this mechanism. These conditions are found in many other emerging markets, which lack the infrastructure of settlement procedures, payment systems, custodial or safekeeping facilities, and regulations.

As a result of these widespread exiting problems, venture capital investors in developing countries often sell portfolio firms to strategic investors, usually a large multinational firm. Things get tricky, however, when the number of potential buyers is small. The purchaser can exploit the venture capitalist's need to exit the investment, and acquire the company for below its fair value. This situation arises most often when the venture capital firm invests in a strategic alliance, where the only feasible purchasers are likely to be the other partners in the alliance.

Several private organizations have explored creative approaches to the exiting problem, including listing shares on an exchange in a developed country, and acquiring a similar firm in a developed country that subsequently merges with the firm in the developing nation. We can expect to see continued innovation in this area in the years to come. Without some solution, the venture capitalization process in these markets can only inch along.

The Bottom Line?

The venture capital revolution is making its way around the globe; in each region, it takes on unique characteristics and faces unique challenges. Countries that create pools of long-term, patient capital, promote economic stability, enact tax policies that encourage entrepreneurship, invest in human capital, and reward risk-taking have the possibility of growing a vibrant venture capital sector. Those nations interested in cultivating a venture industry (or strengthening an existing one) must boost supply by showing institutional and individual investors that venture capital offers an attractive opportunity. Even more important, these nations must stimulate demand for venture funding by creating an environment that encourages—indeed inflames—the entrepreneurial spirit.

Government officials and national leaders who want to stimulate venture capital activity must focus on several important areas. The supply of venture capital can be influenced by:

- Instituting pension reforms. Pools of long-term patient capital are needed for a vibrant venture sector.

- Increasing the supply of experienced venture capitalists to invest the capital.

- Creating accommodating fund structures. Limited partnerships are a particularly effective vehicle for structuring venture capital activity.

- Implementing favorable long-term capital gains tax policy. Lower capital gains tax rates both increase the desire of institutional investors to invest in venture capital funds as well as increase the desire of entrepreneurs to start new companies.

On the demand side, government officials can develop attractive venture opportunities by:

- Decreasing regulations and legal roadblocks to new firms.

- Helping to develop a culture that respects and values risk-taking.

- Developing new public markets for emerging technology companies. Vibrant public markets are an important requirement for exiting venture investments.

- Investing in key infrastructure like telecommunications and transportation.

- Investing in the human capital base of the economy by promoting science and technology training in schools and universities.

- Easing restrictions on various types of incentive compensation. Provision of incentives is a critical element of the venture capital investment process.

Clearly, the international venture capital experience has evolved dramatically over the past decade. In the final chapter, we explore the future of the U.S. venture capital sector. How will the industry change over the next decade? Will the recent shakeout adversely affect future innovation? What types of venture firms are well-positioned in the market? What can others do to position themselves for the coming decade?

10

*Succeeding in the
Next Venture Capital
Revolution*

■

*The next decade will see a dramatic change in the structure of the venture
industry.*

The venture capital industry has experienced dramatic changes during its
relatively short history in the United States. And worldwide, this unique
form of investing is beginning to transform developed and developing
economies alike. But the roller-coaster ride is by no means over. As the
industry continues to grow, venture capital is likely to undergo even more
radical transmutations.

To be sure, investment activity and returns have waxed and waned
many times over the history of this industry—seasoned venture capitalists
are no strangers to these rhythms. And phenomena such as the intensify-
ing competition over transactions, skyrocketing valuations of portfolio
firms, and venture capitalists' reluctance to share transactions with their
peers seen in the late 1990s have appeared many times before. Nor is the
slowdown of the early twenty-first century likely to be the last.

At the same time, we believe that radical change is afoot within the
organization of the industry itself. Indeed, as venture capital undergoes
this profound transition in the next few years, it will leave a whole new
structure in its wake.

Why? As with other industries, the venture industry must occasionally
reconfigure itself in response to growth and broader economic shifts.
These periods manifest themselves in characteristic ways across almost all
industries, including "shakeouts" of less successful players and drastic
restructuring among the survivors. Within the venture industry itself,
three fundamental shifts promise to upset the established order:

- The base of investors who commit capital to venture funds is changing. Whereas the base used to be dominated by a few large institutions, it now contains more and more parties with limited knowledge of and access to the venture fund-raising process.

- Intermediaries in the fund-raising process—such as investment advisors and funds-of-funds—are proliferating.

- Venture capital itself is becoming increasing concentrated in a small number of large funds.

As we'll see, venture capitalists who hope to navigate these changes will need to rethink the way they do business—in three crucial ways.

"Shakeouts" and Industry Evolution

During the nineteenth and twentieth centuries, industries sprouted, matured, and then transmuted in strikingly similar ways.[1] Most of them experienced rapid growth at first, then a shakeout—during which the competitive structure changed dramatically and many weaker firms exited. Though healthy and natural for an industry overall, each shakeout leaves a pile of defunct firms in its wake—companies that couldn't respond quickly enough to the new rules of competition. Even if a number of smaller firms survive, they tend to play a marginalized role in the industry going forward.

As these unfortunate firms fall by the wayside, a few other firms will solidify their position as industry leaders. Many victors from these periods of consolidation were among the earliest firms active in the industry. Having managed to stick around in the past because they successfully adjusted to change, these firms are well poised to handle the shock waves reverberating through the industry. At the same time, new players also enter the arena at these junctures. These companies, unburdened by the "baggage" of long-established industry practices, are particularly nimble at exploiting the emerging dynamics within their industry.

What triggers these reconfigurations of industry structure? A number of events can do the trick; here are just a few examples:

- *New inventions.* An innovation developed outside an industry can drive down the cost of manufacturing a product or providing a service. If firms within the industry adopt the innovation and lower their costs, they can afford to expand their capacity and workforce. As a result, the ideal size of a firm in that industry may increase. Companies that don't adopt the new innovation promptly may wither away.

- A *dominant new industry standard.* New industry standards in the form of technological innovations (for instance, a software operating system) or organizational strategies (such as the "category-killer" super-store) can rewrite the rules of competition for that industry. Firms introducing a standard seek to persuade their suppliers and customers to retool their products or services to favor this standard. If a firm can seize this opportunity quickly enough, it may come to dominate the industry.

- *Ability to adapt to market conditions.* Because of varying levels of management skill or historical happenstance, firms differ in their ability to adapt to rapid change. As we noted above, this adaptive ability may create a self-reinforcing cycle: Once a company successfully responds to shifting events, it may find subsequent adjustments easier.

Investment Banking: A Historical Analogy

To see how these three forces exert their impact, let's step back in time for a moment and look at a venerable U.S. industry: investment banking. In the 1960s, several events rocked the very foundation of this industry—events that left successful *and* unsuccessful players reeling.[2]

In many ways, the industry didn't see the revolution coming. Between the Great Depression of the 1930s and the end of the 1950s, investment banking had achieved an impressive stability. Banks fell into a crystal-clear hierarchy of roles and status. For example, certain top-tier, or "bulge bracket," firms initiated most underwriting activity. They then syndicated transactions with their lower-status peers. The size of each party's allocations—and the profits it pulled in—reflected its position in the pecking order.

Though each kind of bank played a well-defined role, they operated in surprisingly similar ways. The size and scale of a bulge-bracket and a middle-tier bank were not that different in underwriting volume, manpower, or scope. The ranking of the various banks therefore stemmed almost as much from historical social status and tradition as it did from the professional skills of its partners.

We might assume that these operational similarities would present some challenges, as lower-tier banks sought to climb the pecking order or new banks entered the playing field. But surprisingly, the industry saw little such activity during the decades leading up to the 1960s. The reason? Lower-tier banks knew that if they challenged the established leaders, the big banks would cut them out of subsequent syndicated transactions. Though these lesser banks took a modest share of the total profits from these transactions, they didn't believe they could generate enough business by themselves to make up the difference. Equally important, the Glass-Steagall Act of 1933 barred the industry's most natural competitors—the large commercial banks—from entering the underwriting business.

All this changed in the 1960s, when the following developments occurred:

- Underwriting and trading volume ballooned as a result of the robust economy. The potential profits to be made from getting a larger piece of the expanding "pie" tempted lower-tier banks and new entrants to challenge the bulge-bracket firms. The increased volume also strained the existing systems at almost all the banks, which had been set up to accommodate far fewer transactions and trades.

- The banks' corporate clients, caught up in the merger wave that washed over the business world in those years, began demanding more sophisticated services. In particular, they wanted guidance on valuations and deal structuring.

- Regulatory changes internationalized the bond market. Though U.S. investment banks had dominated the New York market for foreign bond issues, the relaxation of capital controls in the early 1960s led to the birth of a truly international EuroDollar market. European banks, particularly the German universal banks, emerged as formidable competitors on this new, wider stage.

- Regulatory pressures began eroding the pricing of brokerage transactions, leading to more competition for trading activities.

These developments had several major consequences for the investment-banking industry. First, the established order of banks was disrupted, and investment banks increasingly began to compete aggressively with one another. Smaller and newer players began clawing their way up the pecking order with increasing success.

Second, the gaps between top-tier banks and others widened. For instance, the twentieth largest bank at the end of the 1950s had one-ninth the underwriting volume of the largest bank.[3] By the end of the 1970s, the twentieth largest bank had only one-fifteenth of the volume of the largest. When we measure the number of investment professionals, net income, and scope of activities, these gaps widen even more.

Finally, the way banking professionals ran their firms changed. By the end of this turbulent period, small banks remained largely informal organizations, with each banker operating autonomously. The largest banks, however, had standardized their most important operations, such as transaction processing and investment-portfolio reviews. Moreover, the banks began exploiting synergies between their securities underwriting, proprietary trading, and market making activities.

How did some previously modest banks and new players successfully achieve higher positions in the industry's pecking order, while others fell back? The "winners" took bold, innovative steps to avail themselves of the new opportunities that these changes presented. For example:

- New entrant Donaldson, Lufkin & Jenrette, sensing corporations' and institutional investors' demand for analytical tools, aggressively built its stable of high-quality research analysts. It funded its expansion by completing an initial public offering in 1970, a time when almost all banks remained private partnerships.

- Merrill Lynch focused on servicing the many well-off individuals who had started investing far more actively in public equities. The bank built a national network of brokerages, at a time when most retail brokers operated on a regional or local scale. Merrill Lynch also acquired the technology it needed to accommodate large trading volumes.

- Salomon Brothers, which had traditionally specialized in the bond market, realized the limitations of the numerous small securities houses that specialized in equity-market-making activities. Sensing that a well-capitalized bank could far more effectively handle the risks entailed, Salomon successfully moved into these markets.

Some leading investment banks, such as Morgan Stanley and Goldman Sachs, also responded to the changing environment with creative strategies. But others didn't budge. Many of these firms deferred investments in computer systems, for instance, and then couldn't keep up with the surge in trading volume that came in the mid-1960s. These firms stuck inflexibly to their core businesses and historical approaches, relying on traditional syndicated transactions rather than branching out into advisory services or novel securities trading. In some cases, the consequences of this rigidity hit with sudden brutality. The bank Halsey, Stuart, for instance, fell from second in total underwriting volume in 1960 to thirteenth just five years later.

Lessons for the Venture Industry

What can the venture industry learn from the investment-banking industry's experience? Though the two industries may seem unconnected in the sweep of history, what happened to investment banking provides a road map for the venture industry—a tool that can help venture firms avoid the fate of those investment banks who failed to change with the times.

The venture industry suffers from a strange paradox. Though its entire purpose is to fund innovation, the industry has made relatively modest innovations in its own structure since the introduction of the limited partnership by Draper, Gaither & Anderson in 1958. Even the recently proliferating publicly traded venture funds are throwbacks to earlier organizations.

Despite the apparent consistency in the venture industry's basic structure, a number of changes are converging that threaten to upend the industry in the same way earlier changes triggered turmoil in investment banking.

A Changing Investor Base. Universities, wealthy families, and corporate pension funds have long dominated venture capital investments. But some new players are increasingly targeting this sector:

- *Public pension funds.* In the 1990s, public pension funds began investing heavily in private equity—more than a decade after their corporate peers joined the party. For instance, in spring 2001 the California Public Employees Retirement System (which had about $169 billion under management at the time) revealed its intention to ultimately up its allocation for private equity from 5 percent to 16 percent.[4] These organizations, which often manage huge investment pools with tiny staffs, make substantial commitments to each fund they select. Initially, they targeted buyout funds, which typically raise immense amounts of capital (and thus welcome large contributions). But in the late 1990s, public pension funds began pouring money into venture capital efforts as well.

▪ *Wealthy individuals.* The robust public markets of the 1990s created a huge pool of wealth that has some unique characteristics. In particular, its owners, many of whom previously ran venture-backed firms, understand the potential of the venture capital process and want to remain involved in it. The relaxation of the "Rule of 99" in 1996, which enabled venture groups to accept funds from up to 499 wealthy investors, also encouraged the emergence of these investors.[5]

▪ *Middle-class individuals.* Some middle-class individuals who are managing their own retirement savings have taken an interest in the venture capital process. During the 1980s and 1990s, the pool of retirement savings has gradually changed its makeup in the United States. Whereas most corporations used to offer defined-benefit plans that mingled employees' savings, more employees are now managing their own savings through separate 401(k) and other defined-contribution plans. (The share of retirement savings in defined-benefit plans, such as major corporate pensions, fell from 84 percent of all pension assets in 1980 to 70 percent in 1988 to about 58 percent in 2000.[6]) More and more individual investors want to put some of their long-term retirement assets in illiquid investments like private equity, just as managers of large pension plans have done for the past two decades. While their interest is likely to wax and wane with market conditions, in the long run individuals will be key players in venture capital.

These changing sources of capital are upsetting the traditional structure in the venture industry. Not only are they leading to greater capital commitments to venture funds, but they also are reconfiguring how these funds are allocated, as we'll see later.

The Rise of Intermediaries. Because these new classes of venture investors are relatively inexperienced in this arena, they need help navigating through the investment process. Intermediaries have stepped in to fill that role, as well as to augment the lean staffs of public pension funds and serve the hugely diverse needs among individual investors. These new professionals come in a variety of shapes:

▪ *Placement agents.* Persuading a public pension fund to invest in a venture fund is exhausting for most venture groups. In particular, the process requires extensive reviews at both the staff and board levels, as well as by outside advisors. To address these demands, venture

groups seeking to raise large funds are increasingly turning to placement agents for assistance. These intermediaries prepare the venture
firm's marketing materials and help raise the fund. Placement agents
affiliated with large institutions such as investment banks have played
increasingly prominent parts in these dealings.

- *Fund-of-funds managers.* Interest in venture investing among wealthy
  individuals has triggered an explosion of funds-of-funds. (These intermediaries gather capital from a variety of investors and then invest it
  in a diversified array of venture groups.) Figure 10-1 captures this
  trend, revealing that funds-of-funds accounted for as much as 20 percent of private-equity investing in 1999.

- *Online private-equity clearinghouses.* Service providers such as Off
  Road Capital seek to match individuals (and some smaller institutions)
  with private companies.[7] These services screen firms seeking financing
  and present their information in a standard format.

- *Publicly traded venture funds.* In response to interest from middle-
  income investors, publicly traded venture funds (e.g., Internet Capital
  Group) have cropped up, as well as public funds-of-funds such as
  MeVC. Joint ventures between mutual-fund companies and private-
  equity groups have also multiplied. For instance, in early 2000, the
  mutual-fund family Putnam Investments provided $450 million to
  purchase an interest in the buyout organization Thomas H. Lee &
  Co.[8] Subsequently, the two organizations jointly sponsored a venture
  capital fund to make Internet investments, which they then marketed
  to Putnam's clients.

Changing Concentration of Funding. The allocation of capital in the venture industry has traditionally followed a cyclical pattern. During boom
periods, small, inexperienced venture groups find it comparatively easy to
raise money. Capital flowing down from institutional investors disperses
fairly evenly throughout the venture industry. During bust times, new venture groups find it much more difficult to raise funds, because investors
concentrate instead on proven groups with established track records. We
can think of this phenomenon as venture capital's "flight to quality."

During the boom period of the 1990s, however, a different pattern
emerged. Though numerous new venture firms flocked to the industry,
capital actually became *more* concentrated in just a few funds. The num-

Figure 10-1   Capital Raised by Funds-of-Funds

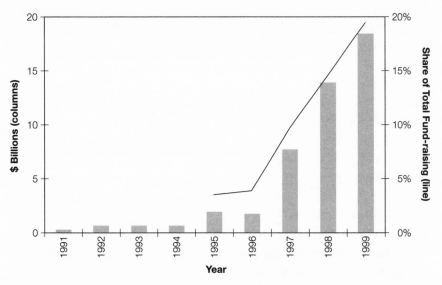

Source: Based on Robert Pease, *Private Equity Funds-of-Funds: State of the Market* (Wellesley, MA: Asset Alternatives, 2000).

ber of active venture firms burgeoned from 374 in 1988, to 468 in 1993, and finally to 727 in 1998.[9] But the share of capital controlled by the largest 5 percent of these firms rose from 32.4 percent to 36.5 percent and then to 42.5 percent during the same period. This concentration likely stemmed primarily from the entry of hefty state pension funds into venture investing (whose minimum investments are typically substantial) and the desire of intermediaries to place their capital with "name" funds.

Then, in April 2000, technology stocks began a dramatic decline in value. This correction will almost certainly accelerate the concentration of funds that began in the 1990s. Numerous examples demonstrate the disproportionate impact that the turbulent market conditions of 2000 and 2001 exerted on small and new groups.[10] For instance, in October 2000 a start-up got a phone call from the venture capitalists that had funded them just four months earlier demanding that the firm return all its remaining capital—even though the young company was exceeding the goals articulated in its business plan. (When the entrepreneurial team members had questioned the inclusion of this provision in the original preferred-stock agreement, the venture firm had reassured them that the provision was never exercised.)

During conversations with the venture group, which was managing its first fund, the entrepreneurs learned that the venture firm's decision to reclaim the capital had nothing to do with the investees' progress. Rather, the venture capitalists had realized that, under current market conditions, they wouldn't be able to raise a follow-on fund unless they could successfully exit at least one investment. They thus decided to concentrate their dwindling resources on the three most mature companies in their portfolio—even if it meant liquidating otherwise healthy investments.

The refinancing of a telecommunications equipment manufacturer offers another illustration. This company had closed a third financing round at a $500 million valuation in February 2000. Though the company's prospects still seemed promising twelve months later, its venture investors realized that they needed to sharply lower the firm's valuation to reflect the severe market correction. The seasoned venture investors who had contributed the bulk of their capital in the first and second rounds (which were pegged at much lower valuations) were willing to reinvest. However, many first-time contributors to the third round got cold feet. These investors included a number of marginal venture firms. They had begun investing in the preceding two or three years and, following a "momentum" strategy, had concentrated on companies about to go public in the hopes of making quick capital gains. When they saw this strategy fail, they froze, unsure of how to proceed. Ultimately, many of the new groups refused to participate. The venture capitalists that participated in the new round structured the transaction such that the holdings of the nonparticipating groups were severely diluted.

Navigating the New Venture Landscape: Guidelines for Survival

How will the many different players in the venturing arena survive these jarring shifts in the industry? Already, some firms have worked out battle plans. Recent headlines in the trade press reveal many examples of creative initiatives:

▪ To enhance the effectiveness of its Internet-related investments, Accel Partners has forged a formal partnership with leveraged-buyout firm Kohlberg Kravis Roberts and encouraged high-tech firms and executives to invest in special commingled funds.[11] Later, the consulting firm McKinsey & Co. became involved as well.

Table 10-1   Billion-Dollar Venture Capital Funds

Year	Name of Fund	Size of Fund ($ billions)
1998	Summit Partners V	1.0
1999	Benchmark Capital III	1.0
	Meritech Capital Partners	1.1
	Oak Investment Partners IX	1.0
	Softbank Capital Partners	1.25
	J.H. Whitney IV	1.0
2000	Accel VIII	1.6
	APA Patricof Excelsior VI	1.1
	Baker Communications Fund II	1.1
	Battery Ventures VI	1.0
	Kleiner Perkins Caufield & Byers X	1.0
	Lightspeed Venture Partners I	1.0
	Mayfield XI	1.0
	Meritech Capital Partners II	1.2
	Menlo Ventures IX	1.5
	New Enterprises Associates X	2.2
	Redpoint Ventures	1.25
	Softbank Technology Ventures VI	1.5
	Sprout Capital IX	1.6[a]
	St. Paul Venture Partners VI	1.3
	TA/Advent IX	2.0
	Technology Crossover Ventures IV	1.7
	THLee, Putnam Internet Partners	1.1
	U.S. Venture Partners VIII	1.0
	Vantage Point Venture Partners	1.62
	Western Presidio Capital IV	1.35
2001[b]	Atlas Ventures VI	1.0
	Austin Ventures VIII	1.5
	Charles River Partnership XI	1.2
	Greylock XI Ltd.	1.0
	Oak Investment Partners X	1.6
	Summit Partners VI	2.1[a]
	Whitney V	1.0
	Worldview Partners IV	1.0

Source: Compiled from various issues of the *Private Equity Analyst,* including especially David M. Toll, "As Giant Venture Capital Funds Proliferate, Other Firms Find Capital Scarcer," *Private Equity Analyst* 10 (May 2000): 1, 50–54; and other press accounts.

[a]Fund had not held final closing as of the end of April 2001. Amount of fund may ultimately be larger.
[b]Through April 2001.

▪ Numerous groups have beefed up their capital under management, raising funds of once-unthinkable amounts. See table 10-1 for a summary of the largest recent funds.

▪ Draper Fisher Jurvetson has sought not only to raise a $1 billion global fund, but also to broaden its network in the United States.[12] To this end, it has established affiliations with other venture groups, typically small, early-stage funds operating in regions other than Silicon Valley (for example, the mid-Atlantic states, the Pacific Northwest, and the Los Angeles region). These groups share some of their profits with the Draper organization. In exchange, Draper helps raise funds and finances selected latter-stage investments that smaller funds may not have enough resources to adequately support.

▪ Many venture capital firms have established "incubators" (physical facilities for new firms, which typically offer a variety of services as well) and "entrepreneur-in-residence" programs to nurture start-up firms.[13] Similarly, numerous groups have invited "venture partners" to join them specifically to make investment decisions for existing portfolio firms.

Which of these approaches holds the most promise for firms that want to emerge as the "bulge-bracket" venture capitalists of the future? Behind the scramble of today's activity, some general principles are clear. In particular, venture firms will have to rethink the way they do business in three key ways if they want to secure a top position for themselves in the industry:

▪ Generate more fee income

▪ Leverage venture capitalists' time

▪ Build venture "brands"

Generate More Fee Income

As a first step, venture firms must increase the fee income that they receive from their limited partners. By pulling in larger fees, they can then use the extra money to leverage strategic resources and build brand identity for themselves.

If we examine changes in compensation across the venture industry over the past few years, we can see that some leading groups have already taken this initial step.[14] However, this process of comparison isn't as straightforward as it might seem initially. Firms calculate their management fees in myriad ways. For example, they might specify fixed fees as a percent of the fund's committed capital (the amount of money investors have agreed to provide over the life of the fund), the value of the fund's assets, or some combination or modification of these two measures. Moreover, both the base used to compute the fees and the percentage paid as fees may vary over the life of the fund.

To spot trends in compensation, we need to untangle these complexities. We started by measuring fee levels in the third year of the fund. Why look at the third year? For one thing, fees often are lower in a fund's first years, which reflects the fact that investment activity is just gearing up in these years. Many firms also *reduce* their fees after a certain number of years or when they raise a new fund (typically after the third anniversary of a fund's closing). Thus, the third year is typically one where fees are highest.

Because fees may not prove uniform across the industry, we need to assess how established the different venture groups are. Of course, reputation is difficult to measure. Instead, we have to examine characteristics of venture capital groups that might *relate* to reputation. Fund size, used in figure 10-2, says a lot about a venture firm's investment track record: Investors feel far more comfortable committing large sums to firms whose partners have had proven success, even if those individuals haven't raised any earlier funds together.

The figure depicts approximately 400 funds raised between 1995 and 2000. As the data shows, fees increased across all fund sizes: The highest fees, as a percentage of committed capital, were paid to the largest funds.

A caution: This measure actually understates the fee pattern. In particular, many changes in fees have occurred in the rates that venture firms charge during just the initial and final years of a fund. To capture this, we need to perform the following calculations:[15]

1. Compute the net present value of *all* management fees specified in the partnership agreements over the lifetime of the fund.

2. Express that value as a percent of committed capital.

3. Discount certain compensation (for example, fees based on committed capital) at a low rate, while applying a higher discount rate to more uncertain compensation (such as fees based on net asset value).

**Figure 10-2 Management Fees in Year 3
(as Percentage of Committed Capital)**

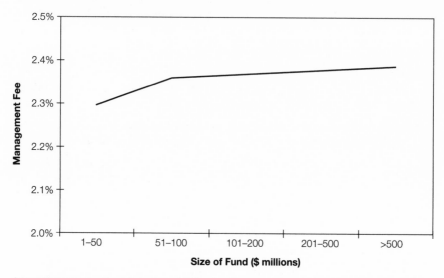

Source: Based on the authors' study of over 1,000 partnership agreements and private placement memoranda
held by a variety of large institutional investors.

Figure 10-3 shows the results of these calculations. The chart reveals that the pattern depicted in figure 10-2 is of relatively recent origin. For funds raised before 1992, experienced venture capitalists actually charged lower fees—probably because they had achieved economies of scale in managing their funds. These firms incur a number of one-time expenses, such as the drafting of the partnership agreement, that remain the same regardless of the size of a fund. Even variable costs, such as the expenses associated with legal fees or due diligence, did not generally increase on a one-to-one basis with fund size. For instance, larger funds usually made larger investments, so that legal fees only increased slightly with capital under management.

After 1993, however, the pattern reversed. The most experienced venture capital organizations began charging substantially higher fees than inexperienced firms do. Interestingly, the trade press has virtually ignored this trend. Instead, it has focused on the well-publicized decisions of a number of top-tier venture groups to raise their share of carried interest, which has actually only increased modestly between 1978 and 2000 once all the venture funds (rather than just the largest, highest profile ones) are considered.

Figure 10-3   Net Present Value of Management Fees Before and After 1993 (as a Percentage of Committed Capital)

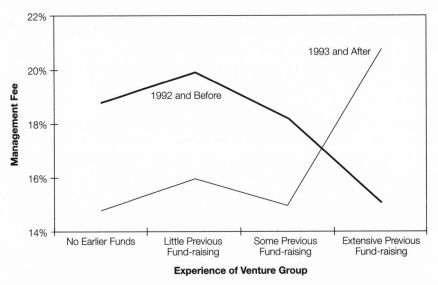

Source: Based on the authors' study of over 1,000 partnership agreements and private placement memoranda held by a variety of large institutional investors.

So, how can venture firms actually boost their fee income? Various firms have tried a number of strategies—each of which has produced mixed results.

Unilaterally Raise Fees. In the red-hot market of the late 1990s, many groups simply informed their investors that the fees had gone up. To be sure, some limited partners complained. After all, whatever the precise terms of the partnership, higher fees are sure to eat into the investors' returns. Moreover, investors worry that large fees might erode the carried interest's power to motivate the general partners; the fees alone will be enough to make those partners rich. And during these years, some venture firms' general partners did put their extra management fees in their own pockets or spent the money on private jets and other lavish expenditures. But times were good, and venture capitalists could easily find other players if a few disgruntled limited partners defected. Many of them bluntly suggested that investors go elsewhere if they didn't like the new terms. However, when supply and demand for venture funds come back into balance, as they inevitably must, unilaterally raising fees will not prove so easy. Groups that do so are likely to find fund-raising much more difficult.

Raise Larger Funds without Building Staff. As another way to increase fee income, firms can raise a larger fund *without* expanding the number of investment professionals who will administer that fund. Many venture groups did this in the late 1990s—though once again, the consequences were often troubling. As we saw in chapter 6, sudden increases in capital under management can disrupt—and even destroy—a venture organization. The success of a venture capital fund is almost inevitably dependent on the skills of the individual venture capitalists. Scaling a venture fund by increasing the number of companies that each investor is responsible for often leads to disappointments.

Even if this approach was desirable, firms will likely have a harder time putting this strategy into action in the years to come. As supply and demand for venture capital comes into balance, venture groups will find it more difficult to make the case that they should get a larger allocation of a given institution's funds: They will need to explain why allocation of another group should be cut in their favor.

Build Stronger Relationships with Limited Partners. To "grease the way" to bigger income, venture firms can also more actively engage their limited partners on a regular basis. Many venture groups today see their limited partners only occasionally: at annual partnership meetings and at two- to three-year intervals when they are in the market to raise a new fund. More frequent interactions may help all parties achieve a meeting of minds—and of needs.

Carlyle Partners provides an example of this approach.[16] This Washington, D.C. group, consisting largely of former senior government officials, first formed in 1987 with a focus on buyouts of defense companies. After pursuing this strategy for a number of years, the group began raising funds more frequently. Instead of simply increasing the rate at which it invested its primary fund, it began raising specialized funds targeted at other areas: venture capital (Carlyle raised the first fund in 1997), real estate (1997), European buyouts (1998), high-yield investments (1999), and so forth. At the same time, the company aggressively built up its central-headquarters staff. By 2000, it had sixty full-time attorneys, accountants, and other professionals, including a number of full-time fundraisers who interacted regularly with limited partners and improved the reporting of their performance. The resulting trust and familiarity among the parties have let Carlyle ask for—and get—bigger contributions from their investing partners. Thus the firm has raised more and larger funds—and earned bigger management fees.

However, this tactic has a downside as well. Venture firms that raise multiple funds may find it difficult to retain talented investment professionals, who conclude that they are not receiving their fair share of the rewards. The sheer scale of the operation may also slow decision-making to a crawl. And if the central organization loses its grip on the firm's operations, one irresponsible fund manager could put the entire franchise in peril.

Pursue Close Collaboration with a Single Limited Partner. As we saw in chapter 5, many first-time funds have recruited special limited partners, who receive a share of the carried interest in exchange for investing in the company. But in recent years, more and more mature private-equity groups have sold a piece of their management company. In exchange, the purchaser (typically a limited partner or intermediary) pays cash to the existing general partners and agrees to make substantial capital commitments to subsequent funds.

A deal between the California Public Employees Retirement System (CalPERS) and Thomas Weisel Partners in January 2000 offers a good example.[17] Weisel, a founder and former chief executive officer of the investment bank Montgomery Securities, was eager to rapidly scale up his venture capital operation. CalPERS, meanwhile, had struggled—sometimes unsuccessfully—to get access to venture capital funds. The two parties struck a deal in which CalPERS bought 10 percent of Thomas Weisel Partners for $100 million. At the same time, the pension fund committed to invest between $500 million and $1 billion in Thomas Weisel venture funds over the next several years.

Once again, these moves can have unintended—and undesirable—consequences. Though the stakes sold are typically small (on the order of 10 or 20 percent of the general partnership), potential limited partners may worry about the implications of these numbers. Because the fraction of carried interest going to the general partners falls, these professionals may have less incentive to work hard. This problem becomes especially worrisome in situations in which the bulk of the proceeds from the sale of the partnership interest goes to the first generation of partners, while the responsibility for the selection and oversight of the investments passes to the next generation.

Return to Negotiated Budgets. Venture firms should consider emulating some of the earliest funds, which did not receive automatic fees each year. Rather than receiving a set 2 percent of committed capital, for instance, these groups prepared an annual budget, which their limited partners reviewed and approved. (A few groups, such as Greylock, still use this arrangement.) A fund's investors will more likely accept a fee increase if they can see how the venture firm plans to use the additional resources.

Venture capitalists will have to make a compelling case for why they should command higher management income. To do this, firms must clearly show investors that nonsalary expenditures—for instance, entrepreneur-in-residence programs, incubators, joint ventures, and other initiatives—are growing. Moreover, they must prove that these costs will directly benefit the investors in the funds.

Warburg Pincus's experience after raising its management fee in 1994 provides a graphic example of how *not* to raise fees.[18] The fundamental rationale behind this firm's fee increase was sound: Warburg's New York location and eclectic investment style translated into higher costs. Moreover, the company ranked as one of the few large venture capital groups in New York at the time. Thus, the group found itself competing for personnel with free-spending investment banks, which were seeking to build up their private equity groups. Finally, Warburg's fee in its previous fund (1 percent of capital under management) had counted among the lowest in the industry. After reviewing all these facts, Warburg raised its fee to 1.5 percent in its 1994 fund.

But Warburg executed the change in a manner that was problematic. Perhaps hoping to assuage limited partners' concerns about the fee increase, the group simultaneously cut its share of carried interest from 20 percent to 15 percent. This move generated considerable attention in the industry and the press. Widely disparate explanations—not all favorable to Warburg—began cropping up in business periodicals. Far from being mollified, some limited partners decried the decision to cut the partners' profit share and increase the fees at the same time. What impact would this "double whammy" have on the general partners' incentives, they wondered? In the fuss, the legitimate rationale behind the decision to raise fees was largely lost.

Venture firms must raise their fees if they hope to respond to the changing environment, but there is no perfect way to do this. Limited partners may resist fee hikes. Boosting fees by substantially scaling the fund—such as through the proliferation of funds offered or the sale of equity in the general partnership—may put undue strain on the venture organization. In most cases, the last alternative we discussed is the best. Limited partners can be persuaded to acquiesce to higher fees if the venture firm can clearly explain to the limited partners why it needs more income—and if the firm takes care to use the increase wisely.

Leverage Venture Capitalists' Time

Simply increasing fee income, however, isn't enough to succeed in the new venture industry. To become a bulge-bracket firm, venture capitalists must *invest* that extra revenue. Groups must also find more efficient ways to deploy their partners' time and energy. All this calls for an overhaul of the way venture firms do business.

While venture capitalists invest in cutting-edge technologies, the late eighteenth-century Industrial Revolution offers some lessons. During that era, many firms in England moved from "craft" to "factory" production. Indeed, the revolution was as much about how producers *organized* work as it was about where they *performed* the work. For instance, even weavers who continued to work out of their homes saw a transformation in the ways in which they produced, distributed, and were paid for materials.

That historical transformation provides an appropriate analogy for the changes in the management of venture capital firms that will occur over the next decade. Traditionally, venture capital has been a craft industry. General partners have played multiple roles, from raising capital and selecting investments to overseeing companies and providing informal advice to portfolio firms. The mixture and quality of these activities have varied widely across venture organizations and individual players.

However, with the recent growth of the venture industry, this craft system has come under severe pressure. Individual venture capitalists are serving on more boards than ever. Meanwhile, demand for their services has mushroomed. And with the flood of new venture money from investors, more companies are receiving funding. Competition among entrepreneurial firms to generate more and better innovations has stiffened, so companies are demanding more assistance from their financiers. These demands are also getting more complex. For instance, in many industries, strategic alliances with large corporations are now essential to small firms' success. These agreements entail complicated, time-consuming negotiations.

Thus, many venture groups are struggling with a tough question: How can they make the most of their partners' scarce time while improving the quality of the assistance they give their portfolio firms? After all, venture firms provide a wide array of support for portfolio firms, including recruiting personnel for start-ups, developing marketing strategies, implementing accounting and information-technology systems, and planning financial strategy.

To ensure the quality of these services, venture groups are increasingly enlisting the help of outside professionals. These individuals, sometimes known as venture partners, provide all the services outlined above—without making any investment decisions.

These arrangements offer venture groups several advantages. First, the firm's partners can focus on what they do best: deciding which firms to finance and providing general oversight. Second, because venture partners are specialists, they often provide far superior service in that specialty. Finally, these partnerships can help build a barrier to entry that delineates top-tier venture capital groups. As happened in the investment-banking industry in the 1960s and 1970s, this trend may further widen the differences between leading and middle-tier venture groups in the years to come.

One illustration of such an effort is Charles River Ventures's CRVelocity.[19] A long-time leader in the venture industry, Charles River has assembled a compelling collection of online and traditional business services that they now offer to portfolio firms. They have gathered a staff of twenty new professionals to administer these services and to help portfolio companies address financial, human-resource, and information-technology issues. Other venture groups, such as Battery Ventures, the Mayfield Fund, and Sequoia Capital, have launched similar initiatives.

In addition to the substantial direct cost, the implementation of such a strategy raises a variety of challenges, such as how to define the roles of each party, ensure timely and accurate information flows, and provide the proper incentives for everyone involved. In this regard, the several hundred stand-alone incubators established in 1998 and 1999 provide a cautionary tale.[20] These incubators aimed to provide a wide variety of services to entrepreneurial firms, including financing, office space, and assistance in recruiting and operations. Yet despite the excitement they initially engendered, most incubators have failed to successfully birth even a single firm.

What went wrong? In many cases, the incubator managers had relatively little experience in working with young firms. They also had unrealistic expectations about how many companies they could help at any one time and the range of firms they could support. Finally, they designed questionable incentive schemes. For instance, some asked for a large share of equity in the portfolio companies—far more than venture capitalists normally seek for an early-stage financing.

All this created a problem for the incubators: The only entrepreneurs who would accept their offers were those who could not raise financing through other avenues; in other words, entrepreneurial firms that weren't exactly on the fast track to success. Even when an incubator did manage to hook an attractive company, its large equity stakes made other investors worry that the entrepreneurs' stakes would prove too small to provide the proper motivation. Few investors committed to follow-on financing rounds for these firms.

The British venture capital industry offers another cautionary tale. These private-equity groups have traditionally relied heavily on intermediaries, such as accounting and consulting firms, to undertake due diligence and even oversee their portfolio companies. Some private-equity groups have gone so far as to describe themselves as "process integrators."

One such group experienced the limitations of this strategy firsthand.[21] Like many of its peers, this organization began shifting its emphasis in 1997 from management buyouts and mezzanine transactions to venture capital opportunities. As the fund navigated this transition, it ran into some unsavory problems. The fees it paid to its outside advisors skyrocketed as the intermediaries struggled to evaluate the new and unfamiliar venture opportunities pouring into the firm. The group also funded numerous technology companies that proved to be failures: In many instances, neither the venture groups nor its advisors identified serious weaknesses in these firms until after several hefty investment rounds. Finally, the three most successful junior partners in the group, frustrated with their small share of the profits, defected and launched a venture firm of their own. In structuring their new organization, they formed collaborations with a number of the same intermediaries with whom the original group had worked for decades.

Thus, the old-line group's core skill—its ability to manage a complex network of relationships—now had little value. Most of the intermediaries couldn't rise to the challenges of the changing market conditions, and the ones that could sought to build on their competitive advantage by creating new relationships with other venture funds.

To escape these problems, venture firms must pursue several strategies to leverage their partners' time:

▪ *Systematize the investment process.* Firms have to clearly define and systematize the investment process. Traditionally, venture groups have been run informally, with the treatment of portfolio companies depending on the whims of the individual general partners. Moreover, many groups haven't codified knowledge about their own practices. Thus, in many cases only senior partners hold the firm's history in their memories. As the number of professionals under the roof of a venture group increases, capturing this information grows even more crucial. For instance, how much—and what kind of—help should the venture group offer its portfolio firms in each stage of their development? How many stock options should an investee's chief financial officer expect to receive? Under what circumstances should the group refinance—or terminate—a lagging firm? Systematizing these procedures can mitigate the ambiguity and confusion that arises when a venture group's staff grows.

- *Knowledge-sharing and account management.* The back offices of many venture groups would shock even the most laid-back entrepreneurs. This informality in part reflects the compensation scheme under which most venture groups operate. Because the general partners retain unspent management fees, administrative expenditures come directly out of their pockets. But as the number of professionals and investors grows, this informal approach is not sustainable. Venture groups have to invest in the same kinds of knowledge-sharing, reporting, and account-management databases that many successful consulting firms have used.

- *Appropriate incentive schemes.* Venture groups also have to develop incentive schemes that adequately reward not only general partners but also others who are not on track to become full-fledged partners. In the past, general partners have been parsimonious toward associates: The promise of a promotion to partner, they believe, constitutes sufficient incentive. Yet, as discussed above, a wider array of professionals have begun participating in the venture industry, many of whom are not on the partner track. To retain them—and reap the benefits of the services they provide—firms need to recognize their contribution.

Build Venture "Brands"

Historically, venture capitalists have had a somewhat wary view of publicity. Many of them feel they have little to gain from press coverage, and a considerable amount to lose. This adversity to publicity reflects the way in which groups have raised funds and identified deals in the past. A relatively small number of endowments and pension funds have contributed the bulk of the capital flowing into venture funds. These limited partners typically have had long-standing relationships with a modest number of venture organizations. Meanwhile, most entrepreneurs are seasoned industry professionals, many of whom seek advice from a few leading law firms specializing in venture capital transactions. Thus innovators have found it relatively easy to identify top-tier venture groups. Venture firms have also avoided publicity because the added scrutiny it brings might erode the informational advantage that's so essential to leading venture groups' success.

But owing to a number of shifts in the venture industry, these professionals' attitudes toward publicity have begun changing in recent years, and will likely continue to do so. The investor base, as we've discussed, has grown more diverse than ever, as has the mixture of entrepreneurs looking for venture financing. And many more intermediaries now provide advice to entrepreneurs. All of these changes make the traditional reliance on word-of-mouth less viable for top-tier venture groups.

The unmistakable success of groups that *have* chosen to market themselves has also caused venture capitalists to rethink the role of publicity. For instance, in the late 1980s, Draper Fisher Jurvetson began aggressively trumpeting its successes—even those in which it may have played only a minor supporting role—in magazine advertisements.[22] The partners have continued to promote themselves and their portfolio companies, on many days issuing two or more press releases about their activities. Meanwhile, the total size of their funds has grown from just under $30 million in 1992 to $1 billion in 2000. The Carlyle Group provides another example.[23] Senior partners of that group state outright that they want to offer investors a "brand"; that is, a consistent approach and quality standards that define each fund.

And last, the proliferation of press coverage and published data about the venture capital industry has also convinced some venture professionals of the value of self-promotion. In earlier years, venture groups believed (with good reason) that if they studiously avoided the media, their activities would remain shrouded in secrecy. But a surge in specialized periodicals, companies such as Asset Alternatives and VentureOne that monitor the venture industry, and journalists who cover the venture industry in general-interest magazines has lifted that shroud.

In short, publicity now offers more benefit than cost for venture capitalists. Moreover, the rewards will only multiply as the industry evolves.

For instance, as individual investors become an increasingly important source of capital, savvy venture firms can capture these potential contributors' attention by cultivating and promoting a unique brand.

A New Landscape

Ten years from now, the venture industry will look far different than it does today. Whereas the industry has evolved slowly since the introduction of the limited partnership in the late 1950s, the pace of change will accelerate in the years to come. And like many other industries, this one will endure a dramatic shakeout that will redefine its contours.

Specifically, a handful of industry leaders will likely dominate the field—leaders who will command far greater financial and human resources than their competitors. Though niche funds will continue to operate, specializing in particular regions and industries, the demarcation between top-level organizations and their competitors will widen even further. In addition, new, agile players will join seasoned groups in jockeying for positions at the top rungs of the hierarchy.

To be sure, many questions about the venture industry remain. How rapidly will this revolution take place? Which survival strategies will prove most successful? How many organizations—and which ones—will make up the new "bulge bracket"? And how will continued globalization shape the international venturing scene?

As with any revolution, only time will answer these questions. Yet one thing seems certain: Success in the new world of venture investing will likely go to those professionals who quickly assess the opportunities and challenges that this new world presents—and who act now to secure their position.

Glossary

∎

agency problem. A conflict between managers and investors, or more specifically an instance where an agent does not intrinsically desire to follow the wishes of the principal that hired him.

agreement of limited partnership. *See* partnership agreement.

angel. A wealthy individual who invests in entrepreneurial firms. While angels perform many of the same functions as venture capitalists, they invest their own capital rather than that of institutional and other individual investors.

associate. A professional employee of a private equity firm who is not yet a partner.

bogey. *See* hurdle rate.

book-to-market ratio. The ratio of a firm's accounting (book) value of its equity to the value of the equity assigned by the market (i.e., the product of the number of shares outstanding and the share price).

bulge bracket. A term frequently used to refer to the top tier of most reputable and established investment banks.

capital under management. *See* committed capital.

carried interest. The substantial share, often around 20 percent, of profits that are allocated to the general partners of a venture capital partnership.

certification. The "stamp of approval" that a reputable private equity investor or other financial intermediary can provide to a company or individual.

closed-end fund. A publicly traded mutual fund whose shares must be sold to other investors (rather than redeemed from the issuing firm, as is the case with open-end mutual funds). Many early venture funds were structured in this manner.

closing. The signing of the contract by an investor or group of investors that binds them to supply a set amount of capital to a venture capital fund. Often a fraction of that capital is provided at the time of the closing. A single venture capital fund may have multiple closings.

coinvestment. *See* syndication.

committed capital. Pledges of capital to a venture capital fund. This money is typically not received at once, but rather taken down over three to five years, starting the year the fund is formed.

common stock. The equity typically held by management and founders of a company. Typically, at the time of an initial public offering, all equity is converted into common stock.

consolidation. A private equity investment strategy that involves merging several small firms together and exploiting economies of scale or scope.

convertible equity or debt. A security that can be converted under certain conditions into another security (often into common stock). Convertible shares often have special rights that common stock does not have.

conversion ratio. The number of shares for which a convertible debt or equity issue can be exchanged.

corporate venture capital. An initiative by a corporation to invest either in young firms outside the corporation or units formerly part of the corporation. These are often organized as corporate subsidiaries, not as limited partnerships.

disbursement. An investment by a venture capital organization into a company in its portfolio.

distressed debt. A private equity investment strategy that involves purchasing discounted bonds of a financially distressed firm. Distressed debt investors frequently convert their holdings into equity and become actively involved with the management of the distressed firm.

distribution. The transfer of cash or shares in a portfolio company (typically publicly traded) from a venture capital organization to each limited partner and (frequently) to itself.

draw down. *See* take down.

due diligence. The review of a business plan and assessment of a management team prior to a venture capital investment.

Employee Retirement Income Security Act (ERISA). The 1974 legislation that codified the regulation of corporate pension plans. *See* prudent man rule.

exercise price. The price at which an option or warrant can be exercised.

first closing. The initial closing of a fund.

first fund. An initial fund raised by a venture capital organization.

follow-on fund. A fund that is subsequent to a venture capital organization's first fund.

follow-on offering. *See* seasoned equity offering.

Form 10-K. An annual filing required by the U.S. Securities and Exchange Commission of each publicly traded firm, as well as certain private firms. The statement provides a wide variety of summary data about the firm.

float. In a public market context, the percentage of the company's shares that is in the hands of outside investors, as opposed to being held by corporate insiders.

free cash flow problem. The temptation to undertake wasteful expenditures using cash not needed for operations or investments.

fund. A pool of capital raised periodically by a venture capital organization. Usually in the form of limited partnerships, venture capital funds typically have a ten-year life, though extensions of several years are often possible.

fund-of-funds. A fund that invests primarily in other venture capital funds rather than portfolio firms, often organized by an investment advisor or investment bank.

gatekeeper. *See* investment advisor.

general partner. A partner in a limited partnership that is responsible for the day-to-day operations of the fund. In the case of a venture funds, the venture capitalists are either general partners or own the corporation that serves as the general partner. The general partners assume all liability for the fund's debts.

grandstanding problem. The strategy, sometimes employed by young private equity organizations, of rushing young firms to the public marketplace in order to demonstrate a successful track record, even if the companies are not ready to go public.

herding problem. A situation when investors, particularly institutions, make investments that are more similar to one another than is desirable.

hot-issue market. A market with high demand for new securities offerings, particularly for initial public offerings.

hurdle rate. Either (1) the set rate of return that the limited partners must receive before the general partners can begin sharing in any distributions, or (2) the level that the fund's net asset value must reach before the general partners can begin sharing in any distributions.

information gap. When, because of his day-to-day involvement with the firm, an entrepreneur knows more about his company's prospects than investors, suppliers, or strategic partners.

in the money. When an option or warrant would have a positive value if it were immediately exercised.

initial public offering (IPO). The sale of shares to public investors of a firm that has not hitherto been traded on a public stock exchange. These are typically underwritten by an investment bank.

insider. A director, officer, or shareholder with ten percent or more of a company's equity.

intangible asset. A patent, trade secret, informal know-how, brand capital, or other nonphysical asset.

investment advisor. A financial intermediary who assists investors, particularly institutions, with investments in venture capital and other financial assets. Advisors assess potential new venture funds for their clients and monitor the progress of existing investments. In some cases, they pool their investors' capital in funds-of-funds.

investment bank. A financial intermediary that, among other services, may underwrite securities offerings, facilitate mergers and acquisitions, and trade securities for its own account.

Investment Company Act of 1940. Legislation that imposed extensive disclosure requirements and operating restrictions on mutual funds. A major concern of publicly traded venture funds has been avoiding being designated an investment company as defined by the provisions of this act.

lemons problem. *See* information gap.

leveraged buyout (LBO). The acquisition of a firm or business unit, typically in a mature industry, with a considerable amount of debt.

leveraged buyout fund. A fund, typically organized in a similar manner to a venture capital fund, specializing in leveraged buyout investments. Some of these funds also make venture capital investments.

limited partner. An investor in a limited partnership. Limited partners can monitor the partnership's progress, but usually cannot become involved in its day-to-day management if they are to retain limited liability.

limited partnership. A contractual arrangement between limited and general partners, governed by a partnership agreement, with a finite lifespan.

lock up. A provision in the underwriting agreement between an investment bank and existing shareholders that prohibits corporate insiders and private equity investors from selling at the time of the offering.

management fee. The fee, typically a percentage of committed capital or net asset value, that is paid to the venture capital fund's general partners by the limited partners to cover salaries and expenses.

market-to-book ratio. The inverse of the book-to-market ratio.

mezzanine. Either (1) a venture capital financing round shortly before an initial public offering or (2) an investment that employs subordinated debt that has fewer privileges than bank debt but more than equity and often has attached warrants.

net asset value (NAV). The value of a fund's holdings, which may be calculated using a variety of valuation rules.

net present value. The expected value of one or more cash flows in the future, discounted at a rate that reflects the cash flows' riskiness.

option. The right, but not the obligation, to buy or sell a security at a set price (or range of prices) in a given period.

out of the money. When an option or warrant's exercise price is above the current value of a share.

partnership agreement. The contract that explicitly specifies the compensation and conditions that govern the relationship between the investors (limited partners) and the venture capitalists (general partners) during a venture capital fund's life. Occasionally used to refer to the separate agreement between the general partners regarding the internal operations of the fund (e.g., the division of the carried interest).

private equity. Private equity includes organizations devoted to venture capital, leveraged buyouts, consolidations, mezzanine and distressed debt investments, and a variety of hybrids such as venture leasing and venture factoring.

placement agent. A financial intermediary hired by venture organizations to facilitate the raising of new venture capital funds.

post-money valuation. The product of the price paid per share in a financing round and the shares outstanding after to the financing round.

pre-money valuation. The product of the price paid per share in a financing round and the shares outstanding before the financing round.

preferred stock. Stock that has preference over common stock with respect to any dividends or payments in association with the liquidation of the firm. Preferred stockholders may also have additional rights, such as the ability to block mergers or displace management.

prospectus. A condensed, widely disseminated version of the registration statement that is also filed with the U.S. Securities and Exchange Commission. The prospectus provides a wide variety of summary data about the firm.

proxy statement. A filing with the U.S. Securities and Exchange Commission that provides information on the holdings and names of corporate insiders, among other information.

prudent man rule. Prior to 1979, a provision in the Employee Retirement Income Security Act (ERISA) that essentially prohibited pension funds from investing substantial amounts of money in venture capital or other high-risk asset classes. The Department of Labor's clarification of the rule in that year allowed pension managers to invest in high-risk assets, including venture capital.

registration statement. A filing with the U.S. Securities and Exchange Commission (e.g., a S-1 or S-18 form) that must be reviewed by the Commission before a firm can sell shares to the public. The statement provides a wide variety of summary data about the firm, as well as copies of key legal documents.

road show. The marketing of a venture capital fund or public offering to potential investors.

roll-up. *See* consolidation.

Rule 10(b)-5. The U.S. Securities and Exchange Commission regulation that prohibits fraudulent activity in the purchase or sale of any security.

Rule 16(a). The U.S. Securities and Exchange Commission regulation that requires insiders to disclose any transactions in the firm's stock on a monthly basis.

Rule 144. The U.S. Securities and Exchange Commission regulation that prohibits sales for one year (originally, two years) after the purchase of restricted stock and limits the pace of sales between the first and second (originally, second and third) year after the purchase.

Rule of 99. A provision in the Investment Company Act of 1940 that exempted funds with less than ninety-nine accredited investors from being designated investment companies. This rule was relaxed in a 1996 amendment to the Investment Company Act of 1940.

seasoned equity offering. An offering by a firm that has already completed an initial public offering and whose shares are already publicly traded.

secondary offering. An offering of shares that are not being issued by the firm, but rather are sold by existing shareholders. The firm consequently does not receive the proceeds from the sales of these shares.

shares outstanding. The number of shares that the company has issued.

Small Business Investment Company (SBIC) program. A federally guaranteed risk capital pool. These funds were first authorized by the U.S. Congress in 1958, proliferated during the 1960s, and then dwindled after many organizations encountered management and incentive problems.

staging. The provision of capital to entrepreneurs in multiple installments, with each financing conditional on meeting particular business targets. This helps ensure that the money is not squandered on unprofitable projects.

syndication. The joint purchase of shares by two or more venture capital organizations or the joint underwriting of an offering by two or more investment banks.

takedown. The transfer of some or all of the committed capital from the limited partners to a venture capital fund.

takedown schedule. The contractual language that describes how and when the venture capital fund can (or must) receive the committed capital from its limited partners.

tangible asset. Machines, buildings, land, inventory, or any other physical asset.

tombstone. An advertisement, typically in a major business publication, by an underwriter to publicize an offering that it has underwritten.

uncertainty problem. A wide dispersion of potential outcomes for a company or project. The wider the dispersion, the greater the uncertainty.

unrelated business taxable income (UBTI). The gross income from any unrelated business carried out by a tax-exempt institution regularly. If a venture partnership is generating significant income from debt-financed property, tax-exempt limited partners may face tax liabilities due to UBTI provisions.

underpricing. The discount to the projected trading price at which the investment banker sells shares in an initial public offering. A substantial positive return in the first trading day is often interpreted by financial economists as evidence of underpricing.

underwriting. The purchase of a securities issue from a company by an investment bank and its (typically almost immediate) resale to investors.

unseasoned equity offering. *See* initial public offering.

valuation rule. The algorithm by which a venture capital fund assigns values to the public and private firms in its portfolio.

venture capital. Independently managed, dedicated pools of capital that focus on equity or equity-linked investments in privately held, high-growth companies. Many venture capital funds, however, occasionally make other types of private equity investments. Outside of the U.S., this phrase is often used as a synonym for private equity.

venture capitalist. A general partner or associate at a venture capital organization.

venture factoring. A private equity investment strategy that involves purchasing the receivables of high-risk young firms. As a part of the transaction, the venture factoring fund typically also receives warrants in the young firm.

venture leasing. A private equity investment strategy that involves leasing equipment or other assets to high-risk young firms. As a part of the transaction, the venture leasing fund typically also receives warrants in the young firm.

vesting. A provision in employment agreements that restricts employees from exercising all or some of their stock options immediately. These agreements typically specify a schedule of the percent of shares that the employee is allowed to exercise over time, known as a vesting schedule.

vintage year. The group of funds whose first closing was in a certain year.

warrants. An option to buy shares of stock issued directly by a company.

window dressing problem. The behavior of money managers of adjusting their portfolios at the end of the quarter by buying firms whose shares have appreciated and selling "mistakes." This is driven by the fact that institutional investors may examine not only quarterly returns, but also end-of-period holdings.

withdrawn offering. An equity issue where a registration statement with the U.S. Securities and Exchange Commission is filed but the firm either writes to the Commission withdrawing the proposed offering before it is effective or the offering is not completed within nine months of the filing.

Notes

■

CHAPTER 1

1. Agnus Campbell and the invention of the cotton picker are discussed in John Jewkes, David Sawers, and Richard Stillerman, *The Sources of Invention* (London: Macmillan Press, 1969).

2. The presentation of Christopher Latham Sholes's invention of the typewriter is based on Darryl Rehr, "The First Typewriter," <http://home.earthlink.net/~dcrehr/firsttw.html> (accessed in November 2000); and "The Typewriter," The Lemelson-MIT Program's Invention Dimension, December 1997, <http://web.mit.edu/invent/www/inventorsR-Z/sholes.html> (accessed in November 2000).

3. Neil Banta and Rob Shultz, interview with author (Gompers), Chicago, IL, March 1995.

4. The description and numbers concerning the angel investing industry are based on J. Freear and W. E. Wetzel, Jr., "Who Bankrolls High-Tech Entrepreneurs?" *Journal of Business Venturing* 5 (1990): 77–89; and J. Freear, J. E. Sohl, and W. E. Wetzel, Jr., "Angels and Non-Angels: Are There Differences?" *Journal of Business Venturing* 9 (1994): 109–123.

5. The discussion of the relative impact of venture capital investing and angel investing is drawn from G. W. Fenn, N. Liang, and S. Prowse, "The Role of Angel Investors and Venture Capitalists in Financing High-Tech Start-Ups" (Washington, DC: Board of Governors of the Federal Reserve System, 1997).

6. The discussion of bank credit outstanding to small businesses is based upon quarterly and annual reports published by the Federal Reserve Bank and compiled at the Web site of the Federal Reserve Bank of St. Louis, <http://www.stls.frb.org>.

7. The Bang Networks venture financing experience is documented in Paul A. Gompers and Sergio Rattner, "Bang Networks, Inc.," Case No. 9-201-074 (Boston: Harvard Business School, 2001).

8. The German government's efforts to promote venture capital are detailed in Organisation for Economic Co-operation and Development, *Government Programmes for Venture Capital* (Paris: OECD, 1995).

9. The discussion of the ATP program is based on Paul A. Gompers and Josh Lerner, *Capital Formation and Investment in Venture Capital Markets: Implications for the Advanced Technology Program,* Report GCR-99-784 (Washington, DC: Advanced Technology Program, National Institutes of Standards and Technology, U.S. Department of Commerce, 1999); and Paul A. Gompers and Benjamin Kaplan, "Torrent Systems," Case No. 9-298-084 (Boston: Harvard Business School, 1998).

CHAPTER 2

1. The story of Don Brooks's development of his Internet browser is based on interviews with Brooks and his colleagues in July 1996.
2. The rise of Netscape and the role of Marc Andreessen, Jim Clark, and Kleiner Perkins Caufield & Byers are drawn from W. Carl Kester and Kendall Backstrand, "Netscape's Initial Public Offering," Case No. 9-296-088 (Boston: Harvard Business School, 1996).
3. The importance of uncertainty in decision making is discussed in Daniel Kahneman, Paul Slovic, Amos Tversky, eds., *Judgment Under Uncertainty: Heuristics and Biases* (New York: Cambridge University Press, 1982).
4. Bill Aulet's experiences at SensAble Technologies are based on discussions with the entrepreneur and other members of the management team in Cambridge, MA in January 1999.
5. The startup of Genset is based on Paul A. Gompers and Amy Burroughs, "Genset: 1989," Case No. 9-298-070 (Boston: Harvard Business School, 1998).
6. Jim Clark and Marc Andreessen's concerns about Microsoft are discussed in Kester and Backstrand, "Netscape's Initial Public Offering."
7. The difficulties faced by Rob Brooker in starting New York Bagel in Budapest, Hungary are drawn from Paul A. Gompers, "New York Bagel: Hungary, April 1994," Case No. 9-297-078 (Boston: Harvard Business School, 1997).
8. The discussion of the biases that entrepreneurs employ when making decisions is based on Antonio Bernardo and Ivo Welch, "On the Evolution of Overconfidence and Entrepreneurs," working paper, Yale University, May 1999; and David Hirshleifer, "An Adaptive Theory of Self-Deception," working paper, Michigan University, 1997.
9. The experiences of Global Digital Utility and Jack Taub are based on Paul A. Gompers, "Global Digital Utilities Corporation," Case No. 9-297-064 (Boston: Harvard Business School, 1997).
10. The effects of risk aversion on decision making are based on Oliver Hart and Bengt Holmstrom, "The Theory of Contracts," in *Advances in Economic Theory: Fifth World Congress,* ed. Truman Bewley (New York: Cambridge University Press, 1987); and Paul Milgrom and John Roberts, *Economics, Organizations, and Management* (Englewood Cliffs, NJ: Prentice-Hall, 1992).
11. Tom Gregory's experience at Ovation Technology is detailed in William A. Sahlman and David H. Knight, "Horizon Group," Case No. 9-286-058 (Boston: Harvard Business School, 1997).
12. The events surrounding the decisions of Hira Thapliyal and Arthrocare are based on Michael J. Roberts, "Arthrocare," Case No. 9-898-056 (Boston: Harvard Business School, 1998).
13. The discussion of the telecommunications switch company is based on discussions with the venture capital investors.
14. The situation concerning Tutor Time is based on Paul A. Gompers, "Tutor Time (A)," Case No. 9-297-064 (Boston: Harvard Business School, 1998).
15. The discussion of private benefits of control is based on Oliver Hart and John Moore, "Property Rights and the Nature of the Firm," *Journal of Political Economy* 98 (1990): 1119–1158; and Raghu Rajan and Luigi Zingales, "Power and the Theory of the Firm," *Quarterly Journal of Economics* 113 (1998): 387–432.
16. The discussion of Kendall Square Research Associates is drawn from Maria Shoe, "Computer Firm Seeks Chapter 11," *Boston Globe,* 31 December 1994, 7.

17. The experiences of Rob Utschneider and Torrent Systems after receiving an ATP Research Grant are based on Paul A. Gompers and Benjamin Kaplan, "Torrent Systems," Case No. 9-298-084 (Boston: Harvard Business School, 1998).

18. The discussion concerning ems and its ability to borrow money is discussed in Paul A. Gompers and Jeffrey A. Ferrell, "Efficient Market Services: August 1993 (A)," Case No. 9-898-009 (Boston: Harvard Business School, 1997).

19. RhoMed's decision to borrow by pledging a patent are discussed in Josh Lerner and Peter Tufano, "Aberlyn Capital Management: July 1993," Case No. 9-294-083 (Boston: Harvard Business School, 1997).

20. The description of events concerning Jim Sims and the founding of Cambridge Technology Partners is drawn from Paul A. Gompers and Catherine Conneely, "Cambridge Technology Partners: 1991 Startup," Case No. 9-098-044 (Boston: Harvard Business School, 1997), and from various news stories.

21. The decision of Elliot Lebowitz to issue shares of BioTransplant in an initial public offering back in 1996 are discussed in Paul A. Gompers and Alexander Tsai, "BioTransplant, Inc: Initial Public Offering, January 1996," Case No. 9-297-095 (Boston: Harvard Business School, 1997).

22. The financial and product market difficulties that befell Don Jones and Star Cablevision are presented in William A. Sahlman and Burton Hurlock, "Star Cablevision Group (A): Harvesting in a Bull Market," Case No. 9-293-036 (Boston: Harvard Business School, 1992).

CHAPTER 3

1. The accounts concerning Felda Hardymon and Bessemer Venture Partners' investments in Securicor are discussed in G. Felda Hardymon, "Securicor Wireless Networks: February 1996," Case No. 9-899-134 (Boston: Harvard Business School, 1999); and G. Felda Hardymon, "Metapath Software: September 1997," Case No. 9-899-160 (Boston: Harvard Business School, 1999).

2. A good discussion of the venture capitalist's due diligence process can be found in William A. Sahlman, "The Structure and Governance of Venture Capital Organizations," *Journal of Financial Economics* 27 (1990): 473–524 and Michael Gorman and William A. Sahlman, "What Do Venture Capitalists Do?" *Journal of Business Venturing* 4 (1989): 231–248.

3. The presentation of Elliot Lebowitz's decision to start BioTransplant is based upon Paul A. Gompers and Alexander Tsai, "Elliot Lebowitz," Case No. 9-297-094 (Boston: Harvard Business School, 1998).

4. Jonathan Guerster's search for a potential investment in edocs by Charles River Ventures is drawn from Paul A. Gompers, "edocs, Inc. (A)," Case No. 9-200-015 (Boston: Harvard Business School, 2000).

5. The description of the investment criteria utilized by Tom Perkins and Don Valentine are based on discussions with venture capitalists. The Arthur Rock description is drawn from "Arthur Rock: Venture Capital's Cornerstone," *New Business*, <http://www.hbs.edu/newbusiness.fall1999/story8.html> (accessed in May 2000).

6. An empirical examination of the staging of venture capital investments is presented in Paul A. Gompers, "Optimal Investment, Monitoring, and the Staging of Venture Capital," *Journal of Finance* 50 (1995): 1461–1489. A theoretical argument for the staging of venture capital is developed in Dirk Bergemann and Ulirich Hege,

"Venture Capital Financing, Moral Hazard, and Learning," *Journal of Banking and Finance* 22 (1998): 703–735.

7. Information about the frequency of venture capitalist's visits to portfolio companies is drawn from Gorman and Sahlman, "What Do Venture Capitalists Do?"

8. The history of staging of venture investments in Apple Computer and Federal Express is drawn from Sahlman, "The Structure and Governance of Venture Capital Organizations," and from both companies' IPO prospectuses.

9. Various types of potential conflicts between outside investors and entrepreneurs are discussed in George Baker, Robert Gibbons, and Kevin Murphy, "Subjective Performance Measures in Optimal Incentive Contracts," *Quarterly Journal of Economics* 109 (1994): 1125–1156; Drew Fudenberg and Jean Tirole, *Game Theory* (Cambridge, MA: MIT Press, 1991); and Bengt Holmstrom and Jean Tirole, "The Theory of the Firm," in *Handbook of Industrial Organization,* eds. Richard Schmalensee and Robert Willig (New York: Elsevier Publishing Co., 1989).

10. The motivations for syndication of venture capital investments is developed in Josh Lerner, "The Syndication of Venture Capital Investments," *Financial Management* 23 (1994): 16–27.

11. The discussion of the start-up of Akamai is drawn from Paul A. Gompers and Howard Reitz, "Cachet Technologies," Case No. 9-200-031 (Boston: Harvard Business School, 2000).

12. An analysis of ownership and compensation of entrepreneurs in venture capital–backed companies is included in Malcolm Baker and Paul A. Gompers, "An Analysis of Executive Compensation, Ownership, and Control in Entrepreneurial Firms," working paper, Harvard Business School, 2000. A good overview of executive compensation can be found in Michael Jensen and Kevin Murphy, "Performance Pay and Top Management Incentives," *Journal of Political Economy* 98 (1990): 225–264; and Brian Hall and Jeffrey Liebman, "Are CEOs Really Paid Like Bureaucrats?" *Quarterly Journal of Economics* 113 (1998): 653–692.

13. An empirical examination of convertible preferred equity is presented in Paul A. Gompers, "Ownership and Control in Entrepreneurial Firms: An Examination of Convertible Securities in Venture Capital Investments," working paper, Harvard Business School, 1998. Theoretical treatments of convertible securities in venture capital are taken up in Francesca Cornelli and Oved Yosha, "Stage Financing and the Role of Convertible Debt," working paper, London Business School, 1998; and Rafael Repullo and Javier Suarez, "Venture Capital Finance: A Security Design Approach," working paper, Center for Economic Policy, 1999.

14. Another reason for the use of convertible preferred equity is that, since the venture firm is investing in a preferred equity stake, the common stock can remain "cheap." The founders of a company usually pay a nominal amount to buy shares of common stock when the company is formed. In this way, they do not owe any taxes on the shares they receive. If they receive the shares for nothing, then they owe ordinary income tax on the value of the stock that they receive because the IRS views this as granting of stock compensation. If the venture capitalist were to invest in common stock, then the price per share paid by the venture capitalist would be the value of the common stock for the entrepreneur's tax purposes. In order to avoid paying taxes on the stock grant, the entrepreneur would have to pay the same price per share as the venture capitalist did. Because the preferred stock gets paid off before the common stock, the entrepreneur can declare a much lower value per share for his common stock than the venture firm pays for its shares of preferred stock. Typ-

ically, the value of the common stock is set to 10 percent or 1 percent of the value of the preferred stock for tax purposes.

For example, if a venture firm paid $1 per share to purchase 5 million shares of common stock and the entrepreneur also received 5 million shares (each owning 50 percent of the firm), in order for the entrepreneur to avoid paying any tax on those shares, he would also have to pay $5 million. Otherwise, he would owe ordinary income tax on $5 million of current income, even though he received no cash. By having the venture capitalist purchase preferred stock, however, the entrepreneur can claim to the IRS that the shares of common stock are actually worth $0.01 for tax purposes. Thus, the entrepreneur needs to invest $50,000 to avoid paying income tax on the shares.

15. A discussion of individual terms in venture capital financing agreements are analyzed in Gompers, "Ownership and Control in Entrepreneurial Firms"; and Steven Kaplan and Per Stromberg, "Financial Contracting Theory Meets the Real World: An Empirical Analysis of Venture Capital Contracts," working paper, University of Chicago, 2000. Some of the legal aspects of these venture capital contracts can be found in Michael J. Halloran et al., *Venture Capital and Public Offering Negotiation* (Englewood, NJ: Aspen Law and Business, 2000); and Jack S. Levin, *Structuring Venture Capital and Entrepreneurial Transactions* (Boston: Little, Brown and Co., 1998).

16. A discussion of the role that venture capitalists play on boards of directors can be found in Malcolm Baker and Paul A. Gompers, "The Determinants of Board Structure and Function in Entrepreneurial Firms," working paper, Harvard University, 2001; and Josh Lerner, "Venture Capitalists and the Oversight of Private Firms," *Journal of Finance* 50 (1995): 301–318. A more general discussion of boards of directors can be found in Benjamin Hermalin and Michael Weisbach, "The Effects of Board Composition and Direct Incentives on Firm Performance," *Financial Management* 20 (1991): 101–112; Benjamin Hermalin and Michael Weisbach, "Endogenously Chosen Boards of Directors and their Monitoring of Management," *American Economic Review* 88 (1998): 96–118; and Barry Baysinger and Henry Butler, "Corporate Governance and the Board of Directors: Performance Effects of Changes in Board Composition," *Journal of Law, Economics, and Organization* 1 (1985): 101–124.

17. A discussion of the decision by venture capitalists to add new directors is presented in Lerner, "Venture Capitalists and the Oversight of Private Firms."

CHAPTER 4

1. A discussion of banking regulations toward loans can be found in Randall S. Kroszner, "Rethinking Banking Regulation: A Review of the Historical Evidence," *Journal of Applied Corporate Finance* 11, no. 2: 48–58; and Phillip Strahan and Randall S. Kroszner, "Obstacles to Optimal Policy: The Interplay of Politics and Economics in Shaping Bank Supervision and Regulation Reforms," in *Prudential Supervision: What Works and What Doesn't*, ed. Frederic S. Mishkin (Washington, DC: National Bureau of Economic Research, forthcoming).

2. The financing history of Akamai Technologies is gathered from Akamai's IPO prospectus, available at <http://www.sec.gov> (accessed in May 2001).

3. The long-run performance of venture capital and nonventure capital–backed initial public offerings is analyzed in Alon Brav and Paul A. Gompers, "Myth or

Reality? The Long-Run Underperformance of Initial Public Offerings: Evidence from Venture- and Nonventure Capital–Backed Companies," *Journal of Finance* 52 (1997): 1791–1821.

4. The relative performance of venture capital investments that go public versus venture capital investments that are either liquidated or get acquired is presented in Venture Economics, *Exiting Venture Capital Investments* (Needham, MA: Venture Economics, 1988).

5. The impact that venture capital has on innovation and patenting rates is explored by Samuel Kortum and Josh Lerner, "Assessing the Contribution of Venture Capital to Innovation," *Rand Journal of Economics* 31 (2000): 674–692.

6. The analysis of states' ability to support innovation and young entrepreneurial firms can be found in Robert Atkinson, Randolf Court, and Joseph Ward, *The State of the New Economy Index* (Washington, DC: Progressive Policy Institute, 1999).

CHAPTER 5

1. The history of early venture capital funds is based on Charles River Associates, Inc., *An Analysis of Capital Market Imperfections* (Cambridge, MA: Charles River Associates, Inc., 1976); Patrick R. Liles, *Sustaining the Venture Capital Firm* (Cambridge, MA: Management Analysis Center, 1977); back issues of the *Venture Capital Journal* and its predecessor publications; and assorted archival material in the collection of Baker Library.

2. The discussion of Draper, Gaither & Anderson is based on interviews with practitioners.

3. Securities law regarding limited partnerships is discussed in Michael J. Halloran et al., *Venture Capital and Public Offering Negotiation* (Englewood Cliffs, NJ: Aspen Law and Business, 2000); and Jack S. Levin, *Structuring Venture Capital, Private Equity, and Entrepreneurial Transactions* (Boston: Little, Brown and Co., 1998).

4. The history of the SBIC program is summarized in Charles M. Noone and Stanley M. Rubel, *SBICs: Pioneers in Organized Venture Capital* (Chicago: Capital Publishing Co., 1970); and U.S. General Accounting Office, *Small Business: Information on SBA's Small Business Investment Company Programs,* GAO/RCED-95-146FS (Washington, DC: U.S. General Accounting Office, 1995).

5. The modern era of venture capital is discussed in George W. Fenn, Nellie Liang, and Stephen Prowse, "The Economics of the Private Equity Market" (Washington, DC: Board of Governors of the Federal Reserve System, 1995); Paul Gompers and Josh Lerner, "What Drives Venture Capital Fundraising?" *Brookings Papers on Economic Activity: Microeconomics 1998* (Washington, DC: Brookings Institution, 1998), 149–192; and many accounts in the business press.

6. The discussion of intermediaries in the venture capital industry is in large part taken from "Investment Managers—A Force in the Venture Capital Industry," *Venture Capital Journal* 29 (September 1989): 10–17; Robert Pease, *Private Equity Funds-of-Funds: State of the Market* (Wellesley, MA: Asset Alternatives, 2000); and David Toll, "Funds of Funds Begin to Specialize as the Field Grows More Crowded," *Private Equity Analyst* 8 (August 1998): 1, 32–39.

7. The emergence of publicly traded venture capital funds and their regulatory difficulties is based on Josh Lerner, "CMGI: Organizational and Market Innovation," Case No. 9-200-064 (Boston: Harvard Business School, 2000).

8. For a more general discussion of the "40 Act," see Louis Loss and Joel Seligman, *Fundamentals of Securities Regulation* (Boston: Little, Brown and Co., 1995).

9. The case of Internet Capital Group is based on "Application Pursuant to Section 3(b)(2) of the Investment Company Act of 1940, as Amended, for an Order Declaring that Internet Capital Group is Primarily Engaged in Businesses Other than that of Investing, Reinvesting, Owning, Holding, or Trading in Securities," File No. 812-11202 (Washington, DC: U.S. Securities and Exchange Commission, 1999).

10. Academic literature on closed-end funds is summarized in Elroy Dimson and Carolina Minio-Kozerski, "Closed-End Funds: A Survey," *Financial Markets, Institutions, and Instruments* 8, no. 2 (1999): 1–41.

11. The story regarding Boston Capital is from Liles, *Sustaining the Venture Capital Firm.*

12. For a discussion of the "grandstanding" problem, see Paul Gompers, "Grandstanding in the Venture Capital Industry," *Journal of Financial Economics* 42 (1996): 133–156.

13. The account of Illinois Superconductor is based on Josh Lerner, "ARCH Venture Partners: November 1993," Case No. 9-295-105 (Boston: Harvard Business School, 1995); and assorted subsequent press accounts.

14. The history of the 20 percent carried interest is based on Raymond Drover, "The Organization of Trade," in *The Cambridge Economic History of Europe: Volume III—Economic Organization and Policies in the Middle Ages,* eds. M. M. Postan, E. E. Rich, and Edward Miller (Cambridge: Cambridge University Press, 1963); and Robert S. Lopez and Irving W. Raymond, *Medieval Trade in the Mediterranean World: Illustrative Documents Translated with Introductions and Notes* (New York: Columbia University Press, 1955).

15. The information on Accel and Matrix's carried interest is based on "Matrix Partners Planning to Raise Carried Interest to 30 Percent," *Private Equity Analyst* 10 (March 2000): 3.

16. The analysis of carried interest is based on the authors' examination of over 1,000 partnership agreements and private placement memoranda held by a variety of large institutional investors.

17. The account of David Silver's legal troubles is based on E. S. Ely, "Dr. Silver's Tarnished Prescription," *Venture* 9 (July 1987): 54–58; and Judge Bernard Weisberg, "Magistrate Judge's Report and Recommendation on Plaintiff's Motion of Summary Judgment," *Lincoln National Life Insurance Company v. A. David Silver,* 1991 U.S. Dist. LEXIS 13857.

18. For detailed discussion of contractual terms in venture partnership agreements, see Halloran et al., *Venture Capital and Public Offering Negotiation;* Levin, *Structuring Venture Capital and Entrepreneurial Transactions;* and Craig E. Dauchy and Mark T. Harmon, "Structuring Venture Capital Limited Partnerships," *Computer Lawyer* 3 (November 1986): 1–8.

19. The account of the Heartland fund is based on "Iowa Suit Tests LP's Authority to Abolish Fund," *Private Equity Analyst* 4 (May 1994): 1, 9.

20. The misadventures of venture groups with buyout investing are described in Liz R. Gallese, "Venture Capital Strays Far from Its Roots," *New York Times Magazine* 139 (1 April 1990): S24–S39. The buyout funds' problems with venture transactions are described in David M. Toll, "LBO Firms Storm into Technology, Trading Leverage for Fast Growth," *Private Equity Analyst* 10 (February 2000): 1, 44–47; and Debra Sparks, "Return of the LBO," *Business Week* (16 October 2000): 130–138.

21. For a detailed analysis of when terms are and are not used in venture partnership agreements, see Paul A. Gompers and Josh Lerner, "The Use of Covenants: An Analysis of Venture Partnership Agreements," *Journal of Law and Economics* 39 (1996): 463–498.

22. The account of Weston Presidio is based on Josh Lerner, "Weston Presidio Offshore Capital: Confronting the Fundraising Challenge," Case No. 9-296-055 (Boston: Harvard Business School, 1996).

23. The tax law requirements regarding capital contributions to venture funds is based on Halloran et al., *Venture Capital and Public Offering Negotiation.*

24. For a discussion of the "crowding out" problem in venture fund-raising, including the issues at Benchmark, see Alistair Christopher, "Piecing Together Limited Partner and General Partner Relations," *Venture Capital Journal* 40 (August 2000): 36–39.

25. For representative discussions of defections at venture funds as a result of senior general partners failing to yield control, see "Family Planning," *Venture Capital Journal* 39 (June 1999): 41–43; and Michael Gannon, "How Burr, Egan Decided to Split into Three Firms," *Private Equity Analyst* 5 (April 1994): 1, 11.

26. Sequoia's decision to invest in Bang Networks is documented in Paul A. Gompers and Sergio Rattner, "Bang Networks, Inc.," Case No. 9-201-074 (Boston: Harvard Business School, 2001).

27. The account of Adams Capital Management is based on Felda Hardymon and Bill Wasik, "Adams Capital Management: March 1999," Case No. 9-899-256 (Boston: Harvard Business School, 1999).

28. The dissolution of Burr, Egan is discussed in Gannon, "How Burr, Egan Decided to Split into Three Firms."

CHAPTER 6

1. Mayfield's fund-raising history is summarized in "X Marks the Spot: Mayfield First to Reach Milestone," *Private Equity Analyst* 9 (June 1999): 4; and "A Tale of One Venture Fund," *Private Equity Analyst* 10 (May 2000): 54.

2. The supply and demand framework discussed here for analyzing venture capital was introduced in James M. Poterba, "Venture Capital and Capital Gains Taxation," in *Tax Policy and the Economy*, ed. Lawrence Summers (Cambridge, MA: MIT Press, 1989); and refined in Paul A. Gompers and Josh Lerner "What Drives Venture Capital Fundraising?," *Brookings Papers on Economic Activity: Microeconomics 1998* (Washington, DC: Brookings Institution, 1998): 49–192.

3. The information about fund-raising in the period after the October 1987 crash is based on an analysis of an unpublished Venture Economics database.

4. The difficulties that the 2000–2001 market decline has posed for institutional investors is discussed in Laura Kreutzer, "Many LPs Expect to Commit Less to Private Equity," *Private Equity Analyst* 11 (January 2001): 1, 85–86.

5. The problems with the accounting schemes used by venture capital groups are discussed in Paul A. Gompers and Josh Lerner, "Risk and Reward in Private Equity Investments: The Challenge of Performance Assessment," *Journal of Private Equity* 2 (Winter 1998): 5–12; Walter M. Cain, "LBO Partnership Valuations Matter: A Presentation to the LBO Partnership Valuation Meeting" (New York: General Motors Investment Management Co., 1997); and Jesse E. Reyes, "Industry Struggling to

Forge Tools for Measuring Risk," *Venture Capital Journal* 30 (September 1990): 23–27.

6. The discussion of the problems with B2B and B2C investments is based on numerous discussions with practitioners.

7. The discussion of the disk drive industry is based on Josh Lerner, "An Empirical Exploration of a Technology Race," *Rand Journal of Economics* 28 (1997): 228–247; and William A. Sahlman and Howard Stevenson, "Capital Market Myopia," *Journal of Business Venturing* 1 (1986): 7–30.

8. The account of the biotechnology industry is based on the authors' analysis of unpublished Venture Economics databases.

9. The discussion of Schroder Ventures is based on Kate Bingham, Nick Ferguson, and Josh Lerner, "Schroder Ventures: Launch of the Euro Fund," Case No. 9-297-026 (Boston: Harvard Business School, 1996).

10. The discussion of Palladium and Redpoint are based on David G. Barry and David M. Toll, "Brentwood, IVP Find Health Care, High Tech Don't Mix," *Private Equity Analyst* 9 (September 1999): 1, 29–32; and other press accounts.

11. The discussion of Summit Partners is based on "Summit's Jacquet Departing to Form Own LBO Firm," *Private Equity Analyst* 8 (May 1998): 3–4.

12. The Foster Capital Management story is related in "Foster Management Moves to Dissolve Consolidation Fund," *Private Equity Analyst* 8 (December 1998): 6.

13. Information on patent applications is discussed in Samuel Kortum and Josh Lerner, "Stronger Protection or Technological Revolution: What Is Behind the Recent Surge in Patenting?" *Carnegie-Rochester Conference Series on Public Policy* 48 (1998): 247–304.

14. The calculation about the relative size of the venture capital market in various nations is based on European Venture Capital Association, *EVCA Yearbook* (Zaventum, Belgium: European Venture Capital Association, 2000); *Venture Capital in Asia: 2000 Edition* (Hong Kong: Asian Venture Capital Journal, 2000); and World Bank, *World Development Indicators* (Washington, DC: World Bank, 2000).

CHAPTER 7

1. The history of corporate venture capital is based on Norman D. Fast, *The Rise and Fall of Corporate New Venture Divisions* (Ann Arbor: UMI Research Press, 1978); G. Felda Hardymon, Mark J. DeNino, and Malcolm S. Salter, "When Corporate Venture Capital Doesn't Work," *Harvard Business Review* 61 (May–June 1983): 114–120; Venture Economics, "Corporate Venture Capital Study" (1986); and assorted press accounts.

2. The disappointing returns from independent venture investments are documented in Blaine Huntsman and James P. Hoban, "Investment in New Enterprise: Some Empirical Observations on Risk, Return, and Market Structure," *Financial Management* 9 (Summer 1980): 44–51; and Phillip Horsley, *Trends in Private Equity* (San Francisco: Horsley | Bridge Partners, 1997).

3. The Xerox case is documented in Brian Hunt and Josh Lerner, "Xerox Technology Ventures: March 1995," Case No. 9-295-127 (Boston: Harvard Business School, 1995); and Josh Lerner, "Xerox Technology Ventures: January 1997," Case No. 9-298-109 (Boston: Harvard Business School, 1998).

4. The Analog Devices discussion is based on David H. Knights, "Analog Devices Enterprises/Bipolar Integrated Technology," Case No. 9-286-117 (Boston: Harvard Business School, 1985); Rosabeth Moss Kanter et al., "Engines of Progress: Designing and Running Entrepreneurial Vehicles in Established Companies," *Journal of Business Venturing* 5 (1990): 415–430; Bruce G. Posner, "Mutual Benefits," *Inc.* 5 (June 1984): 83–92; and various press accounts and securities filings.

5. The discussion of the large-sample patterns of success is based on Paul A. Gompers and Josh Lerner, "The Determinants of Corporate Venture Capital Success: Organizational Structure, Incentives, and Complementarities," in *Concentrated Corporate Ownership*, ed. Randall Morck (Chicago: University of Chicago Press for the National Bureau of Economic Research, 2000): 17–50.

6. The account of Dell Ventures relies on Paul Gompers, Carin-Isabel Knoop, and Cate Reavis, "Dell Ventures," Case No. 9-200-062 (Boston: Harvard Business School, 2000).

7. The discussion of Exxon Enterprises is based on the Venture Economics, "Corporate Venture Capital Study."

8. The account of the Java Fund relies on Lawrence M. Fisher, "$100 Million Fund Will Finance Java-Based Ventures," *New York Times* (22 August 1996): D4; and "Past Initiatives—Java Fund," Kleiner Perkins Caufield & Byers, <http://www.kpcb.com/keiretsu/initiative_old_list.php?initiative=10> (accessed in May 2001).

9. The BlueLight fund is discussed in Henry W. Chesbrough and Mary Teichert Rotelli, "Hotbank: Softbank's New Business Model for Early Stage Venture Incubation," Case No. 9-600-100 (Boston: Harvard Business School, 2000).

10. The eLoyalty fund is documented in Alissa Leibowitz, "Bain, Sutter and TCV to Invest eLoyalty Fund," *Venture Capital Journal* 40 (September 2000): 16–18.

11. The Intel experience is discussed in David G. Barry, "Raids on Corporate Venturing Teams Bring Compensation Issue to Fore," *Corporate Venturing Report* 1 (May 2000): 1, 19–21; G. Felda Hardymon and Ann Leamon, "Intel 64 Fund," Case No. 9-800-351 (Boston: Harvard Business School, 2000); and "Intel Declines to Give Investment Team a Share in Profits," *Corporate Venturing Report* 1 (October 2000): 1, 17–18.

12. The sources of the Xerox and Dell cases discussed in this section are: Hunt and Lerner, "Xerox Technology Ventures: March 1995"; Lerner, "Xerox Technology Ventures: January 1997"; and Gompers, Knoop, and Reavis, "Dell Ventures."

13. The sources of the Xerox and Intel cases discussed in this section are: Hunt and Lerner, "Xerox Technology Ventures: March 1995"; Lerner, "Xerox Technology Ventures: January 1997"; Barry, "Raids on Corporate Venturing Teams"; Hardymon and Leamon, "Intel 64 Fund"; and "Intel Declines to Give Investment Team a Share in Profits."

14. The S.R. One fund is described in David G. Barry, "S.R. One's Gavin Urges Newcomers to Stay in Game," *Corporate Venturing Report* 2 (January 2001): 1, 22; and "Portfolio Profiles: S.R. One," *Venture Capital Journal* 36 (October 1996): 39–41.

15. Fireworks Partners's experience is described in Leslie Cauley, "IBM Multimedia Star Cashes Out," *USA Today* (26 May 1993): 2B; Laurence Hooper, "IBM Launches 'Fireworks' Unit to Form Joint Ventures for Multimedia Projects," *Wall Street Journal* (21 January 1993): B8; Kevin Maney, "IBM Multimedia Executive Joins Blockbuster Venture," *USA Today* (16 March 1994): 2B; and "Sound and Vision—IBM's Lucie Fjeldstad has $100 Million: What's She Going to Do With It?" *InformationWeek* (15 February 1993): 22–24.

16. The efforts at Cambridge Technology Partners are described in Paul A. Gompers and Catherine Conneely, "Cambridge Technology Partners: Corporate Venturing," Case No. 9-297-033 (Boston: Harvard Business School, 1997).

17. The rethinking of R&D in large corporations is described in Richard S. Rosenbloom and William J. Spencer, *Engines of Innovation: U.S. Industrial Research at the End of an Era* (Boston: Harvard Business School Press, 1996).

CHAPTER 8

1. The information about the SBIC program is from Charles M. Noone and Stanley M. Rubel, *SBICs: Pioneers in Organized Venture Capital* (Chicago: Capital Publishing Co., 1970).

2. The calculation of the size of public venture capital financing in 1995 is from Josh Lerner, "The Government as Venture Capitalist: The Long-Run Effects of the SBIR Program," *Journal of Business* 72 (1999): 285–318.

3. The public venture-backed companies were identified through Noone and Rubel, *SBICs;* and Roland Tibbetts, "50 Examples of SBIR Commercialization" (Washington, DC: U.S. National Science Foundation, 1996).

4. The material on the SBIC program and infrastructure-building is from Noone and Rubel, *SBICs;* and Susan Rosegrant and David R. Lampe, *Route 128: Lessons from Boston's High-Tech Community* (New York: Basic Books, 1992).

5. The data regarding venture financing in 2000 is from National Venture Capital Association, "Venture Capital Investments Achieve Record Levels in 2000," <http://nvca.org/Vepress01_29_01.htm> (accessed in April 2001); and from unpublished Venture Economics databases.

6. The Canadian Labor Fund Program is discussed in Andrew Carragher and Darren Kelly, "A Comparison of the Canadian and American Private Equity Markets," *Journal of Private Equity* 1 (Spring 1998): 23–39.

7. The estimates of the size of R&D spillovers are reviewed in Zvi Griliches, "The Search for R&D Spillovers," *Scandinavian Journal of Economics* 94 (1992): S29–S47.

8. The SBIR program is discussed in Lerner, "The Government as Venture Capitalist," and in Josh Lerner, "The Problematic Venture Capitalist," *Science* 287 (2000): 977–979.

9. The discussion of the ATP program is based on Paul A. Gompers and Josh Lerner, *Capital Formation and Investment in Venture Markets: Implications for the Advanced Technology Program,* Report GCR-99-784 (Washington, DC: Advanced Technology Program, National Institutes of Standards and Technology, U.S. Department of Commerce, 1999); and Paul Gompers and Benjamin Kaplan, "Torrent Systems," Case No. 9-298-084 (Boston: Harvard Business School, 1998).

10. The federal R&D numbers are based on the National Science Board, *Science and Engineering Indicators—2000* (Washington, DC: Government Printing Office, 2000); earlier publications in this series by the National Science Foundation; and National Academy of Sciences, *Applied Research in the United States* (Washington, DC: National Academy Press, 1952).

11. The Doriot quote is from Patrick R. Liles, *Sustaining the Venture Capital Firm* (Cambridge: Management Analysis Center, 1977).

12. Gregory Gardiner, "A Presentation to the Board of the Yale Corporation," Yale Office of Cooperative Research, February 1997, <http://www.yale.edu/ocr/indust_studies/strategies.html> (accessed in May 2001).

13. The Boston University experience is based on Seragen's filings with the U.S. Securities and Exchange Commission, available at <http://www.sec.gov> (accessed in May 2001).

14. The Martin Marietta case is discussed in U.S. General Accounting Office, *Energy Management: Problems with Martin Marietta Energy Systems' Affiliate Relationships*, GAO/RCED-87-70 (Washington, DC: U.S. General Accounting Office, 1987); and U.S. General Accounting Office, *Energy Management: DOE/Martin Marietta Earnings Limitation Agreement*, GAO/RCED-87-147 (Washington, DC: U.S. General Accounting Office, 1987).

15. The ARCH Venture Partners experience is documented in Josh Lerner, "ARCH Venture Partners: November 1993," Case No. 9-295-105 (Boston: Harvard Business School, 1995).

16. The Idaho National Engineering and Environmental Laboratory experience is discussed in Adam B. Jaffe and Josh Lerner, "Reinventing Public R&D: Patent Law and Technology Transfer from Federal Laboratories," *Rand Journal of Economics* 32 (2001): 167–198.

CHAPTER 9

1. "European Private Equity Continues to Show Strong Return in 2000," European Venture Capital Association, 15 March 2001, <http://www.evca.com/pdf/Press Rel00.pdf> (accessed in April 2001).

2. The survey of U.S. institutional investors' attitudes towards international private equity is presented in Goldman, Sachs & Co. and Frank Russell Capital, Inc., *1999 Report on Alternative Investments by Tax-Exempt Organizations* (New York: Goldman, Sachs & Co. and Frank Russell Capital, Inc., 1999).

3. The experience of venture capital funds and the role of privatization is analyzed in Anthony Aylward, "Trends in Venture Capital Finance in Developing Countries," IFC Discussion Paper 36 (Washington, DC: International Finance Corporation, 1998).

4. The discussion of the French government's efforts to promote biotechnology investments is drawn from Paul A. Gompers and Amy Burroughs, "Genset: 1989," Case No. 9-298-070 (Boston: Harvard Business School, 1998).

5. The experience of the Japanese Development Bank's venture capital initiative is presented in Josh Lerner, Lee Branstetter, and Takeshi Nakabayashi, "New Business Investment Company: October 1997," Case No. 9-299-025 (Boston: Harvard Business School, 1999).

6. The Israeli Yozma program and its ramifications for the Israeli venture capital industry are presented in Paul A. Gompers and Jeff Anapolsky, "Advent Israel Venture Capital Program," Case No. 9-298-072 (Boston: Harvard Business School, 1998).

7. The discussion of the development of the Irish venture capital sector are drawn from Paul A. Gompers and Catherine Conneely, "Venture Capital in Ireland: Getting their ACT Together," Case No. 9-298-001 (Boston: Harvard Business School, 1998).

8. The difficulties encountered by the USAID venture capital programs is examined in James W. Fox, "The Venture Capital Mirage: An Assessment of USAID Experience with Equity Investments," Center for Development Information and Evaluation, working paper (Washington, DC: U.S. Agency for International Development, 1996).

9. Discussion of French regulation of the biotechnology sector is drawn from Gompers and Burroughs, "Genset: 1989."

10. The presentation of Hungarian policy towards new firms and its effect on the overall entrepreneurial environment is based upon Paul A. Gompers, "New York Bagel: Hungary, April 1994," Case No. 9-297-078 (Boston: Harvard Business School, 1997).

11. The importance of the initial public offering market for the development of a venture capital sector in non-U.S. markets is discussed in Bernard Black and Ronald Gilson, "Venture Capital and the Structure of Capital Markets: Banks Versus Stock Markets," *Journal of Financial Economics* 47 (1998): 243–277; and Leslie Jeng and Philippe Wells, "The Determinants of Venture Capital Funding: Evidence Across Countries," *Journal of Corporate Finance* 6 (2000): 241–289.

12. The discussion of the development of the Easdaq market in Europe is drawn from Josh Lerner, "The European Association of Securities Dealers: November 1994," Case No. 9-295-116 (Boston: Harvard Business School, 1995).

CHAPTER 10

1. Steven Klepper and Kenneth L. Simons, "Innovation and Industry Shakeouts," *Business and Economic History* 25 (Fall 1996): 81–89; and Steven Klepper and John H. Miller, "Entry, Exit, and Shakeouts in the United States in New Manufactured Products," *International Journal of Industrial Organization* 13 (1995): 567–591.

2. The history of the investment banking is drawn from Vincent P. Carosso, *Investment Banking in America: A History* (Cambridge: Harvard University Press, 1970); Samuel L. Hayes, III, A. Michael Spence, and David Van Praag, *Competition in the Investment Banking Industry* (Cambridge: Harvard University Press, 1983); and Robert Sobel, *Salomon Brothers, 1910–1985: Advancing to Leadership* (New York: Salomon Brothers, 1986).

3. The statistics are taken from Hayes, Spence, and Van Praag, *Competition in the Investment Banking Industry.*

4. The information about CalPERS's asset allocation policy is taken from Ricki Fulman, "CalPERS' Alternatives Program Shoots to Triple Assets Invested," *Pensions and Investments* 29 (April 2, 2001): 19–20.

5. The relaxation of the "Rule of 99" is discussed in Kevin A. Jones, "The National Securities Markets Improvement Act of 1996: A New Model For Efficient Capital Formation," *Arkansas Law Review* 53 (1997): 153–174.

6. The changes in the retirement savings system are documented in *Flow of Funds of the United States* (Washington, DC: Federal Reserve Board, various years).

7. OffRoad Capital, "Company Profile," About OffRoad, <http://www.offroadcapital.com/about/index.html> (accessed in May 2001).

8. The Lee-Putnam transaction is described in Erica Copulsky, "Thomas Lee Co. Gets $250 Million—Twice—In Its Deal with Putnam," *Investment Dealers' Digest* 65 (19 July 1999): 5–6; and David M. Toll, "Management Firms Suddenly Become Assets Themselves," *Private Equity Analyst* 9 (August 2000): 1, 37–39.

9. The changing patterns in funding concentration are documented in David J. Ben-Daniel, Jesse E. Reyes, and Michael D'Angelo, "Concentration in the Venture Capital Industry," *Journal of Private Equity* 3 (Summer 2000): 7–13.

10. The accounts of recontracting by venture capitalists after April 2000 are based on conversations with practitioners.

11. The Accel-KKR joint venture is described in "Accel, KKR to Jointly Manage Internet Fund," *Private Equity Analyst* 10 (March 2000): 4.

12. Draper Fisher Jurvetson's affiliate structure is described in "Latest Affiliate of Draper Fisher to be Established in New York," *Private Equity Analyst* 9 (November 1999): 3.

13. The establishment of incubators by venture groups and the hiring of venture partners are documented in Lynnley Browning, "Venture Capitalists, Venturing Beyond Capital," *New York Times* (15 October 2000): C1; and David M. Toll, "Boom in Business Incubators Brings Marked Change to VC Landscape," *Private Equity Analyst* 10 (October 2000): 1, 69–72.

14. The management fee analysis is based on the authors' study of partnership agreements and private placement memoranda held by a variety of large institutional investors.

15. For a detailed account of the net present value calculation methodology, see Paul Gompers and Josh Lerner, "An Analysis of Compensation in the U.S. Venture Capital Partnership," *Journal of Financial Economics* 51 (1999): 3–44.

16. Carlyle Partners' strategy is discussed in Steven P. Galante, "Carlyle Is Putting Finishing Touches on Global Strategy," *Private Equity Analyst* 10 (April 2000): 1, 60–62.

17. The CalPERS-Weisel transaction is described in "CalPERS Acquires 10 Percent Share of Thomas Weisel Partners," *Private Equity Analyst* 10 (February 2000): 3–4.

18. The experience of Warburg, Pincus is discussed in Steven Galante, "Warburg Points the Way to a Lower Carry," *Private Equity Analyst* 4 (July 1994): 7; Jennifer L. Reed, "Warburg, Pincus Seeks Only 15% Carry," *Venture Capital Journal* 34 (May 1994): 6; and "Warburg Pincus Preps Huge Fund Launch," *Buyouts* 7 (4 April 1994): 1.

19. CRVelocity is discussed in Paul A. Gompers, Ann Leamon, and Josh Lerner, "CRVelocity," Case No. 9-201-092 (Boston: Harvard Business School, 2001).

20. The experience of stand-alone incubators is documented in Morten T. Hansen, Jeffrey A. Berger, and Nitin Nohria, "The State of the Incubator Marketspace," *Harvard Business Review* Report (June 2000).

21. The experience of the British venture capital group is based on conversations with practitioners.

22. Draper Fisher Jurvetson's branding strategy is discussed in Scott Harris, "The Education of Tim Draper," *The Industry Standard* 3 (16 October 2000): 172–192.

23. Carlyle's branding strategy is discussed in Galante, "Carlyle Is Putting Finishing Touches on Global Strategy."

Index

■

About the Authors

∎

Paul Gompers, Professor of Business Administration and Director of Research at the Harvard Business School, specializes in research on financial issues related to venture capital and private equity funds as well as start-up, high growth, and newly public companies. He received his A.B. *summa cum laude* in biology from Harvard College in 1987. After spending a year working as a research biochemist for Bayer Chemical AG, he attended Oxford University on a Marshall Fellowship where he received an M.Sc. in economics. He completed his Ph.D. in business economics at Harvard University in 1993.

His research focuses on the structure, governance, and performance of private equity funds; sources of financing, incentive design, and performance of private firms; and long-run performance evaluation for newly public companies. His papers have been published in many academic journals including the *Journal of Finance,* the *Journal of Financial Economics, Brookings Proceedings on Economic Activity, Journal of Private Equity,* the *Quarterly Journal of Economics,* and the *Journal of Law and Economics.* He is the coauthor, with Josh Lerner, of *The Venture Capital Cycle* and the author of *Cases in Entrepreneurial Finance,* forthcoming.

Professor Gompers is currently on the advisory board of several companies. He has served as a consultant for many large corporations, top private equity funds, and institutional limited partners. He is also a Faculty Research Fellow in the National Bureau of Economic Research's Corporate Finance Program.

Josh Lerner is a Professor of Business Administration at Harvard Business School, with a joint appointment in the Finance and Entrepreneurial Management units. Before obtaining a Ph.D. in economics from Harvard, he worked for several years on issues concerning technological innovation and public policy at the Brookings Institution, for a public-private task force in Chicago, and on Capitol Hill. His undergraduate degree is from Yale College.

Lerner is also a Research Associate in the National Bureau of Economic Research's Corporate Finance and Productivity Programs. In addition, he is an organizer of its Innovation Policy and the Economy Group. He is the coauthor, with Paul Gompers, of *The Venture Capital Cycle* and the author of *Venture Capital and Private Equity: A Casebook*. His work has also been published in a variety of leading academic journals.

In the 1993–1994 academic year, he introduced an elective course, "Venture Capital and Private Equity," for second-year M.B.A.s, which has become one of the five largest elective courses at Harvard Business School. He serves as the School's representative on Harvard University Patent, Trademark, and Copyright Committee and as Faculty Chair of the Focused Financial Management Series, a set of targeted executive education courses on current issues in finance.